Welch

Welch

An American Icon

Janet Lowe

John Wiley & Sons, Inc.

New York • Chichester • Weinheim • Brisbane • Singapore • Toronto

Published by John Wiley & Sons, Inc.
Published simultaneously in Canada.

Library of Congress Cataloging in Publication Data:

ISBN 0-471-41335-6

Printed in the United States of America.

10   9   8   7   6   5   4   3   2   1

Contents

Preface

AS THE PUBLISHER, JOHN WILEY & SONS, and I began work on this book in the summer of 2000, we had every reason to believe that John F. Welch, chairman of General Electric Corporation, would be retiring in the spring of 2001. Actually, we had expected him to retire when he turned 65 on November 19 of 2000. That is GE's rule, and Welch had always said he would comply. Nobody was surprised when Welch signed a contract for a postretirement book in late summer, although his author's advance blew the tires off everyone else on the highway. But we hadn't seen nothin' yet. By the end of October Welch had pulled a switcheroo that left most of the business world standing with their mouths agape, and one that sent this writer frantically back to her computer. I had just completed the first draft of this book when Welch rushed the company into the largest merger in GE history and also the largest industrial merger ever. The publisher and I passed *Welch: An American Icon* back and forth for many months making last-minute updates as the deal progressed. Thanks, Jack. More trouble and strife, but a more interesting experience.

This is my second book on the irrepressible Welch. When I was preparing to write the first book, I contacted him at General Electric and told him of my plans. He said he did not see any purpose in anyone writing yet another book about him. I persevered, and in our correspondence promised to write a small but serious book, and although I would pull no punches, the book would be fair. Welch telephoned the subject of one of my earlier books, Warren Buffett, to check my credentials, and in the end agreed to be interviewed. When *Jack Welch Speaks: Wisdom from the World's Greatest Business Leader* was published, Welch sent a note in his famous scrawling, bold penmanship: "You promised to be fair, and you were."

Welch: An American Icon is a far different work from my earlier book. Again, it is thoroughly researched, pulls no punches, and at the same time, takes a fair and balanced look at Welch's life, work, and what it means to all of us. The first book focused on what Welch had to say for himself and about his career. This new effort is an analysis of how the Jack Welch legacy came to be—how he made himself into a global icon representing American business in its most powerful, most impressive, most efficient, and most admired incarnation.

By the time I started this second book, Welch had begun to write his own memoirs, and he could not agree to additional interviews. However, I still had extensive notes from our previous meeting, and the corporate communications staff at GE answered questions and were helpful. Happily a number of other GE experts and former GE employees were willing to be interviewed. The book also involved hundreds of hours of library and Internet research, as the endnotes will show.

Jack Welch isn't an easy man to anticipate or to understand, but his company, GE, is even more complex. The number of business units, the financial clout, and GE's geographic scope are almost impossible to fathom. I encourage readers to take a moment before starting to read to review the material at the back of the book, and to refer to the information liberally while reading. The chronology, the list of GE businesses, and the 19-year stock performance information will help put the events covered here in perspective.

When he leaves office, it is with mixed feelings that I will say good-bye to Welch as GE's chairman. On the positive side, he's had a good run and left a powerful legacy. It will be intriguing to see what his successor will be able to do with the company he inherits. On the flip side, Welch will step down from his post at a time the world is facing many interesting dilemmas and consequences of the ever-burgeoning size of business and of globalization. He leaves a lot of work unfinished. I'm betting that Welch admirers and critics alike will miss his spunkiness, his enthusiasm, his right-is-right attitude. There is always the possibility that Jack Welch will devote his considerable intellect and talents to either government policy or good causes. Either of these arenas would benefit from a strong dose of Jack Welch.

JANET LOWE

Del Mar, California
November 2000

Acknowledgments

AS IS ALWAYS THE CASE, WRITING A BOOK takes the generous cooperation and contributions of many people. I would like to thank you all for your efforts:

At John Wiley, Joan O'Neil, publisher, Debra Englander, editor; and Meredith McGinnis, marketer; my literary agent, Alice F. Martell; Beth Comstock and David Scheffer at General Electric; Austin Lynas for reviewing the manuscript.

Special thanks to the following people for the time they spent talking to me about General Electric, and the Jack Welch legacy: Michael G. Allen, president, The Michael Allen Co., Westport, Connecticut; Professor Joseph Bower, Harvard Business School; Graef Crystal, corporate compensation consultant, San Diego, California; Gerald Gunderson, professor of American business and economic enterprise, Trinity College, Hartford, Connecticut; Curtis Lang, editor, OnMoney.com; Edward Morgan, president, Christian Herald and Bowery Mission, New York; Charles T. Munger, vice chairman, Berkshire Hathaway Inc., Omaha, Nebraska and Los Angeles, California; Daniel Natarelli, chief executive officer, Specialty Silicone Products, Ballston Spa, New York; Brad Sperber, director of outreach, the CERES Foundation; Jack Welch, chief executive officer, General Electric Corporation, Fairfield, Connecticut.

Part I

The Jack Welch Legacy

I am captivated more by dreams of the future than the history of the past. — Thomas Jefferson

Every artist dips his brush into his own soul, and paints his own nature into his pictures. Henry Ward Beecher

*B*usiness reporters from every imaginable news outlet rushed to a hastily convened press conference at General Electric Corporation's New York City offices in the former RCA Building. Jack Welch, GE chairman and chief executive officer, a globally powerful business leader, stood at the lectern, his bald head shimmering in the television lights. He was a little pissed off that anyone should dare to suggest that he'd suddenly decided to pull off the largest industrial merger in history just so that he would have an excuse to postpone his pending retirement. "It ain't anything to do with 65 or hanging on," he insisted, his ordinarily high-pitched, scratchy voice rising a little. "There is a lot of psychobabble out there about me to the effect that 'Is this guy hanging on to the building? He can't go home?' This is *not* a story of the old fool who can't leave his seat, who loves the job so much he can't go home. Don't write that story. That story is stupid. In the paper I called it 'B' with a bunch of dashes."[1]

Welch, diminutive and feisty, went so far as to promise to punch any reporter in the nose who said so, and few reporters did, though Welch, and the reporters, and everyone else knew that there was a lot of truth to the so-called psychobabble. But most shareholders were dreading the day Welch would leave GE, so they were prepared to accept Welch's explanation of what happened. At any rate, his version of the story was plausible. It made a lot of sense.

"It would have been nice if this whole thing could have happened a year ago," said Welch. "It might have been nice if this happened 18 months from now. But it didn't. I was standing in the pit at the stock exchange on Thursday night at 4:30 trying to sell some stock for a partner of ours called Wipro, which went public on the New York Stock Exchange. I was trying to get them some PR and get them on CNBC and CNN and everything else. I'm standing in the pit and I see Honeywell up top, going across, up 10 points. I damn near dropped. I didn't know what the hell happened. So Bob [the reporter] sticks a mike in my face and says, 'Have you heard two minutes ago that UTC just bought or just merged with Honeywell?' I said no. And I didn't. I said it was interesting. And my next reaction was, well, what are you going to do about it? I said I'm going home and think about it."[2]

That was Thursday, October 19, 2000. Welch's announced retirement was less than five months away. The next morning, Welch was in his office early conferring with bankers, lawyers, and his own staff. Late Friday morning Welch called Honeywell International chief executive officer Michael Bonsignore. He could not reach Bonsignore, who was in a board meeting. That really threw Welch into a panic. He convinced Bonsignore's secretary to take a note in and hand it to the boss. The board was about to vote to accept a $40 billion merger offer from United Technologies Corporation, but that bit of business came to a halt.

"When you get a call from Jack Welch and he says, 'Don't do anything because I'm prepared to meet you and top the bid,' you don't have to wonder if he's serious," said one Wall Street insider. "No one is going to say, 'You're not serious; you can't do it.' " If any company has the financial might to make a speedy, high-priced bid, it is GE. And if any CEO has the guts to do it, it's Jack Welch. Welch scribbled GE's preemptive offer on a sheet of paper and faxed it to Bonsignore: $44 billion in stock or $55.12 a share, plus assumption of some of Honeywell's debt. But Honeywell's board (which incidentally included two GE board members: Ann Fudge and Andrew Sigler) had reservations. To soothe their fears, Welch made an offer that sent a bombshell through GE corporate headquarters and rattled the nerves of the candidates who anxiously awaited a decision on who would replace Welch when he retired in April 2001. Welch told the Honeywell board he would stay on through the end of 2001 to make sure the deal went through smoothly. Since a merger that would increase GE's revenues from $131 billion to $156 billion and expand its employee base from 340,000 to 450,000 persons is likely to take a little time, there are hints Welch might stay even longer.

Some GE executives were quietly miffed that Welch thought they couldn't get the Honeywell merger integrated into GE without him. But Welch wasn't about to take chances with his own and his family's fortunes.

"The guy that owns more GE stock, I think, than most of you is me," he told reporters at a press conference. "I don't own anything else. GE stock going up is all my kids and I got. So If you think I'm running out on that, you're wacky."[3]

IT'S ABOUT MONEY, IT'S ABOUT POWER, IT'S ABOUT THE FUN OF MAKING THINGS HAPPEN.

Earlier in the same year, when Welch made headlines by signing a record $7.1 million autobiography deal, consumer polling showed that most people didn't even know who Jack Welch was. Those who don't should check him out. Welch is a guy who makes a lot of things happen, all kinds of things that affect the lives of all of us, even when we aren't aware of it.

Even if Welch's name isn't a household word, it is treated with reverence in the business press. Larry Bossidy, a respected GE veteran who later served as chief executive of AlliedSignal, has said Welch is the "management oracle of the past 50 years."[4] Incidentally, Bossidy was responsible for merging AlliedSignal with Honeywell in 1999, forming another link in the web of connections and influence that Welch has woven during his long career at GE. During his 20 years as GE's chief, Welch guided the transition of one of the most venerable of American companies from an old-economy manufacturing company with a market capitalization of $13 billion into a $525 billion global conglomerate that is involved in everything from major household appliances to high finance to high-tech medical scanners.

Once called the toughest boss in America, Welch has added some of the most feared words to the business lexicon: restructuring, downsizing, right-sizing. Welch wasn't too happy about the nickname he was given—"Neutron Jack," a CEO who kills off the people but leaves the buildings standing. But other executives liked what he was doing and followed his lead. He ignited a movement based on cost reduction and enhanced efficiency that spread like wildfire throughout the corporate world.

By the end of the twentieth century, the negative nicknames had given way to praise. Eventually he was dubbed "Krypton Jack," something of a bullet-proof superman. *Newsweek* called Welch America's boss who towers above all other bosses—its *uberboss*. He has been called the alpha-male of the corporate world, the Vince Lombardi of business. Welch's admirers and imitators are legion. Bob Ulrich, chairman and chief executive of Dayton Hudson Corporation, which among other retail chains owns Target stores, strives to reenergize his company using Welchian principles. Jürgen Schrempp, who became CEO of DaimlerChrysler in 1995, has claimed Welch as his hero in his restructuring and expansion of the German conglomerate formerly known as Daimler-Benz.[5]

Kichisaburo Nomura, president of All Nippon Airways Co., considers himself a student of Welch and quotes the American business leader when addressing his employees. "The secret of success is changing the way you think."[6]

The Rand Corporation, dedicated to research on national defense, has suggested that the U.S. Department of Defense should follow Welch's lead in restructuring the military services, especially as it relates to developing and using human talent. "In the words of a DoD working group: 'In preparing for the future, the single most valuable contribution of the current leadership is to build a learning organization which is devoted to increasing the effectiveness of initiative and ingenuity of commanders and highly skilled employment teams, in effect, put into motion a mechanism of continuous improvement.' "[7]

Even the so-called new-economy companies look to Welch for inspiration and ways to keep on a high growth curve. At Microsoft's 2000 annual meeting, chief executive Steve Ballmer said that he had been "spending a reasonable amount of time . . . studying GE's results."

When *Fortune* named Welch the manager of the century, the editors explained, "Welch wins the title because in addition to his transformation of GE, he has made himself far and away the most influential manager of his generation . . . As the most widely admired, studied, and imitated CEO of his time, Welch has enriched not only GE's shareholders but the shareholders of companies around the globe. His total economic impact is impossible to calculate but must be some staggering multiple of GE performance."[8]

THE POWER OF GENERAL ELECTRIC

But again, simply managing a company expertly seems an inadequate explanation for the cult hero status Welch has achieved within the business community. Since when did corporate executives become cultural icons? To understand the power and influence of Jack Welch, you must first comprehend GE, its behemoth size and the height, width, and depth of its economic reach.

Although it is regarded as an extremely lean corporation

considering the scope of its business, before the Honeywell acquisition GE had more than 340,000 employees. Afterward, that number grew to about 460,000. If all of those people were gathered in one place, they would make up a city the size of Tuscon, Arizona. Only 35 of the world's 191 nations have gross domestic products (GDPs) higher than the new GE's revenues. In fact, when GDP and revenues are compared, GE is roughly about the size of Vietnam. Nine of GE's 12 divisions are big enough to be included individually on the Fortune 500.

In the book *Built to Last: The Successful Habits of Visionary Companies*, authors James C. Collins and Jerry I. Porras include GE among the world's transformational companies, those that distinguish themselves beyond mere success or ability to endure. They ranked GE with 3M, American Express, Boeing, Ford, Hewlett-Packard, IBM, Johnson & Johnson, Procter & Gamble, Sony, Wal-Mart, and Walt Disney. Visionary companies, explained the authors, have woven themselves into the fabric of society with their products, Scotch tape, Tide detergent, Band-Aids, Mickey Mouse, and General Electric lightbulbs and appliances.[9]

General Electric is omnipresent, even though at times people don't realize it. Anytime you see a plastic part on your car or any piece of equipment, you may be looking at a GE product, since the company is a leader in the plastics industry. When you flip a light switch in your home or office, not only is the lightbulb likely to be manufactured by GE, GE also probably made the turbine at the electric generating plant that supplies the power. When you watch television, GE is there, with full ownership of the NBC television network and 200 affiliated stations. On top of that, GE shares ownership of the MSNBC cable network with another giant, Microsoft. (But as is explained in more detail in Chapter 3, even if your television set carries the GE logo, GE didn't make it.) When you take a commercial airline flight, there is a good chance that GE designed and manufactured the engines on the airplane, and may very well own the airplane itself. Through GE Capital, it owns more commercial aircraft than American Airlines. If you travel by train, GE most likely built the locomotive motor. If you go to a medical center for a CAT scan or an X-ray, GE may have made that equipment and will be servicing it. Furthermore, GE probably financed all the aforementioned equipment through GE Capital, the largest finance operation in the world.

THE GIANT THAT IS GE

During its 123 years of operation, GE has become so large that the question arises: Is GE's performance affected by the U.S. economy or is it the other way around? Even at the time Welch took charge, the company was so big that sales equaled about 1 percent of America's gross domestic product, and once GE swallows Honeywell, that percentage will grow. In fact, it is expected that the new GE will comprise about half a percent of world economic output. Many experts considered GE a proxy for the U.S. economy as a whole, rising and falling with the tide of economic well-being. For years there was an American saying, "As goes General Motors, so goes America." GM is still an influential company, but its power has been diminished by foreign competition. A different general is in charge now. As goes General Electric, so goes the nation, and perhaps even the world.

THE GE TRANSFER OF VALUES

Perhaps the most astounding thing is the impact that Jack Welch has had on the world economy and even world culture as both become increasingly globally integrated. Welch has pushed GE—

the most American of all corporations—into a decisive and irreversible world dominance. As a result, the rest of the world has been driven to be more like GE and hence more like the United States. Some of Welch's influence stems from GE's might, but not all of it. Simply because of its size and financial power, GE is an economic, political, and social force unto itself. Yet Welch's strong will and dominant personality have left their mark.

Welch, in his management style, epitomizes the American ideal: big, bold, egalitarian, democratic, energetic, creative, driven by the work ethic. Welch is both an evangelist for capitalism and an enforcer of capitalist precepts. At the same time, the values that he so energetically espouses—meritocracy, dignity, simplicity, speed, a hatred of bureaucracy—touch on universal longings that are not limited to North America; they translate almost anywhere, and he knows that.

"When everyone asks me over and over again, 'How do you transfer GE values somewhere?' I tell them we can do it because they are really the most simple values of all. It's human dignity and voice," said Welch. "What our managers try to do is let everybody raise their hand and say what they think. And if people have a voice and they have a say in things, they respect it and like it. Now, that dignity and voice may be a little different in Beijing than in Pittsburgh. But it's nothing other than giving people the treatment that you would already want for yourself in that culture."[10]

THE SHORTFALLS OF CAPITALISM

Nevertheless, Welch has many critics, especially among environmentalists and idealistic and religious organizations dedicated to improving the human condition everywhere. To decide whether

Welch has been a positive or negative influence on society, it is necessary to face several realities: Without the complex machinery for technical advances that a company such as GE provides, we are stuck in the present. Because a sound economic base is essential to the well-being and progress of mankind, Welch has made a significant positive contribution. But life is never as simple as that.

While Welch's notions seem to make sense and have a special allure, his business revolution brings with it problems. No great change to society comes without a price, without a turbulent transition. The trouble Russia and its former satellite nations have had moving from communism to capitalism is a prime example of how the process can stumble and even break apart. Yet, just as there was no chance of stopping the industrial revolution, the Pandora's box of electronic commerce and globalization has been opened. Fast and cheap transoceanic flight, satellite telephone and television communications, and especially the Internet have made globalization inevitable. When television viewers in Calcutta and Cincinnati watch the same report on the Cable News Network (CNN) at the same time, their view of the world quite naturally draws closer together.

This book explores how Welch shaped and influenced GE, how he pushed and prodded both a company and a nation into global power, and how the global vision of one man, an individual who has never been elected to a single government post or ever led a great church or populist movement, is impacting the lives of everyone everywhere, even though they don't know quite who he is.

Welch is an individual of high energy and intelligence who holds true to his beliefs, but to assume that he always knows what is right or that he has made no mistakes is incorrect. As extraordinary as GE is, the visionary companies with far-flung, complicated operations never have unblemished records.[11]

The impact of the thrust of General Electric and Welch—both American icons—into the international arena should be open for discussion:

* GE's economic clout, like that of Microsoft Corporation, raises many questions about the role of antitrust regulation in the global economy. Do the old American rules of fair play still apply in a worldwide setting? If they do not, what new rules do apply? How should these rules be written, and in what court of law should they be enforced?

* Welch has fine-tuned and revved up the workplace to such a fervid pace that workers are concerned about the impact on their family life and their communities. Has the work ethic been pushed too far?

* What checks and balances are or should be in place to protect other citizens from the corruption that sometimes arises from power on the scale wielded by Welch and future GE chief executives?

* Welch is a leader among chief executives who have raised their own salaries to a mind-boggling level, while at the same time moving jobs out of the United States in order to reduce worker pay to the lowest possible level. Is this fair? If not, what can be done about it?

* GE is accused of polluting the environment, neglecting worker safety, and abandoning towns where it once had factories. Has GE been a good corporate citizen at home, and how can we ensure that GE will be a responsible global citizen?

According to GE's charter, a chief executive must retire at age 65, and Welch, who reached that milestone on November 19,

2000, will stay a little longer and leave office after 2001. The remaining questions are these: What kind of corporation will his successor Jeffrey Immelt inherit, and what is Immelt likely to mean to the company, the nation, and the world? Finally, what will Jack Welch, who seems to have plenty of energy and enjoys good health, do with the remainder of his life? In what new way will the irrepressible and indomitable Jack Welch be with us?

chapter one

The House of Magic: How Welch Became an American Icon

Optimism, leadership, and productivity have been three of the characteristics that have moved this country to a special place in front of the nations of the world.[1]   Jack Welch, 1992

Opportunity is missed by most because it is dressed in overalls and looks like work.   Thomas Edison

WHY AND HOW HAS JACK WELCH, A GUY WHO works in an office and talks a lot on the telephone, captured the imagination of the type of people that once looked to the likes of Winston Churchill or Dwight D. Eisenhower or John F. Kennedy for inspiration? It was a matter if circumstances. "People tend to pick out heroes for each era," said Gerald Gunderson, professor of American business and economic enterprise at Trinity College in Hartford, Connecticut. "The world quieted down. In the 1980s and 1990s business became more important in people's minds again. Politicians seem less vital."

A man for the time in which he lives, Welch could not have achieved anonymity if he wanted to, claimed Gunderson. "Society would not allow it. Leaders are adopted as symbols or mental shortcuts to explain an otherwise complex and confusing world."[2]

But to describe Welch as merely a lucky traveler in history is to sell his own contribution to success short. Welch ascended in GE because of his charisma and ability to lead, and brought remarkable vision to the job. Edward Morgan, who worked on the "GE Brings Good Things to Life" campaign and later left GE to head the organization that runs New York's historic Bowery Mission, said that he learned from Welch the importance of motivation. "You tell your people, 'We're going to create a shining goal.' That goal needs to be inspirational. It needs to be broad enough that it excites people inside and outside the organization."

Welch worked at GE for 40 years—in fact, he never had a full-time job anywhere else—but that isn't to say his thinking stayed in one place. He had to change. During Welch's career the public image of a chief executive officer was subject to several incarnations and reincarnations. In the 1970s the CEO was seen as a bumbling bureaucrat who couldn't even build a car that would hold together, and certainly could not produce a small, fuel-efficient automobile that could compete with Japanese models. In the 1980s the CEO was a rapacious plunderer, accused of laying off loyal workers so that he could buy a racier corporate jet or capitalize on his own stock options. Now, as one century ends and another begins, CEOs are regarded as a celebrity class, an aristocracy, visionaries with exceptional powers to create wealth through innovation, enlightened management, and manipulation of assets.

Indeed Welch's life and career have been shaped by the time in which he lives, just as they have been influenced by the place where he was born and raised. Welch's life has turned out the way it is supposed to in America—he's the walking, talking American dream come true.

WHO *IS* HE? A CLASSIC AMERICAN SUCCESS STORY.

General Electric surely is the most typically American of all companies, and Welch, the son of John F. Welch Sr., a Salem, Massachusetts, railroad conductor, is the most blatantly American of any chief executive in the world. In the predictably American way, Welch has little patience with tradition for its own sake, and, as might be expected, he is unintimidated by trappings of social class. Welch, who stuttered for most of his life, gives his mother, Grace Welch, much of the credit for his self-confidence. "She told me I didn't have a speech impediment," he recalled. "Just that my brain worked too fast."[3] His tongue just couldn't keep up.

An energetic, imaginative self-starter who grew up in the historic port town of Salem, Massachusetts, Welch thrives on confrontation and is outspoken to the point of being brash. Yet he also is a captivating ruffian who still speaks with the accent and cadence of a Boston-area kid who's playing a tough game of sandlot baseball. His high school classmates called him the "most talkative and noisiest boy." Sports were always central to Welch's psyche. Since his school days Welch has been known as an aggressive hard worker, and as a kid he was able to incorporate work and play when he earned $3 a day caddying at the golf course near his home.

Welch was the first in his Irish-American, working-class family to attend college, though he was not able to attend an Ivy League school as he'd hoped. The college he attended, the University of Massachusetts, did not have the prestige of nearby Amherst and Smith Colleges, but it has had many other distinguished graduates, including Jack Smith, who is chairman of General Motors. The spartan UMass campus sits like an old New England mill town in the midst of rolling green hills, but it was fertile soil for young Welch.

When their son took off for college in the fall of 1953 it was a new experience for the Welches, though the $50 a semester cost seemed a small sacrifice for their only child. Jack's usually taciturn father had simple advice for the boy: "Work really hard, and don't mess up."

CHEMISTRY RATHER THAN THE CHURCH

Welch's mother, a devout Catholic, had enormous influence on her son. She had been trying to have a child for 16 years with no luck; then, when she was 40, Jack was born. Grace Welch hoped her wonderful bright boy would study to be a priest or physician, but Jack followed his own course. He chose chemistry because he loved it. Welch played hard and lived in the rowdiest fraternity house on campus, but he also studied, and he graduated with honors.

"All of my professors—many of them have died now—were my friends until the day they died," recalled Welch. "I was sort of like their child. They pushed me through . . . They just liked me, and they took care of me, boosted me."[4]

THE SECRET TO SUCCESS?
ONE WORD: PLASTICS.

After graduating from UMass with high enough grades that he was offered graduate school fellowships, Welch moved on to the University of Illinois for a Ph.D. in chemical engineering. In 1960, Welch and his young bride loaded up the new Volkswagen Beetle he got for graduation and drove off to Pittsfield, Massachusetts, where he reported to his first real job. There, at a salary of $10,500 per year, Welch was given the opportunity to create a business in a field that was just starting to have significance— plastics.

"I was lucky enough to join GE in a place where I was, like, the only employee. So I hired my first technician. I was emperor, king, prince—you pick the title, okay?" Welch not only had a chemistry lab on his hands, he had a management lab. "We started a pilot plant, and when we got a little more money, we hired two, and three, and then four. So it was a rare break—starting with a piece of chemistry and saying, 'Go make something out of this, Jack.' "[5]

Dennis Dammerman, GE vice chairman, said that when he and Welch began their careers at GE, most of the young executives were reminded incessantly that they were "stewards" of whatever department, division, business, or product line they ran. "We were entrusted with relics, sometimes Edisonian relics, on a velvet pillow. Growth and activity were fine, but stability and risk-avoidance were paramount. The ancient physician admonition applied: 'Above all, do no harm.' "

Dammerman said GE employees often talked about the company as a giant supertanker that needed miles and miles of water to turn once the wheel was spun. It was an oft-repeated analogy that implied stately ponderousness. But, he continued, the plastics division wasn't burdened with a past. "Welch and his team in the embryonic plastics business in the sixties and early seventies were regarded as wild men and bomb throwers. They felt no mandate to be 'stewards' of anything, because they hadn't been given anything to be stewards of."[6]

Thanks to a flair both for technical details and for marketing, Welch rose to be head of the plastics division. As had happened when he was a boy playing baseball at the sandpit near his home, Welch found himself on a team, and he was the chosen leader. By age 37, Welch became a group executive for the $1.5 billion components and materials group. This included all of plastics, plus GE medical systems.

By then the management game was in his blood, and in 1981, at the age of 45, a dark horse, Welch became General Electric's youngest chief executive ever. From the start, GE-ers called Welch "someone who colored outside the lines," even a "wild man." And yet the previous CEO, Reg Jones, liked Welch. "We need entrepreneurs who are willing to take well-considered business risks— and at the same time know how to work in harmony with a larger business entity," explained Jones. "The intellectual requirements are light-years beyond the requirements of less complex organizations."[7] In a business world where most top executives lose their effectiveness in 10 years or less, Welch has been an exception, staying on the job and driving GE to loftier levels of accomplishment for 20 years.

Part of Welch's magic touch is a trait he developed as he worked his way up through the ranks. He gave employees a sense that he knows them. Even people way down inside the system relate to Welch on a personal level. Brian Nailor, a marketing manager of industrial products who attended a management session at GE's Crotonville training center, said, "He's able to get people to give more of themselves because of who he is. He lives the American dream. He wasn't born with a silver spoon in his mouth. He got himself out of the pile. He didn't just show up."[8]

THE COMPANY HE INHERITED

Welch had the unusual knack to be simultaneously a maverick and a company man. This ability can be attributed to both luck and his basic nature. The company man aspect of his life has been central to his success, since no leader functions in a vacuum. CEOs inherit corporations with both tangible and intangible assets. Some say corporate leaders should be judged on the difference between what they inherit and what they bequeath. Welch did indeed inherit an impressive canvas on which to paint.

In terms of longevity alone, the 123-year-old GE is exceptional. GE is the only one of the companies among the original 12 stocks in the Dow Jones Industrial Average that remained there on the Dow's 100th anniversary. The average life expectancy of a U.S. multinational corporation, a Fortune 500 or its equivalent, is between 40 and 50 years. At least one-third of the companies listed in the 1970 Fortune 500 had vanished by 1983—acquired, merged, or broken into pieces. Even people tend to live longer than corporations. Of the 9 million companies in the United States, about 74 percent are 25 years old or less. Only 2.5 percent are more than 75 years old. GE is in a class with such ancient and influential Japanese conglomerates as Matsushita and Sumitomo, the European corporations Unilever and Nestlé, and deeply rooted American giants DuPont and the Coca-Cola Company.

Since its inception, GE has endured 20 American presidents, 25 recessions, the Great Depression, six wars, and countless changes to the tax code. During that same time, GE was awarded more patents than any other company in the United States, and expanded its business operations to more than 100 countries.[9]

Though the company traces its roots back to 1878, the General Electric we know today was founded by a consolidation of Thomson-Houston and Edison General Electric in 1892. GE counts among its forefathers Thomas Alva Edison, perhaps the most prolific and world-changing inventor of all time. He was the holder of more than 1,300 patents; his creations include the light-bulb, the phonograph, and the motion picture camera. Edison's impact on the twentieth century and the way we live even now is profound. Although Edison is the best-known name in GE's history, the inventor Charles P. Steinmetz is credited with building America's first major industrial research lab. Steinmetz started GE's lab in a carriage house in 1900, but within 15 years the lab had 300 researchers and was churning out innovations in X-ray equipment, radio, lighting, and more. Steinmetz's research facilities soon came to be called the House of Magic.

THE GE VALUES

Not only has GE been a pioneer in one of the most revolutionary eras of human history—the application of electrical energy to everything from lighting up the night to traveling long distances to looking inside the body to diagnose disease—GE was innovative in the creation of the modern corporation and the contemporary workplace. *Forbes* magazine reported in 1929 that "General Electric is the latest large American enterprise to grant all classes of workers vacations with pay. This news should interest many executives. Few corporations are more progressive or better managed than General Electric. Briefly, all classes of the company's

75,000 wage-earners are to be given a week's vacation after three years' service, an arrangement which will include 75 percent of the workers."[10]

Not only was GE well managed; the company Jack Welch inherited was, at least financially, one of the strongest in America. With a triple-A debt rating, $2.2 billion in cash and marketable securities, and a 19.5 percent return on equity, it sat on solid bedrock. Furthermore, GE's core ideologies were firmly in place. These often articulated values include:

* Improving the quality of life through technology and innovation
* Interdependent balance between responsibility to customers, employees, society, and shareholders, with no clear hierarchy
* Individual responsibility and opportunity
* Honesty and integrity[11]

Just because a company has values, however, doesn't mean the company or its employees don't stray from the values, either accidentally or intentionally. GE has been accused of being a major polluter, dumping both chemicals and radiation into the environment; of abusing antitrust laws; of unethical business practices both at home and abroad; and, especially under Welch's leadership, of treating longtime employees badly for the sake of higher profits. One of the main complaints about GE is simply that it is so large that it overwhelms many of the people, governments or other companies it encounters.

"GE, of course, is a very different company than when it was founded," said Trinity College professor Gerald Gunderson. "It came about in the last part of the nineteenth century, when the unifying theme was coming together around some element of science. Union Carbide, U.S. Steel, and the railroads are examples of such companies. In GE's case the science was electricity. That meant the company always had to have a divisional structure. You had a lot of difference between people in lightbulbs and people in transformers, because each draws on electrical theory or knowledge, but each requires special applications. So the company was naturally structured to move into the modern era. That said, an awful lot of things could have happened differently. GE has carried on. It has a shrinking base in electrical products compared to the total. Now it is big in financing, jet engines, and so forth. It made a transition. Others haven't done as well."

SEEING THE NEED FOR CHANGE

But the 1980s, when Welch took charge, also were times of technological change, economic stress, and challenges from outside the United States. Many old-line companies were slipping down. GE prior to Welch had the goal of simply growing a little faster than the economy as a whole, which was less than inspiring. When Welch became CEO in 1981, GE's outgoing chairman Reg Jones was voted the best CEO by his peers among the Fortune 500 companies, and GE was voted the best-managed company. Nevertheless, Welch saw that the company, indeed the entire nation, could and should be better, and must be better to maintain its momentum in the last two decades of the century and to propel itself into the twenty-first.

On the December day when his promotion was announced, the U.S. prime rate rose to 21.5 percent; the economy was slowly coming out of one recession and was about to drop into another; the Dow Jones Industrial Average was at 937, a level it first reached 15 years earlier. Stocks had just experienced their worst decade since the 1930s. GE's own stock had lost half its value over the previous 10 years.

Not just at GE, but everywhere in America, old management

ideas were clearly worn out. Technology was on the move; Europe and Asia had recovered from the cataclysm of World War II, and the United States itself was ready to recover from the Vietnam War. Japan was sweeping the world with its commitment to quality, and W. Edwards Deming was calling attention to the U.S. deficits in that particular realm.

"We were dealing with Asian threats across every business," explained Welch. "It was a reminder that we'd better get a lot better, faster. So I guess my message in our company was, 'The game is going to change, and change drastically.' And we had to get a plan, a program together, to deal with a decade that was totally different."[12]

THE COMPANY HE RUNS

Welch set out on a mission to see GE become the world's most valuable company, and he achieved that goal. In 1997, GE became the first company in the world to exceed $200 billion in stock market value. With a share price that rose an average of 23.5 percent per year, by 2000 GE's market value exceeded $500 billion. With the Honeywell merger, GE's market capitalization is expected to rise to at least $520 billion. GE and Microsoft often trade places as the corporation with the highest market value. The Honeywell acquisition, finally and firmly, put GE ahead of Microsoft. These two archetypal U.S. companies juggled back and forth in the top slot, and when taken together, their impact on the economy is incredible.

In the first three months of 1998, the rise in share prices of Microsoft and General Electric created more wealth than was added by the entire growth in the nation's output of goods and services. The stock market value of Microsoft and GE together rose $102 billion, beating an estimated $92 billion increase in the country's annual gross domestic product. This of course could mean several things: Perhaps GE's and Microsoft's share prices were overvalued; maybe their growth was just a spurt, making up for (or to be evened out later) by underperformance. It could mean other producers in the U.S. economy were lagging very badly, and the country's weight was being carried by two extraordinary companies. Late 2000 brought a stock market correction indicating that the prices of many stocks were too high, but the correction notwithstanding, GE has been a stellar investment.

NO WONDER INVESTORS LIKE WELCH

If you bought $10,000 worth of General Electric shares in March 1981—when Welch was elevated to chief executive—never sold, and reinvested your dividends each quarter, your stake would have been worth more than $640,000 at the end of 1999. (During that time, there were four two-for-one stock splits.)

Berkshire Hathaway chairman Warren Buffett often laments that it has become increasingly difficult for Berkshire's stock price to beat the market as the company grows. Yet Welch has bested the S&P 500 index in most of the past 30 years. For the period between March 31, 1981, and December 31, 1999, GE beat the S&P 500 index by a factor of 1.4 times. For the most recent three years of that period, the factor was 1.8.[13]

General Electric's underlying numbers seem to justify its share price. By 1999, GE was the ninth largest and second most profitable company in the world. Since Welch took over in 1981, GE sales rose more than sixfold (from $27.2 billion to $173.22 billion); profits also grew more than six times (from $1.6 billion to $10.72 billion). Measured by sales, it is second in the nation after Exxon Mobil. In terms of profits, GE also is second only to Hutchison Whampoa.

Welch agrees with Buffett that size is a burden unless you make it work for you by using the size for leverage, and that is exactly what he has done.

"The two greatest corporate leaders of this century are Alfred Sloan of General Motors and Jack Welch of GE," says Noel Tichy, a longtime GE observer and University of Michigan management professor. "And Welch would be the greater of the two because he set a new, contemporary paradigm for the corporation that is the model for the twenty-first century."[14]

THE WAY WELCH RUNS GE

The Canadian magazine *Maclean's* reported that in addition to being the most admired corporate leader in the world, "He is also, by near-universal agreement, a tough and foulmouthed SOB," who conducts meetings so aggressively, using criticism and demeaning ridicule, that people tremble.[15] This description leans toward the truth, but is somewhat extreme. Welch is direct, plainspoken, and decisive, and does not suffer fools gladly. He demands a lot from GE employees and, in doing so, does not use words as if he were in church school on Sunday. He would never have been able to change GE as much as he did without a forceful personality. And yet, say the people closest to him, he listens to others and he is consistent and fair.

Certainly Welch can be impatient. Tom Peters recalls hearing a story about when Welch asked some purchasing people to work on some tasks. "Weeks later, he met with them to review their progress. To his dismay, they had none to report, only weighty analyses and half completed efforts at coordinating with various departments. Welch was furious. He called the meeting to an abrupt halt, then ordered it reconvened only four hours later. The agenda? To report on progress. He got it, too. More was done in those four hours than had been done in several weeks preceding them."[16]

Even with acknowledgment of Welch's strong spirit, there are differing ideas as to what accounts for his success. Writers at *Forbes* say that the secret to Welch's accomplishments is not a series of brilliant insights or bold gambles, but rather fanatical attention to detail.[17] Some say his greatest talent is matching technologies to markets; others say it is that of a change agent. Most agree he truly Americanized GE—bringing the democratic process, the voice of the ordinary worker, into the corporate arena—while at the same time pushing GE into global leadership.

Management experts say Welch's reputation as a leader can be attributed to four key qualities:

1. He is a skillful, intuitive portfolio strategist.
2. He's willing to change the rules if necessary.
3. He's highly competitive.
4. He is a great communicator and motivator.

The Strategist

As a portfolio strategist, Welch knows what he likes and doesn't like. He is focused and analytical, but after his homework is done he trusts his instincts. He demonstrated this skill immediately after becoming CEO by restructuring GE from 350 businesses down to two dozen core activities, and either expanding internally or making acquisitions to position all GE's businesses as either number one or number two in their fields. The last-minute, high-intensity Honeywell acquisition was Welch's last and largest strategic strike, and it is one that will be redefining GE for years to come.

Seizing the Opportunity to Change

The Honeywell acquisition and Welch's postponed retirement are examples of how boldly and swiftly Welch can readjust course, but his attitude toward change goes deeper than any specific event. It is a philosophy. When Welch instructs his managers to "hate bureau-cracy and all the nonsense that comes with it,"[18] he is shifting from top-down to outside-in orientation. He is saying, basically, let ex-ternal demands, not internal management, guide your productive behavior. That makes intuitive sense to workers. They don't need to commission a management study to confirm what he says.

Running a Business Like a Feisty Little Hockey Player

Nothing has demonstrated Welch's competitive nature as clearly as the day he realized that one of GE's major competitors, United Technology Corporation, was about to acquire Honeywell, giving UTC control over some of the most advanced and forward-thinking technology in the aviation industry. Welch's reaction was swift and effective. From the start of his career until the Honeywell incident, Welch injected his own competitive nature into GE's very fiber. He set painfully high standards for huge growth margins, market leadership, and near-flawless quality for his divisions, stan-dards he calls stretch goals because they require employees to reach as high as possible—but he also expects the standards to be met and maintained. While there is no doubt about who is in charge at GE, the nature of Welch's leadership is flexible and constantly adapting. Rather than planning and controlling the operations of GE divi-sions from corporate headquarters, Welch sets performance targets and lets each business unit run itself. He exudes faith in his employ-ees, but as one NBC worker explained, he also instills a little fear. "When the chairman speaks, you'd better listen."

Even though he puts a touch of tyranny into his leadership, Welch has transformed himself into the most influential manager of the century. Beyond a CEO, he is seen as a management role model, an oracle, an icon for those people who hope to ascend to the mountaintop of management.

The Masterful Communicator

Welch became a teacher, a guru, within GE by actually stepping into the classroom. At Crotonville, GE's acclaimed management academy, Welch has led more than 250 class sessions in his two decades as chairman, engaging more than 15,000 GE managers and executives in a dynamic dialogue about the company, its functions, and its future. Welch's hell-bent-for-leather sessions sometimes last up to four hours.

Even so, communicating to large numbers of people was something Welch had to learn. Welch says that he was five years into his term as CEO when he realized that his message wasn't getting across to the entire company and he wasn't always as convincing as he hoped to be.

"I was intellectualizing the issues with a couple of hundred people at the top of the company, but clearly I wasn't reaching hundreds of thousands of people," he recalled.[19]

The company's powerful in-house communications machine does its part. After Jack Welch gave a rousing leadership speech at GE's January management meeting in Boca Raton, Florida, the next day 750 video copies of the speech were dispatched to GE locations around the world. The tapes were prepared in eight different languages, including Mandarin and Hungarian.[20]

Many people have tried to condense the Welch philosophy into bullet points, and Welch himself likes to use simple concepts to sell big ideas. They almost always distill to the following concepts:

* Face reality, but don't be afraid to envision big results.
* Be forthright and candid with everyone.
* Lead rather than manage.
* Change before you are forced to do so.
* If you don't have a competitive advantage, get out of the game.
* Control your own destiny, or someone else will.

"For me," explained Welch, "good communication is simply everyone having the same set of facts. When everyone has the same facts, they can get involved in shaping the plans for their components. At the Corporate Executive Council, everyone in the room sees the entire company and can draw his or her own conclusions about its performance, its environment, where it's going for the next 90 days, where it's going for the next two years, and where the vulnerabilities are, where the strengths are."[21]

IS WELCH A GE AVATAR?

As some see it, Welch wasn't entirely in control of his own destiny once he started up the management ladder at GE. He soon became an avatar, the embodiment of the GE ideal, a reincarnation of previous GE leadership, simply adapted to his own time and conditions. Welch was the eighth chairman of GE and the youngest GE chief executive in the company's history, but he wasn't an anomaly. Each of the previous eight GE chairmen captured the spirit of his own era. Gerald Swope, Ralph Cordiner, Fred Borch, and Reg Jones have been legends, although perhaps not to the extent that Welch has been. Collins and Porrras insist Welch did not inherit a grossly mismanaged company, that in fact the opposite was true. The challenge for Welch was to spot trouble before it occurred, to take preventive measures, and to make the most of GE's tremendous momentum.

Welch was a Yankee revolutionary; but, once again, he wasn't GE's first revolutionary. In 1913, GE hired Owen D. Young, a reputable lawyer, to help protect the company from government Sherman Antitrust Act probes that had started in 1911. When he reported for work at the company, Young was amazed by the potential he saw there. He lived in a world mostly lit by kerosene lantern and moved by hydro and animal power. "Electricity was then a new art and the notion that great machines could move without belt or other visible ties opened my eyes and mouth with wonder."[22]

Young quickly learned the business, and when GE purchased the Wireless Telegraph and Signal Company Ltd. and renamed it the Radio Corporation of America, Young became RCA's first chairman. There he supervised David Sarnoff, a daring thinker in the radio and television industry. Young first became chairman of GE in 1922, with Gerald Swope serving as president. Young served as chairman until 1940, and then briefly again between 1942 and 1945. Young and Swope believed that electrifying the home was the key to GE's future success. Demand for household goods would grow dramatically when they were cheap and reliable, and in turn, use of electricity would expand. Young was the first person to reinvent and reengineer GE, and he did it 70 years before the terms became catchwords in the business vocabulary. He was hailed as a new breed of manager—a scientific one.

To the public, Young pledged "either a better product at the old price or the same product at a lower price." To employees he promised, "We must aim to make the earning power of human beings so large as to supply them not only with a living wage, but a cultural wage."[23] In other words, the company's wealth would be shared so that everyone could have the opportunity to develop their intellect and enjoy life more. Young had grown up poor on a farm, and he didn't wish poverty on anyone. The shareholders didn't necessarily like Young's attitude, but he, like Henry Ford, realized that satisfied workers were not only more productive workers they were consumers of GE's products. Young also understood business cycles, though the concept did not enter the lexicon until 1919. His president, Swope, introduced the concept of "enlightened management."

Other GE change agents were Fred Borch and Ralph Cordiner. Cordiner (1950 to 1963) pushed GE into a vast array of new industries. He restructured and decentralized the company and created Crotonville, GE's famous management training and indoctrination center. Fred Borch (1964 to 1972) took GE into many new bold, risky ventures such as jet aircraft engines and computers.

"Borch let a thousand flowers bloom," observed Welch. "He got us into modular housing and entertainment businesses, nurtured GE Credit through its infancy, embarked on ventures in Europe, and left Aircraft Engines and Plastics alone so they could really get started. It became evident after he stepped down that GE had once again established a foothold into some businesses with a future."[24]

IMPECCABLE TIMING

What makes Welch seem different, argue some observers, was propitious timing. Not only did Welch come aboard at such a low point in the economy that any recovery would be hailed as heroic, he became GE's CEO at a time when the importance of business to the American culture was ascending. He has benefitted from two great eras of prosperity, that which occurred late in Reagan's first term and stretched through his second, and the long Clinton-era prosperity. While it could be said that Welch was able to take advantage of these economic windfalls, it equally can be argued that GE contributed to them as well, since as a single company it represents more than 1 percent of the U.S. gross domestic product.

Allan Sloan, a *Newsweek* business columnist who describes his journalistic role as that of "a skunk at the garden party," is one who makes that claim. Sloan concedes that Welch is very, very, very good at what he does, but that to some extent, Welch's success can be credited to the superior economic times in which he has served. The economy was dead in the water and interest rates were above 20 percent when Welch took over GE. Even so, GE's stock price rose from $4^{3}/_{16}$ (adjusted for four stock splits) on March 31, 1981, the day before he took over, to $133.75 in November 1999. That's a 3,200 percent increase, more than triple the Standard & Poor's 500 900 percent rise during the same period. GE stock rose 20.5 percent per year, compounded, compared with 13.2 percent for the S&P.

As the economy continued to expand at a healthy rate and as Welch gained experience and saw his programs mature, the results got better and better. The average total return on GE shares since 1980 has been about 27 percent, and as the years passed the return grew. The total return for 1999 alone was 54 percent.[25]

Financial writer Alan Abelson, a columnist for *Barron's* and other publications, cast himself as a second skunk at the garden party. He agrees that Welch's stature and skills are indisputable, but that to some extent, GE has cleverly managed earnings so as to make them smooth and predictable, something that gives investors confidence. GE has reported 100 consecutive quarters of increased earnings from continuing operations, a pattern that is extremely rare in the business world. An example of how earnings can be manipulated, says Abelson, is right there in GE's annual report, although it is buried in fine print. The footnotes in GE's annual reports show that in 1997, pension fund income contributed $331 million to GE's total earnings of $8.2 billion. In 1998, pension income accounted for $1.01 billion of the company's total earnings of $9.3 billion, when the money's leverage value is taken into consideration. If pension fund earnings were subtracted from GE's total, earnings growth would be about 5.1 percent, versus the reported 13 percent. Abelson then uses a multiple of 25, which was the going rate for the Dow Jones Industrial Average at the time, to estimate how much of a boost GE's stock price was getting from the addition of retirement fund income to total earnings.

"By this reckoning, the $685 million more in pension-plan income GE took into earnings last year than it did in 1997 added a tidy $179 billion to its market capitalization. Man, that's leveraging to a fare-thee-well!" wrote Abelson.[26]

There are other ways to measure performance besides increase in share price or growth in earnings. Using pretax return on equity (ROE) as a benchmark of financial performance, it becomes evident that Welch's predecessors performed as well as Welch did in his first 10 years. From 1915 to 1980, ROE was 28.29 percent. For his first decade, Welch's ROE was 26.29 percent.[27] Among his fellow GE CEOs, Welch ranked fifth out of seven. ROE isn't a completely objective yardstick, however, since it doesn't take into account recessions, depressions, wars, and so forth.[28]

But still, however GE's performance is measured, Welch had to play his cards just right to maintain and improve GE's overall position, and he did so. Professor Joseph Bower of the Harvard Business School believes that "GE is thoughtful and innovative in the way it approaches managing a company. In that sense GE must have shaped Jack Welch. Now Welch then shapes GE, because he did so much with his inheritance that he made it radically different in many ways."

AN AGENT OF CHANGE

A superior CEO like Welch has been compared to sports legends. Like a Michael Jordan, a Tiger Woods, or a Florence Griffith Joyner, not only does he win, he changes the way the game is played. Although there are divergent opinions on the specific key to Welch's success, it is widely agreed that he rewrote GE's playbook in several ways: First, Welch conquered the company's diversity, making it a strategic asset rather than a liability. Additionally, he made bureaucratic GE quick-thinking and entrepreneurial by accelerating all of its activities to warp speed. Finally, capitalizing on GE's fraternal nature, Welch got his managers to feel like business was a game and they were headed for the Super Bowl. *Forbes* magazine explained, "His greatest achievement is that having seen [what needed to be done], he faced up to the huge, painful changes it demanded, and made them faster and more emphatically than anyone else in business."[29]

Welch has characteristics in common with other business leaders as well. Like CNN founder Ted Turner, he wanted his company always to be a contender. Like Microsoft founder Bill Gates, Welch has been keenly in touch with the future. Like Berkshire Hathaway's Warren Buffett, he shared his ideas with anyone who would listen, and plenty of people did.

The British magazine *The Economist* concurred that Welch's greatest accomplishment was getting GE to confront three big external shocks: globalization, the move from manufacturing to services, and the Internet. These were big challenges, requiring vision, energy, and time. The first two accomplishments—globalization and the shift to services—are well worth exploring, and we will do so in the chapters ahead. Welch's role in the third—integration with the Internet—may be more perception than reality, an issue that will be discussed in the third section of this book. It will become evident that Welch succeeded because he was the right person to lead the company at the time. He indeed took charge of GE during an era when the economy was in crisis, the automobile industry was being redefined by the Japanese, conglomerates like GE were out of favor, and business leaders were responding miserably to a number of threats. Welch applied a group of expansive, positive ideas to the unique challenges of the time.

Not everyone is convinced that the company was completely transformed by Welch, or rather just highly groomed so that it could continue to maintain its prodigious heritage. And yet, "Welch's GE," claims Victor Vroom, a professor at the Yale School of Organization and Management, "is a model for the promise—and the problems—of creating the modern industrial company."[30]

chapter two

The Gospel of Good Management

In life there are simplifiers and complicators. The simplifiers have a great advantage.
> Professor Joseph Bower, Harvard Business School

If you are thinking one year ahead, you plant rice. If you are thinking twenty years ahead, you plant trees. If you are thinking a hundred years ahead, you educate people.
> Chinese Proverb

CROTONVILLE SITS HIGH ABOVE THE HUDSON
River on a woodsy, well-groomed 52-acre estate. Deer and other
wildlife meander on the former farm just north of Tarrytown, New
York. On a clear day, New York City's World Trade Center glimmers
on the horizon, some 30 miles away. The exterior of General Electric's Management Development Institute bespeaks the gentility of
an understated but pricey camp for adults. Vases bursting with fresh
flowers, and bowls brimming with grapes, plums, apples, and bananas
grace the tables in every building. Coffee bars are scattered strategically and the java is constantly refreshed. Every restroom has a bottle
of mouthwash and stacks of tiny disposable cups. It seems so relaxed.
Inside the classroom building, however, it's a different matter. The
halls are quiet because students are spending long, intense hours in
seminars, huddled over textbooks, spreadsheets, and computers. In
Crotonville's famous "pit" there is more of a commotion as senior
management and the company's younger upstarts noisily and aggressively debate issues facing their company.

Throughout its life General Electric has been known for initiating or adopting the latest management concepts. GE embraced
management by objectives, decentralization, and the notion of employee empowerment at very early stages. In 1956, the company
published and distributed to all of its managers a two-volume
work entitled *Some Classic Contributions to Professional Managing*.
The volumes contained 36 papers representing the most significant leadership principles up to that time. The books were intended to spread powerful management ideas throughout GE—a
company where doing business in the most businesslike way possible had long been a priority.[1]

Ralph Cordiner, who served as GE's chairman in the 1950s
and under whose guidance the book was published, realized that
the company's management training needs were unique and
would continue to be so. He purchased the estate of the Hopf In-

stitute, which once had been a historic farm in Ichabod Crane country. There Cordiner built the first private corporate training center in the world. GE's Management Development Institute at Crotonville soon gained a reputation as "the Harvard of corporate America" and had many imitators, including IBM's Sands Point School and Hitachi's Management Development Institute in Japan. At Crotonville and other spin-off academies that GE has built in Europe and Asia, the company spends close to $100 million a year training employees. Those same employees also get plenty of high-quality on-the-job training.

"GE is the greatest leadership school in the world," said Michael Allen, a former GE strategist who now runs his own corporate strategy consulting firm. "I would say Jack's legacy has been that he's used that system to build a five-star management team. GE exports managers to other corporations. It did 25 years ago and Welch is still doing it. The vultures are swarming around those who might not get the top jobs, or juicy jobs, in the next transition."

LET THE REVOLUTION ROLL AT CROTONVILLE

Almost immediately after Welch became chairman he went to work expanding Crotonville's contribution to GE life, lifting it above its function as a training facility. The school evolved into a cauldron of change, was enlivened as a corporation-wide nerve system where big, broad ideas are expressed and sent flying out to all the organs and limbs of the company. It became a brew pot for the new culture that would permeate the company. Students who spend a week or longer at Crotonville take their experiences back to businesses of vastly diverse natures—businesses that are scattered in more than 100 countries worldwide. When Welch pushed for a speed and pitch of change that virtually pulled GE apart at the seams, Crotonville, he said, was the glue that held everything together. Right from the outset Welch declared, "I want a revolution, and I want it to start at Crotonville."[2]

Welch continued to emphasize the central role of Crotonville and push for innovative management right up to the time he named his successor. At the year 2000 annual meeting, Welch reminded the audience that his management ideas were based on the principle of realism, seeing the world the way it is, not the way we hope it will be or wish it to be: "Seeing reality for GE in the '80s meant a hard look at a century-old portfolio of business, insisting that every business at GE be number one or number two in their global markets or that they must be fixed, sold or closed. Taking action on this number one or number two reality brought us to where we are today: the owners of the most exciting and powerful array of global businesses in the world. Seeing reality today means accepting the fact that e-business is here. It's not coming. It's not a thing of the future. It's here." Welch challenged GE workers to transform the existing business practices into a digital format and to do it pronto. "Any company—old or new—that does not see this technology as literally as important as breathing could be on its last breath."[3]

Though the challenge was fresh, Welch said the goal at GE was the same as it had been for years "The number one thing we're trying to achieve is to create and nourish a high-performing team. That's what leadership is. It isn't someone on a horse commanding the troops. It's the ability to succeed through other people's successes," he explained.[4]

THE GREATEST ROLE IS THAT OF A TEACHER

For generations GE has been known for its powerful and progressive chief executives, but Welch expanded the job, becoming a celebrity spiritual guide through the dark and difficult canals of the modern business world. Welch has made himself the Socrates of commerce, a teacher who asks deep questions then challenges the answers until the student gets it right. Half a dozen books have been published explaining Welch's management approach and principles. Slogans and catchphrases like "Get better or get beaten," best practices, stretch goals, and smart bomb marketing (it zeros right in on a specific target) are linked to his name. Welch popularized the concept of "work-out," where employee teams get together and solve problems. He preached simplicity: "At GE, we're driving to be lean and agile, to move faster, to pare away bureaucracy. We're subjecting every activity, every function, to the most rigorous review, distinguishing between those things which we absolutely need to do and know versus those which would be merely nice to know."[5]

Welch spoke passionately of "bullet train change" and the necessity of speed. "Speed is everything. It is the indispensable ingredient in competitiveness. Speed keeps businesses—and people—young. It's addictive, and it's a profoundly American taste we need to cultivate."[6]

Though Welch does not write about management and seldom lectures except at Crotonville, books, newspapers, and magazine articles on business and management quote Welch right along with contemporary gurus the likes of Peter Drucker, Stephen Covey, Tom Peters, and Ken Blanchard. Welch's annual message to shareholders and his speeches at GE's annual meeting are studied for guiding principles and for new ideas.

Professor Joseph Bower of Harvard said the key to Welch's popularity has been his plain but powerful rhetoric. "He was able to explain what he was doing, both inside and outside the company." Bower noted that Welch's predecessor, Reg Jones, began implementing the "portfolio" way of thinking, emphasizing the importance of market share, relative market position, and cash flow. He turned out thick books on the importance of getting out of businesses in which GE was not willing to invest at a rate that would allow the company to win big. "What does No. 1 or No. 2 mean?" asked Bower. "Exactly the same thing. The only difference is, 200,000 people can understand it."

Dr. Steve Kerr, a former professor at the University of Southern California and the dean of Crotonville, said that although it would have been a waste of his time, Welch would be a great professor.[7]

THE POWER OF ORDINARY PEOPLE

One of the marks of a great leader is the ability to recognize talent. Great leaders assemble a team, and then supply both a vision of what is possible and a genuine sense of urgency about getting things done. This has the effect of galvanizing the talent and creativity of large groups of people. GE has had a reputation for selecting a particular type of talent, mostly avoiding Ivy Leaguers for top graduates of lesser schools or the armed forces, whom it picks more for their confidence, competitiveness, and dedication to hard work than their exam results.

"It is a terrible mistake to think of creativity and imagination as the exclusive province of the gifted few," explained Harry C. Stonecipher, president and CEO of the Boeing Company, in a 1998 speech. "Jack Welch does not make that mistake. He is a passionate believer in the power of ordinary people to do extraordinary things, if they are both 'liberated' and 'empowered,' to use two of his favorite words."[8]

TEMPERED IN THE JACK WELCH KILN

Welch often is described as a difficult boss with an abrasive personality. But those who get along well with Welch see his personal style as one way he decides who can cut it at GE and who cannot. One GE employee explained: "You can't even say hello to Jack without it being confrontational. If you don't want to step up to Jack toe to toe, belly to belly, and argue your point, he doesn't have any use for you."[9]

An unnamed former GE executive said that for those who understand what is going on, it's like the hockey games that absorbed Welch in his youth. "Jack will chase you around the room, throwing arguments and objections at you. Then you fight back until he lets you do what you want—and it's clear you'll do everything you can to make it work. It's a ritual. It's like signing up."[10]

THE CEOS WELCH HAS SENT OUT INTO THE WORLD

Executives from General Electric often leave the company to take choice positions elsewhere, a situation that provides something of a GE network or brotherhood throughout the business world. Often when Welch or other GE people go out to work out a deal—whether it be the sale of a GE product or the acquisition of a new company the size of Honeywell—they are dealing with a former colleague or someone who has a connection to GE. When Welch became CEO, the losers in that race fled the company to head GTE, Rubbermaid, Apollo Computers, and a company that Welch brought back into the GE fold, Radio Corporation of America (RCA). Those executives left because they were primed to direct their own companies, and it was clear they wouldn't be running GE. GE-trained executives can always find high-level jobs elsewhere. Headhunters are constantly plotting to recruit GE managers to fill slots at other companies. More GE alums have become CEOs at American corporations than alums of any other company.[11]

Larry Bossidy is perhaps the best-known GE expatriate, a man of approximately the same age and with the same amount of GE experience as Welch. Before leaving GE, Bossidy was Welch's right-hand man. Bossidy was named chief executive officer at AlliedSignal at the end of June 1991. He retired in 2000, the year AlliedSignal merged and became Honeywell. Although Honeywell encountered problems very shortly after the merger, Bossidy's performance at AlliedSignal was admired by investors. For every dollar's worth of AlliedSignal stock a shareholder held the day before he took office, the investor would have more than $10 when Bossidy retired, assuming dividends had been reinvested. That is a compound annual growth rate of about 30 percent. It is surprising to realize that this rate was not attained with a so-called growth stock or within the computer or Internet-related business sector. AlliedSignal manufactured auto parts, aerospace equipment and specialty chemicals. When Bossidy arrived, Allied's return on equity was 10.5 percent; when he left it was 28 percent. Corporate debt fell to just 30 percent of capital from 44 percent. Free cash flow grew at 44 percent a year, compounded. Operating margins tripled, with about half the increase coming from AlliedSignal's existing businesses. Though viewed as industrial companies, the former AlliedSignal and Honeywell, like GE, have used extremely sophisticated and scientific technology in much of their manufacturing businesses.

A SMALLER SUCCESS

Daniel Natarelli worked at GE for 26 years and was a contemporary of Welch's. "I'm presently running a little company I started in 1990 after my career at GE," said Natarelli. "A lot of what I'm doing here I learned at GE and from Jack Welch, the Jack Welch way of doing things."

Natarelli said that among the things he gleaned from Welch was to be decisive. GE always had a truckload of young, brilliant Ph.D.s out of impressive schools, said Natarelli, but what set Welch apart was his ability to make quick, almost instantaneous decisions, and to be right the great majority of the time.

"You could approach him anytime. Say we're at a ski resort, having a little R&R, just came down the slope and might be talking about skiing. If you bring up business in an environment like that, the guy or lady you're trying to talk to might say, 'Gee, that's a good idea, Let's talk it about it when we go back. We're doing this now; we'll do what you want to do later.' If Welch was interested he listened right there. You tell him what you want to do and how much you need to do it. If he didn't like it, he'd tell you right there. Or, he'd say, 'Do it.' Once he says that, you've got it. It used to make us laugh—he was just a young guy and he'd do that. After he gave you an approval, it was as formal and binding as any document. He'd ask you an hour later, 'How's it going?' You'd say, 'We're still at the bar.' He'd say, 'Didn't you call anyone, get them going?'"

THE GE ROLE MODEL

When Welch huddles with other corporate leaders to consider projects, he's often working with a former colleague. Such is the case with Harry Stonecipher, who started his career at GE, has been CEO of both Sundstrand and McDonnell Douglas, and is now president of Boeing. Stonecipher is so influential that some Boeing workers claim there was a reverse takeover when Boeing and McDonnell Douglas joined, with the culture of the weaker, failing McDonnell taking dominance. Stonecipher still hearkens back to what he learned at GE, as well as what he gained in stock options.

"We study GE more than anything. We want the GE culture and style to define the new culture and style of Boeing," said Stonecipher. He then took the time to thank Welch for GE's stock market performance. "I am very fond of Jack Welch. He made me a lot of money."[12]

When Stonecipher created a leadership center outside St. Louis, he modeled it after GE's Crotonville. Construction on the center was started when McDonnell was independent, but was finished after the company merged with Boeing.

SECULAR SKILLS, SOCIETY'S GAIN

Edward Morgan, who spent 20 years in corporate communications at GE and at one time was a speechwriter for Welch, left the company and became president of the Christian Herald Association, where he applied GE management principles to charitable work. Morgan, a deeply religious person, said he left his job at GE headquarters because he was increasingly restless: He had come to a point in his life where he wanted to work more with his family so that they could achieve some of their spiritual goals. After serving on the Christian Herald Association board for a while, in 1993 Morgan took full-time charge of the staff of the financially strapped nonprofit.

Among other activities, the Christian Herald operates New York's 121-year-old Bowery Mission. The Mission and its children's after-school and camp program were well regarded, but the mission work was being dragged down by two unprofitable divisions, the *Christian Herald* magazine and the Christian Herald Book Club. The magazine, a money loser for 15 years, would have required a heavy investment in cash to turn around. The book club was marginally profitable, but was outclassed by its growing, for-profit competitors who offered a similar service.

"I made the strategic decision with our board that our remaining resources would be concentrated on a 'growth market.' Unfortunately, that [growth market] is the epidemic of hurting people, broken families, women in crisis, and homelessness in America," said Morgan. "As a nonprofit, we would bring in resources to help problems, transform lives, and make a difference in our society."

Morgan moved the headquarters out of a suburban mansion and into the city, canceled the organization's ailing *Christian Herald* magazine, and discontinued the book club. With grants from the City of New York and the U.S. Justice Department and the generosity of a donor list that has ballooned from 4,000 to 30,000, the organization made major changes at the Bowery Mission, renovated its run-down homeless shelter on the Bowery, and started several new ventures, including an effective drug and alcohol rehabilitation center. After Morgan became president, annual contributions from individuals, foundations, and corporations leaped from $1.7 million to $3.9 million, more than half of the operating budget of $6.5 million.

Morgan still expresses a sense of wonder that he—someone with no experience in running a nonprofit organization, but who had worked with Welch for 20 years and watched him turn GE into something new—could take that knowledge and successfully apply it to social problems.

"The most important things I brought to the Christian Herald and the Bowery Mission were soft things; not financial management, but a tremendously valuable attitude."

He said Welch described the attributes—the three E's—exactly in the 1999 annual report. "Energy—a can-do attitude; the GE Edge—if something can't be accomplished, try a creative alternative. The edge I'm talking about is the hunger to be the best at what you do. Execution—there are a lot of idealistic dreamers out there, and here's where the techniques come in. The Six Sigma, stuff like that, are specific techniques. You can't make anything happen if you don't have the Execute."

Morgan said his goals for the Christian Herald were more difficult to achieve than he ever dreamed they would be, and it took about three times as long as he expected to accomplish them.

And yet, said Morgan, "Today I never look back. There were times when I thought it wouldn't work, but even if it didn't work, it was the right thing to do. It did work—we're now in double-digit revenue growth, a surplus position, and growing the ministry."

In 1999, the Christian Herald's mission addressed the needs of thousands of clients. The mission served 250,186 meals, provided (in aggregate) 57,743 nights of shelter, and distributed 32,020 clothing items. Additionally, 216 children participated in the after-school program, and 819 youngsters attended Christian Herald's camp.

FLOURISH OFF

Not everyone leaves GE on the positive note that Morgan did. Welch raised hackles within the company in the late 1980s when he included in a manifesto that people who didn't buy into the company's values should "flourish elsewhere." The "flourish off" statement was removed from the value statement, but it came back to roost at the 1992 corporate meeting in Boca Raton, Florida. It had been a spectacularly successful year for GE financially, and everyone was in a celebratory mood. Then Welch delivered one of his chilling reality checks:

"Look around you: There are five fewer officers here than there were last year. One was fired for the numbers, four were fired for [lack of] values."[13]

John Trani, who left GE to become the CEO of Stanley Works, made this observation: "The Welch theory is that those who do, get; those who don't, go."[14]

Gary Wendt, who built GE Capital into a financial power-house, at one time was considered a contender for the GE throne, but he and Welch never seemed to get along. There was specula-tion that Welch was unhappy that Wendt had built GE Capital into his private empire, but because the financial services business was such a success, Welch was reluctant to let him go. Wendt is said to be the only man to have shouted back at Welch in public.

Wendt once said of Welch, "He's very difficult on me, I find."[15]

Strategy consultant Michael Allen figures that Wendt, in his 20 years at GE Capital, outperformed M. R. (Hank) Greenberg at American International Group (AIG), the highest-performing fi-nancial group ever. "If we could break GE Capital out of GE, we probably would find that Wendt created more at GE, in terms of earnings growth and share price growth."

Wendt became involved in a messy, nationally publicized di-vorce when his wife of 31 years, Lorna Jorgenson, said she was entitled to half the couple's assets as compensation for her duties as a corporate wife. A judge ordered Wendt to pay her $20 mil-lion. Shortly after that Wendt left GE and became chief executive at Conseco, an insurance company that was in trouble because of unmanageable investments in the managed medical care business. Conseco is a large company with a book value of $5.4 billion and $98.6 billion under management. Welch has shown that his man-agement principles can take a healthy company and improve on it. Wendt will have the chance to prove whether GE's manage-ment skills can rescue and revive an ailing company.

Glen Hiner, who now heads the problem-plagued Owens Corning, was among the executives who left GE under something of a cloud. Once seen as one of GE's brightest lights, Hiner's career seemed less golden after he headed up the ill-fated acquisition of Borg-Warner's chemical division, which is described in Chapter 4. Since leaving GE, Hiner has become something of a specialist in troubled companies. The fundamentally healthy Owens Corning was forced to file for Chapter 11 bankruptcy in the fall of 2000 to meet a $1.2 billion legal settlement related to the decades-old disastrous use of asbestos in building construction material.

THE BROTHERHOOD

Whatever the circumstances surrounding a departure from the company, training at GE puts shine on a resume and makes a manager part of a fraternity whose members keep in touch and network long after leaving GE. John Trani appointed John D. Opie, former GE vice chairman of the board and executive officer, to Stanley Works' board of directors. Even a partial list of GE alums is impressive. In addition to those already mentioned there are:

* Joaquim Agut—executive chairman of Terra Networks, SA.
* Kaj Ahlman—vice chairman of E. W. Blanch.
* Bruce Albertson—president and CEO of Iomega.
* William A. Anders—former CEO of General Dynamics, where he took the company apart but in three years achieved a cumulative total return of 175.5 percent.
* Stephen Bennett—president and CEO of Intuit.
* James G. Berges—president of Emerson Electric Co.
* Norman Blake—has run both Heller Corp. and U.S. Fidelity and Guaranty (USF&G), an insurance company that later merged with St. Paul Companies.
* John B. Blystone—CEO of SPX Corp., where in four years he posted a 647 percent stock gain.

* Mark P. Bulriss—CEO of Great Lakes Chemical.
* Robert Collins—chairman of Scott Technologies.
* David Cote—chairman of TRW.
* Judy B. Curry—vice president and controller of Tupperware.
* Genaro Diaz—chief operating officer, Mercantil.com, Latin America's largest business-to-business portal.
* Paolo Fresco—chairman of Fiat SpA.
* Warren Jensen—CFO of Amazon.com.
* Kevin McMullen—chief executive officer of Omnova Solutions Inc.
* Daniel Natarelli—in 1990 founded his own company, Specialty Silicone Products Inc.
* Jim Rogers—chairman of Alliant Exchange Inc., a food-service company.
* Tom Rogers—chairman and CEO of Primedia.
* Paula Skokowski —vice president of marketing at the computer voice application service General Magic.
* Thomas C. Tiller—CEO, Polaris Industries.
* John Weber—president of Vickers Inc., a company that makes hydraulic pumps, motors, cylinders, and other equipment.
* Dennis Williams—president and chairman of IDEX Corp.

SOME TRACK RECORDS AREN'T SO HOT

At times, the company that lures someone away from GE is disappointed due to expectations that are too high. "Stars at GE often fail in their first job outside," said Phil DeCocco, a former GE human resources executive now running Sturges House Inc., a consulting firm in Westport, Connecticut. The former GE executives, said DeCocco, "don't realize how good they had it and how well-oiled a business machine GE is."[16] It takes a little time and mental adjustment before they are able to apply their skills in a different environment. As a result, some recruiters hire former GE executives only for their second job away from GE, where they tend to do better, at least most of the time.

Some of the best-known GE alums fail to measure up, especially when it comes to GE's specialty—total return to shareholders. In the three years he has been at Stanley Works, Trani has delivered a *minus* 14.2 cumulative total return to shareholders. Sales growth has been almost flat, though annual earnings growth at Stanley Works has come in at slightly more than 16 percent. The company says it is rebuilding, and stronger results are yet to come.[17]

In the case of Glen Hiner at Owens Corning and David Cote, a former contender for Welch's job, who now serves as chairman of TRW Inc., lower comparative performances stem from the fact that their companies had deep and abiding troubles before they came on board. The jobs they have now are nothing like their jobs at GE, which basically involved squeezing "more juice" from an already juicy "productivity lemon." Thomas Tiller, who left GE to run Polaris Industries, a maker of snowmobiles, motorcycles, and all-terrain vehicles, finds that he now works with sparser resources. Unlike a lot of other companies, GE, Tiller notes, has "infinite cash."[18]

WATCHERS FROM ABROAD

Employees come from GE facilities, and even GE customers, suppliers, and business partners come from all around the world to study at Crotonville, creating such a dissonance of time and place that the dormitories at the school have compact kitchens on each floor stocked with frozen pizzas, TV dinners, ice cream, and other foods so that students can fix themselves a meal anytime of the day or night that an empty stomach wakes them up. When Paolo

Fresco, former GE vice chairman and right-hand man to Welch, left to become president of Fiat, Welch's influence on managers in Europe became undeniable. Long before Fresco left, however, Welch had dedicated followers outside the United States.

Welch's actions have been tracked as carefully in the British, German, Japanese, Indian, and other foreign press as they have by the media in the United States.* *L'Expansion* in France acknowledged him as the most imitated business leader anywhere. "If Jack decided to start walking on his head one morning, everyone would do likewise."[19] The *Financial Times* of London asked the question that people everywhere were asking about Welch: "If his approach does work, can it outlast him?"[20]

Although Welch has influenced the thinking of many corporate managers, not all of them have been able to do things the way he did—at least not so far. Heinrich von Pierer, CEO of the German industrial company Siemens, like other German executives, has taken Welch as a role model. Siemens, for example, now strives—like GE—to be first or second in any of its lines of business, to be fast and lean. But, due to local laws, some of Welch's methods, such as mass layoffs, won't work in a German company. "I would not get very far with a nickname like 'Neutron Jack,'" conceded von Pierer.[21]

Corporate leaders in Asia face similar obstacles. "As odd as it may seem," wrote the *Wall Street Journal*, "John F. Welch Jr. strikes a deep chord in the land that invented lifetime job security; he took a conglomerate (Japan's favorite form of business) that makes big metal things (Japan's great passion), turned it around (the Japanese

---

*My earlier book on him, *Jack Welch Speaks: Wisdom from the World's Greatest Business Leader* (John Wiley & Sons, 1998), thus far has been translated from English into the Chinese, Indonesian, Japanese, Korean, Swedish, and Portuguese languages.

dream of the new century), and, like most Japanese chief executives, he's over 60 years old."[22]

Kichisaburo Nomura, president of All Nippon Airways Co., ad-
mires Welch, even though Nomura has not laid off thousands of
workers, sold off traditional subsidiaries, or cut costs enormously.
In fact, at the end of the 1990s his company had lost money for
eight years in a row.

But even in Japan some right-sizing has been necessary. "It's
difficult to be as drastic as [Welch]," said Sadao Kondo, 62, president of Sanyo Electric Co., which in 1999 announced it was cutting 6,000 jobs through attrition and early retirement. "But we've
turned the rudder in that direction."[23]

When asked what he thought of the adulation by the Japanese,
Welch demurred. "It's not my place to tell others how to run their
businesses. Japanese business leaders are very capable and ingenious. The last thing they need is help from Jack Welch." He
added that the teacher role in that country is particularly awk-
ward for him because he's long been a student of Japanese management techniques.[24]

VOLUNTEER MANAGEMENT

Recently General Electric has explored the ways that managers
still with the company can share their expertise with charitable
organizations through Elfun, the global organization of GE employees and retirees. Elfun—a contraction of the words "electrical
funds"—was founded in 1928 as a way for GE's top brass to make
financial investments and get together for fraternal activities. For
the first 50 years, it was an elite group and membership was considered a rite of passage into senior management at GE. Welch encouraged Elfun to make its membership more egalitarian and to
shift its focus to volunteerism. Now, 80 chapters of Elfun have

been established around the globe, with a total of 35,000 members. The chapters have done everything from sponsoring blood drives to collecting holiday toys to cleaning up beaches. The club places special emphasis on adopting schools and tutoring students in the communities where GE has operations.

About seven years after he left GE, Edward Morgan was called back to his former workplace to address a worldwide conference for GE Elfun chapters. "The manager of the Elfun invited me to come back and talk about how GE employees can transfer their skill sets to nonprofits," said Morgan. "That's a little broadening of the work of Elfun, which has been to transfer labor, give one-on-one help, work individually on community projects. They're saying, let's not just volunteer, clean up the beach. Let's take GE skills and culture and transfer them to nonprofits where it might be a help."

THREE PRIORITIES

Jack Welch takes personal responsibility for three business processes at GE: sharing knowledge, allocating resources, and developing the talents and skills of people who work for GE. Considering how Welch focuses his time, it is no mystery why GE has such powerful managers under its roof and that they are in demand around the world. The most important chief executive Welch will have trained is Jeffrey Immelt, the man who is to replace him as the head of General Electric, but more about that in future chapters.

Part II

General Electric Then and Now

Both tears and sweat are salty, but render a different result. Tears will get you sympathy. Sweat will get you change.
Jesse Jackson

Give me a place to stand, and I will move the earth.
Archimedes

*W*hat did Jack Welch do to put General Electric in overdrive and traveling the express lane? He took the company through steps of change that the rest of the business world hadn't thought of yet. First, he restructured the company from within, routing out layers of management and reducing the employee ranks to only the absolutely necessary. He then went to work on the businesses within GE themselves, vowing to make GE either first or second in each of its ventures. He pushed the efficiency concept further by introducing the Six Sigma quality program, and finally, he committed GE to globalization and integrating the Internet into every aspect of the company, both to reduce costs and to expand markets. All the while, he used GE's amazonian cash flow to acquire companies to fill in gaps in existing sectors and to expand GE both at home and abroad.

When Welch first took charge at GE and started talking about a fast pace of change, many people wondered what he was thinking. Why uproot a company with GE's stability? "There's a whole set of phrases that are designed to wait until disaster strikes," explained Welch. "Phrases like: 'If it ain't broke, don't fix it,' or 'Don't be a solution in search of a problem,' or 'Don't break up a winning team.' We all use these over and over—a dismissal of someone trying to change something that's going just fine. But in truth, the wisdom may lie in changing the institution while it's still winning—reinvigorating a business, in fact, while it's making more money than anyone ever dreamed it could make.[1]

Welch made GE bigger than anyone dreamed it could be as he moved toward globalization on a grand scale. As fast as he went and as wide-ranging as GE's purchases were, Welch said his most difficult challenge was to resist sprinkling GE's money everywhere, but rather to put money on the right gambles and to put no resources into the wrong ones. The transformation of

GE has been enormous, with its $405.2 billion worth of businesses falling into the category of either services, technology, or manufacturing.

THE TRANSFORMED GENERAL ELECTRIC

"I wouldn't call GE an electric company anymore," said Gerald Gunderson, professor of American business and economic enterprise at Trinity College, Hartford, Connecticut. "They're a general company, but an electrical company? That's a misnomer. They're really equivalent to what we used to call a merchant bank, not one that works with consumers, or even an underwriter bank like Salomon Brothers, but a bank that provides tailored financial assets, leases airplanes, supplies working capital."

Indeed, when the Fortune 500 companies were being assembled for 2000, the magazine editors realized that GE—for the first time ever—got more revenues from financial services (51 percent) than from electrical equipment (43 percent). Its own rules required *Fortune* to classify the conglomerate as a financial services company. "When CEO Jack Welch heard about the change, he attempted, through a series of e-mails and phone calls, to persuade us to retain GE's classification as an electrical-equipment maker." He didn't get his wish.[2]

Gunderson said that without question, Welch has created a company that is innovative in its structure. "They've done what a lot of people think of as ideal. You push responsibility down into the ranks to energize people. A lot of people say this—some do it better than others. In some cases, when you poke around in the company you see it's still a hierarchical place. GE has done a better job than most. It is the best among the large companies in sparking entrepreneurship in each of the divisions."

STUTTERING STRAIGHT TO THE MENTAL WARD

Dennis Dammerman recalls the moment when he and other GE executives first got the clue that Reg Jones's replacement would live up to his reputation as nonconformist. No sooner was Welch appointed than he spoke to his 500 general managers and asked, "How do you like having a stuttering overachiever as CEO?"[3]

It didn't sit well with some. They were used to a sedate, gentlemanly approach to business and were uncomfortable with a leader in Fairfield who seemed driven and overreaching. Someone walked into the local watering hole near corporate headquarters, called the Hi-Ho, in 1981 and overheard one of the old-timers sadly repeating into martini number two, "I'll give him two years—then it's Bellevue."[4]

Although it seemed to everyone else that Welch rushed into transforming GE on the very first day he took office, he claims he was too slow in initiating certain changes. "I took way too long to de-layer GE and take its costs down to where they had to be to get us globally competitive," says Welch. "Everybody back then was calling me Neutron Jack, but the truth was that as a guy in my mid-to-late 40s I lacked the confidence to move as decisively as I should have. I was too afraid of breaking the glass."[5]

THE GLASS SHATTERS

Nevertheless he broke a lot of glass. With few of the legal, political, or social limitations that inhibit European and Asian companies, he took drastic action. In 1981, GE had 440,000 employees worldwide. By 1993, that number had shriveled to less than half—just over 200,000 worldwide. The numbers declined even though Welch was acquiring hundreds of additional companies.

(Because of the pace of acquisitions, GE's employee level, before it took on Honeywell, stood at around 340,000.)

Few places were the layoffs more wrenching than in Schenectady, New York, the birthplace and spiritual home of GE. After Edison established his Machine Works there, the operation grew into a city within a city, covering a square mile of downtown—roads connecting factories, warehouses, a hospital, its own police and fire service. At the peak, GE had employed 29,000 people in and around Schenectady, and GE virtually defined the community. A total of 3,500 GE workers lost their jobs when the gas turbine manufacturing division was moved to South Carolina, and then the motor department and the foundry went. Nevertheless, by communicating and working with employees and the labor unions and by offering generous layoff packages, the downsizing was accomplished with minimum strife and without a labor strike.

Welch's next big chore was to crank GE itself—the corporate structure—around to make it a tight machine. Management professor Noel Tichy says Welch's greatest commandment to the GE team was to fix a unit, close it, or sell it off. If GE was not the first or second contender in a business segment, Welch expected managers to correct the situation or to cash out.[6] In his first two years as CEO, Welch spent his energy on what he called the "hardware revolution," selling companies that didn't fit and acquiring companies with the technologies that boosted the strength of the companies he would keep. Additionally, Welch put GE into some entirely new businesses.

It was the "industry leader" philosophy that dramatically changed GE's product mix and strong volume growth. Welch dumped various birthright GE businesses like small appliances and television manufacturing, concentrating instead on more profitable operations like medical equipment, turbines, and jet engines.

"To the hundreds of businesses and product lines that made up the company," explained Welch, "we applied a single criterion: Can they be number one or number two in whatever they do in the world marketplace? Of the 348 businesses or product lines that could not, we closed some and divested others. Their sale brought in almost $10 billion. We invested $18 billion in ones that remained and further strengthened them with $17 billion worth of acquisitions. What remained [in 1989], aside from a few relatively small supporting operations, are 14 world-class businesses."[7]

Next, Welch embarked on what became known as the "software revolution," grooming GE's management style to make the most of its assets. Welch has often said that there is an "endless amount of juice in the productivity lemon," and with that in mind, in the late 1990s he adopted the Six Sigma quality program. The rigorous measurement-based method of quality control was developed at Honeywell and gained favor among top executives when AlliedSignal confirmed its success.

GE had highlighted four key growth initiatives: globalization, services, Six Sigma quality control, and its latest—the Internet or e-business. In a last-year-before-retirement push for even greater efficiency and productivity, Welch announced in 1999 that GE would pursue an all-out online initiative. "Getting into Asia or out of Asia or onto the Internet aren't fundamental strategies, they're tactics to respond to change," explained Welch.[8]

SHOOTING AT THE RIGHT TARGETS

From a financial perspective, what Welch did at GE was easier to explain than it was to execute. The efficient use of capital has been a driving force, considering that the capital was applied to the acquisition of 900-plus companies at a cost of $150 billion. The last-minute Honeywell International deal added another $44 billion to the acquisition pot. "I would say our whole thrust here was to get into the right businesses, find businesses with growth, get an organization that could respond to change quickly, and get as much out of the capital we employed as we possibly could," said Welch. "We didn't understand EVA (economic value added) or MVA (market value added) or any of these other things, okay? But if you look at the Cokes and the GEs of the world, they've both gotten a lot out of their capital."[9]

MVA was devised by the New York City financial consulting firm Stern Stewart. Not only is it a measuring stick for management, many investors use it to predict a stock's future performance. To calculate a company's MVA, add up the total lifetime capital a company has gleaned from equity and debt offerings, bank loans, and retained earnings. Make further adjustments, such as capitalizing research and development (R&D) spending as an investment in future earnings and amortizing it over an appropriate time period. This number is compared to the current value of the company's stock and debt. The difference between the total market value (the amount investors can take out of the business) and investment capital (the money they put in) is MVA. A positive MVA shows wealth has been created, while a negative MVA indicates money has been depleted.

EVA is the after-tax net operating profit in any given year, minus a company's cost of capital in that year. Using this concept, a company that consistently achieves a positive EVA will see its MVA soar. A negative EVA over a long period of time drags down MVA as the market loses faith that the company will provide an acceptable return on capital.

In fact, both MVA and EVA reduce business to the long-understood basics of banking—you take money into the business at one rate, invest it for a higher rate of return, and the difference is what you put in your own bank account.

THE FLEXIBLE STRUCTURE OF GE

"Obviously, nothing is permanent," says Welch. "I sold many businesses and bought many businesses. But the concept of an operating system with social architecture that shares learning is inbred in every person that's here."[10]

The result of all this activity for a while meant a shift in GE's business mix from industrial businesses to service businesses. In 1980 the mix was 85 percent products and 15 percent services. In 2000 GE had a mix of 25 percent products and 75 percent services. By 2000, GE Capital Services alone accounted for 40 percent of its parent's income and 33 percent of its employees.[11] Welch calls this a transformation from a product company to a solutions company.[12] GE may still be a "solutions" company, but the Honeywell merger—which seemed more opportunistic than strategic—tipped GE's business mix back toward industrials.

Nevertheless, GE can be expected to continue toward an expanding service component, providing GE a bigger and more reliable income stream. For every $1 billion in turbines sold at GE Power Systems, for example, the company expects to develop services businesses with a net present value of $2 billion. The medical business recently won a $2.5 billion contract to look after all the equipment in Columbia/HCA hospitals, the United States's biggest hospital chain. Analysts claim these long-term contracts alone justify GE's high stock market premium, which sometimes runs as high as 42 times expected earnings.

Involvement in services fills another need. It is a way to bury GE so deeply into the customers that they cannot survive without it. If a power plant uses GE engines and has a GE maintenance contract to go with it, things go more smoothly, but the plant also is more dependent on the manufacturer. Competitors find that making good equipment isn't enough anymore; the equipment is so technologically advanced that customers want and need the services that go along with it.

What Welch has succeeded in doing is creating a company very like a Japanese *keiretsu*, or complementary financial, manufacturing, and trading group. A *keiretsu* is a federation of old-line Japanese companies that work together to support each other's business models. Usually the members exist as separate corporations, though they may have substantial cross-ownership through stock holdings. In Japan, *keiretsus* were a tradition that took hundreds of years to develop and mature. At the end of the twentieth century, some Japanese keiretsus began unraveling, mainly because their attention was too focused on Japan, a country with its economy in repose. The companies in Japan and other nations that fare the best are those, like GE, in global markets. The benefits of a global *keiretsu-under-one-roof* have been amplified by the Internet, which allows GE to bid on such basics as office supplies and equipment as a single unit, rather than as a bunch of separate divisions.

As shocking as the changes were when he first started making them, GE under Welch has been more evolutionary rather than revolutionary, pushing growth through trimming, grooming, and goading the giant that is GE. The company has produced fewer genuine innovations in the past two decades than it did in its early years.

TEND THE CASH COWS, LET THE DOGS RUN LOOSE

Welch collected critics along the way, and there are individuals and groups that he has never been able to win over. Management expert Tom Peters was appalled at what Welch was doing at GE, but was one of the people who changed their tune in the mid-1990s. "The chairman was spouting 'liberation,' 'small and beautiful,' and something called 'workout' in the '90s, but the '80s was his decade.

He turned his dogs into dog food (selling off the likes of Utah International) and coined (literally as well as figuratively) his Boston
Consulting Group look-alike approach: All GE businesses would
be number one, or number two, or number three in their industry,
or out they'd go. Michael Porter didn't like it. (And I wasn't that
keen on it either.) Except it worked. Good advice for the '90s.
Milk the cows, harvest the dogs, and worry not whether linguist
supreme Bill Safire pillories you for metaphorical mayhem."[13]

One of Welch's less humorous critics has been Thomas O'Boyle,
author of *At Any Cost: Jack Welch, General Electric and the Pursuit of
Profit*. Boyle says historians will "wonder why GE was hailed as
such a success, when it was unable to grow anything new, other
than financial services, and while growth in its core manufacturing
business was at best anemic. They will wonder why a company that
owed its very existence to technology lowered its research and development spending 19 percent, in real terms, in the 1990s, even
while it continued to post record profits."[14]

A STAGGERING SIZE

Although employee levels are down, assets and sales have risen at
GE. The result has been an ever-increasing trend toward largeness,
something that not only affects GE, but is affecting other companies as well. "The numbers on the size of these big companies, I
can't even imagine," said Professor Gunderson. "When you get
capitalization like GE or Cisco Systems, it's overwhelming to me.
They're huge."

But, adds Gunderson, putting on weight is a limiting factor in
the growth of any company, and GE may be no exception.
"When you're first starting up [in] a market it's easy to get massive
gains, if you have a good product that meets unmet demands. In
the early stages of a start-up, you can make huge cost reductions

resulting in diminishing costs over time. It's much easier to achieve cost reductions when you are a $100 million company than when you are a $1 billion company."

The chapters in this section will explore in greater depth what Welch did at GE, how and why he did it, and what the results have been.

chapter three

The Companies
General Electric Dumped

I do everything for a reason—most of the time the reason is money.   Suzy Parker, fashion model and actress[1]

The question is not "who is going to let me," it's "who is going to stop me?"   Ayn Rand, *The Fountainhead*

WHEN REG JONES BOUGHT UTAH INTER-
national for General Electric in 1976, the deal was celebrated as
the biggest U.S. merger ever. Jones was gone for less than two years
when his successor, crusty Jack Welch, sold Utah International, a
mining company whose primary assets were coal properties in
Queensland, Australia. Broken Hill Proprietary Company, Ltd.
(BHP), an Australian industrial and natural resources operation,
bought the coal-mining operation for $2.4 billion. It seemed a pe-
culiar thing to sell since Utah had turned a profit of $318 million
the year before it was sold, but there seemed to be trouble on the
horizon. Utah's main market, coking coal for steel mills, was depressed. One part of Utah, Ladd Petroleum, was kept within GE
because the product could be used as a reserve supply for the plastics division. Welch made good use of the proceeds, deploying
some of the Utah International cash to acquire Employers Reinsurance Corporation for $1.1 billion. This was an early clue that
Welch was giving GE a new and different focus. Welch was letting
the world know he did not intend to sell commodities such as coal
and that he had a more than passing interest in financial services.

Again, when Welch embarked on his selling spree in the
1980s, he did so with a sense of urgency. The GE workforce began to understand that Welch meant it when he said that any GE
holding that didn't have the requisite market share, and wasn't
likely to achieve it, would be sold. To Welch, hesitation carried a
punishing cost:

"U.S. business today finds itself challenged by aggressive overseas competitors. National productivity has been declining, and in
industry after industry, product leadership is moving to other nations. Companies that refuse to renew themselves, that fail to cast
off the old and embrace new technologies, could well find themselves in serious decline in the 1990s. We are determined that this
shall not happen to General Electric."[2]

The strategy to stick to businesses with a dominant market share grew out of Welch's conviction that when a market enters a down cycle, the industry leaders may suffer, but competitors who rank third or fourth are either destroyed or seriously damaged.

In the first three years Welch occupied the sprawling corner office at GE headquarters in Fairfield, Connecticut, he sold more than 100 operations, collecting for GE a cash account of $3.5 billion plus change. As the divestitures continued and the proceeds were used to expand other businesses, the new GE, one that would lick the competition in everything it did, took shape.

At least among the earliest divestitures, Welch said, "The businesses I eliminated were not simply in the red for two or three years; they had been depressed for 30 years or 50 years in the long history of GE, and their employees had consciously become underdogs."[3]

Some of the businesses GE sold actually fared well under new owners; some have not.

HOUSEHOLD APPLIANCES WERE PART OF GE'S IDENTITY

In 1982 the television show *60 Minutes* took GE to task for shutting down a 50-year-old clothes iron plant in Ontario, California, that seemed to be profitable. The year before, the plant had turned out four million metal steam irons, but GE felt that the metal product would no longer sell well and that it had to switch to plastic irons. Overhauling the Ontario facility would be too costly, so the new-model irons would be manufactured in Mexico, Brazil, and Singapore.

This was distressing news for the people of Ontario, since the plant was its major employer, and surprising to many Americans, who were just beginning to realize how many so-called home-grown products were now imported from overseas. The president of the plant's union local explained that Ontario residents had sometimes waited two or three years to be hired at the plant. "It was a job that you could have pride in. We had a product we could have pride in. A person, when they were finally able to get on in that plant, they felt that they were secure and then they could go and build a secure life for themselves. It's a hard thing. It's an emotional thing because we felt that the plant doesn't belong to General Electric. It belongs to us, the people in the community."[4]

That same year the Ontario plant was closed, GE's air-conditioning business went. Welch unloaded housewares early, at about the same time he sold Utah International. Because of the intense competition from the Japanese, in 1984 Welch sold GE's signature housewares business to Black & Decker, a company well-known for its power tools. That $300 million sale also included the consumer products business GE took possession of in 1986 when it acquired RCA. A trend was clearly unfolding, and that upset GE old-timers who valued the tradition of Edison, Steinmetz, and all the engineers who transformed the homes and especially the kitchens of the world.

"I became CFO (chief financial officer) during this period," said Dennis Dammerman, "in 1984, and I can still remember the howls when some of these family heirlooms were unceremoniously disposed of: 'How the hell could he sell the electric potato peeler business?' "[5]

Unfortunately, the electric housewares business didn't survive all that long with its new owners, either. Ten years after buying the housewares business from GE, Black & Decker repositioned itself to focus on its core products, and sold those operations that were underperforming or were peripheral to the company's mission. As a result, Black & Decker passed its household products business along to Windmere-Durable Holdings for $315 million.

THE NAMES MAY BE DECEIVING

Like the small appliance cadre, employees of the National Broadcasting Company were miffed when in the summer of 1987 Welch sold the long-treasured NBC radio network to Westwood One for $50 million. Westwood One, a Los Angeles firm that also owned the Mutual Broadcasting System, was best known for its youth-oriented music stations. The indignation was amplified by the realization that GE had allowed the valued name NBC News to go along with the network.

The dispositions continued despite the wails of despair. GE's television set manufacturing arm, which was ranked fifth, sixth, or seventh worldwide, was traded to Thomson Consumer Electronics, the U.S. division of the French company Thomson Multimedia, in return for Thomson's European medical imaging operation. Again, GE's branding was so valuable that Thomson licensed the name to allow the sets to display the GE logo. Thomson has built the consumer electronics group it received into a prospering business, although it took time. For several lean years in the television set industry, no producers made money. But Thomson stuck with it, investing $400 million into the endeavor. Thomson met success with the introduction of its Digital Satellite System, a pizza-size dish that delivers crystal-clear television signals via satellite and bypasses cable television. The dish became the fastest selling consumer electronics product in history. In 1995 Thomson introduced a "smart" VCR that skips past recorded commercials, and its introduction of R&D-based products continues.

Thomson's medical imaging operation was added to GE's

medical business, which was already ranked number one globally, and although Thomson did well with the television business, as is described in more detail in Chapter 4, GE had one
heck of a time getting the medical imaging business on a fast
and smooth track.

NO TO NUCLEAR POWER

Welch was inspired to get GE out of certain businesses not only
because of their problematic economics, but also because the businesses themselves were a thorn in GE's side. The nuclear power
and military weaponry divisions both fall into that category.

GE helped usher in the nuclear age with the development of
America's first atomic bomb during World War II. In the postwar
years, the company saw the potential of applying nuclear energy
for numerous other uses. The company helped the U.S. Navy
build nuclear power systems for aircraft carriers and submarines,
and also created a whole new industry in generating electricity
with nuclear reactors.

Yet from the very beginning of atomic research, antinuclear
sentiment ran strong in the United States. The attitude gained
ground when citizens of some Western states realized they'd
been radiated by fallout from the above-ground nuclear tests in
the Nevada desert during the 1950s. After the frightening 1971
Three Mile Island nuclear accident near Harrisburg, Pennsylvania, the nation's citizens seemed to say they'd had enough. The
American market for power-generating nuclear reactors deteri-
orated rapidly. No new orders for nuclear plants have been
placed since then, and when aging U.S. reactors go off line,
they have not been replaced. Western Europe and Asia stayed
with their nuclear energy strategy longer than the United
States did, but following the 1986 Russian explosion at the

Chernobyl nuclear reactor that killed hundreds of people and sent a cloud of radioactive dust across Europe, the public worldwide expressed grave doubts about the wisdom of nuclear power generation.[6]

Not only did GE (like many other companies in this experimental industry) have a questionable safety record at the nuclear facilities it operated, it became clear that capital costs would remain high and revenues would diminish for utility companies who generated and distributed the electricity. Despite early hopes and promises, nuclear power did not turn out to be low-priced in relation to other sources of electricity. The final 20 nuclear reactors built in the United States cost $3,000 to $4,000 per kilowatt of capacity each to build. By contrast, wind turbines are being installed at less than $1,000 per kilowatt and new gas-fired combined cycle plants using the latest jet engine technology cost $400 to $600 per kilowatt.[7]

Soon after Welch took office he laid it on the line with GE's nuclear operation. Society, he said, had decided against nuclear energy and there was no point in pursuing the business any further. Downsizing was painful for employees at GE's nuclear power division. Not only did workers feel rejected by the entire nation, they felt worthless to their own company. Welch said he understood how they felt. "Our people were the best and the brightest. When I said, in 1981, that there was not going to be another nuclear plant built in the United States, they were upset, they were angry, they were writing letters. Even today, if you ran a survey of nuclear, and asked, 'How do you like our strategy?' they'd say they don't like it. Not because of anything wrong with GE strategy. They just don't like what's happened to their situation. They don't like reality. I feel for them. It's a tough deal. But the world decided nuclear power was not what it wanted."[8]

Welch announced that the company would maintain the nuclear equipment and facilities it already had built, and it has done
so. For example, GE continues to provide power management
services to the Diablo Canyon Nuclear Plant in Avila Beach, California. In spite of the early impression that GE would be completely out of the nuclear business, the company maintains a
foothold. GE has a joint venture business in Japan with Toshiba to
work on nuclear energy technology. Japan and other Asian countries are still building nuclear facilities, though it appears that nuclear energy is losing acceptability there as well.

In a move that was emotionally and politically charged, in the
year 2000 Taiwan's government abruptly ended construction of
the island's fourth nuclear power plant. Taiwan's premier, Chang
Chun-hsiung, said his nation's inability to dispose of nuclear waste
or deal with any nuclear accident in an island setting made him
shelve the $5.5 billion project. He said the government would
honor contracts and compensate foreign suppliers, including GE
and Japan's Mitsubishi Heavy Industries Ltd.

Even with drastic cutbacks in the nuclear sector, problems from
old business activities have continued to hound GE, as employees
and former employees contend that management has been negligent in the handling of nuclear material at the Wilmington, South
Carolina, plant. When that case went to court, GE was found in-
nocent of negligence. From other people comes the demand that
GE make a greater contribution to nuclear waste cleanup at sites
around Troy, New York, and Hanford, Washington, communities
where many current and former GE employees live.

NO MORE WEAPONS OF WAR

During the 1980s and 1990s, some groups of GE shareholders
lobbied the board of directors over and over to get out of the

business of military arms. When GE sold its weapons business in 1993, Welch was motivated by two factors: First, the cold war had come to an end and military procurement would be shrinking. But additionally, that business always had been fraught with government investigations, legal action, and fines. Between 1985 and 1992, according to the federal government's General Accounting Office, GE was involved in 15 criminal convictions and civil judgments, which was a large number when compared with other defense contractors. Teledyne, which had the second most strikes against it in the 11-year period covered by the GAO report, had only seven convictions and civil judgments.[9]

In November 1993, GE made an exit from the defense business by selling its aerospace division to Martin Marietta for $4 billion in cash and preferred stock. Consolidation among defense contractors went hell for leather in the early 1990s, with General Dynamics dismantling most of its assets and other companies either merging with a competitor or closing their doors. In 1995 Martin Marietta merged with the Lockheed Corporation to become Lockheed Martin. Though the shrinkage of an entire industry was tumultuous, by 2000 Lockheed Martin seemed financially solid. GE has made a substantial profit on the shares it received when it sold its defense businesses, and the prospects for future share price appreciation look good for Lockheed Martin, which has predicted long-term earnings per share growth of between 15 percent to 20 percent.

OVERALL, DIVESTITURE WAS SMART

By the time he retires, Welch will have sold about 350 of GE's businesses, netting the company a total of $23.8 billion. Although dispositions of GE property slowed down in the 1990s, some analysts say the job isn't finished. Honeywell planned to sell off some of its underperforming companies before GE entered the picture, specifically its automotive products division, which includes the Prestone, FRAM, and Autolite brands. While those divestiture plans have been canceled for now, over the long haul GE will sell some units. Analysts also recommend that GE bite the bullet and get out of its appliance manufacturing altogether, no matter how unsavory it is to sell the $5.6 billion major appliance division in Louisville, Kentucky. Several attempts have been made to maximize earnings at Louisville, but by Welch's exacting standards the plant remains a sporadic performer. More about that in Chapter 5.

The critics of Welch's so-called "hardware revolution" claim he took GE out of some of the business segments where the pace of technological innovation is the greatest, and therefore the competitive risks and rewards are the greatest. These include semiconductors, consumer electronics, mobile communications, and ceramics, technologies that have netted other companies enormous amounts of money. The semiconductor business was sold to Harris Corporation, and GE swapped RCA Global Communications for $160 million and five radio stations for $122 million. To some GE stakeholders, it was disappointing that GE would be less of an innovator, and instead would mobilize its financial resources to buy the needed technology when it falls behind.

As was the case with RCA Global Communications and its television manufacturing business, GE made divestitures to clean house of activities that simply didn't fit with the company's image or within its big blueprint. Another example was an interest in a company that operated prisons. The prison management business came with the RCA package, and Welch sold it almost immediately.

For the most part, the subsequent performance of companies that were Welch's divestitures worked to GE's advantage. Though some companies prospered after they were sold, that is not to say that they would have done as well at GE, a company without a commitment to their success.

Certainly, given GE's 20 years of positive results, shareholders have not complained about the companies that GE shuttered or sold. Investors reacted happily to the sale of underperforming assets from the start. When it got rid of Utah International, GE's long inactive stock hit $50 a share, nearly twice the price of a year earlier.

Welch readily admits that the interests of stockholders (i.e., the need for profits) was never far from his mind as he unloaded business after business. "A proper balance between shareholders, employees, and communities is what we all try to achieve. But it is a tough balancing act because, in the end, if you don't satisfy shareholders, you don't have the flexibility to do the things you have to do, to take care of employees or communities. In our society, like it or not, we have to satisfy shareholders."[10]

chapter four

The Companies
General Electric Acquired

Do not follow where the path may lead. Go instead where there is no path and leave a trail.

George Bernard Shaw

Business, taking it very broadly, is not unlike a Jacquard loom. If the pattern card be right and the yard be right and the machine be in order, then we may be reasonable sure that the product will be what we intended to be. That is, our plans will work out.

Owen D. Young, chairman, General Electric, 1922[1]

OCTOBER IS THE MONTH OF STOCK MAR-
ket surprises, and Jack Welch definitely seemed surprised by what
he was seeing on the big board when he visited the New York
Stock Exchange on October 19, 2000. The share price of Honeywell International, a company that competed with General Electric in several arenas, had jumped $10. The spike in share price
caught Welch's attention, because he is good friends with Larry
Bossidy, who had merged AlliedSignal with Honeywell just 11
months earlier. Before that merger, Welch had considered acquiring AlliedSignal. Later, he and the GE team had studied the combined company, Honeywell, as an acquisition option, but decided
it was trading too high. Now, despite the 10-point jump, Honeywell was selling in the high 30s, with an offer on the table for $50
per share.

In the spring, when Welch took a serious look at Honeywell,
the share price was as much as $60 per share. "Market conditions
had changed a lot since we last looked at it," said Welch. "Last
time I looked, I think the price of the joint company was $67 bil-
lion. It was $35 billion this time."[2]

While the lower price tag presented an opportunity for GE, it
also points up a risk. Honeywell has been through a very bad
year, and its troubles could drag GE down. AlliedSignal and
Honeywell launched their $16 billion merger in June of 1999
with high optimism. AlliedSignal was actually the dominant
company in the partnership, and although the combined company would operate from AlliedSignal's headquarters in Morris-
town, New Jersey, it would assume the well-known and
respected Honeywell name. Additionally, since Bossidy was
planning to retire anyway, Honeywell's chairman, Michael Bonsignore, would become chairman. The two men figured that in
no time they could boost the new company's earnings per share
by at least 20 percent, and Wall Street analysts bought into that,

sending Honeywell's stock spiraling up. When Bossidy retired in April as scheduled, first-quarter earnings looked good, and for a while Honeywell seemed on track. But just one week after an upbeat annual meeting, Bonsignore announced that second-quarter earnings would not meet expectations. He adjusted his growth prediction from 20 percent down to 12 percent, and after that expectations dwindled even lower. Honeywell's share price dove 24 percent in two days after Bonsignore delivered the bad news.

Things didn't get better for a company than less than a year earlier had been described by the *New York Times* as "a merger made in heaven." Third-quarter 2000 earnings dropped by 49 percent. Higher oil prices, a general economic slowing, and a weak euro added pressure. Bonsignore pledged that Honeywell would bounce back by cutting almost 6,000 jobs, by selling off up to $4 billion of noncore assets and by buying back its own stock. These fixes would take 18 months to two years to work, and in an impatient investment environment, that was too long. Bonsignore entered acquisition talks with United Technologies, and a $40 billion, $50 per share deal with the longtime GE nemesis seemed imminent.

In rushes Jack Welch, 90 days short of his retirement, with an offer from GE calculated at about $55 per share. The move was uncharacteristic of GE. Though the company has bought growth through acquisition, most of the companies it acquired were small and could be readily and rapidly assimilated into an existing unit. Putting GE and Honeywell together requires the blending of two complex companies. In fact, from what was going on before the merger, it is clear that even the Honeywell and AlliedSignal marriage was still in an adjustment stage.

Welch's offer seemed impetuous and left unanswered questions. There were times earlier in the year when Honeywell

traded as low as $34 per share. Why didn't Welch jump then?
Welch never answered that question. But the deal also has some
attractive elements. Mergers between companies in the same
business have a higher rate of success than companies in disparate
fields. GE and Honeywell, said Welch, were a perfect fit that presented minimal antitrust problems. "We're buying a $25 billion
high-technology company. It has 90 percent overlap with the
things that we do, and yet with virtually every single activity
there is no product overlap."[3]

In the biggest deal of his career, Welch doubled the size of GE's
already large aircraft engines and servicing businesses and added
to its plastics, chemicals, and industrial control units. Welch
promised that the merger, basically a pooling of interests, would
contribute an additional $24 billion to GE's revenue base of $112
billion. Better yet, the acquisition would keep Honeywell out of
the hands of GE's aerospace archrival, United Technology's Pratt
& Whitney.

Jack Welch says he got his first taste of leadership from the
scrappy, aggressive kids in his neighborhood as they played endless games and sports in an abandoned gravel pit near his home.
He gained experience organizing games, choosing teams, looking for a competitor's vulnerability, and going for the score.
Running a business is much like playing a game, except that the
score is kept in dollars—in GE's case, billions of dollars. The
winner is the company that ends up with the most assets and
highest earnings. In 1999, said Welch: "We've made $10 billion
to $15 billion of acquisitions every year for the past five years.
Most don't even make the papers. A billion here, a billion there,
two billion here. That's what a big company's balance sheet allows it to do: keep playing."[4]

STAYING IN THE GAME

Not counting Honeywell, Welch made about 900 acquisitions worth a total of $105.8 billion in his nearly 20 years at the helm of GE. That breaks down to a $464 million acquisition almost every week that he was CEO. He started buying slowly, but by the end of the century, GE was making more than 100 acquisitions each year, an allocation of capital that has been the biggest contribution to GE's growth.[5] Its $6.3 billion purchase of the Radio Corporation of America (RCA) alone, the giant electronics firm whose crown jewel was the National Broadcasting Corporation, in 1983 catapulted the conglomerate from 16th up to 10th on *Fortune's* list of the 500 biggest industrial companies in the United States. It was the largest nonoil merger to date *and* GE bought the company with cash.

Welch was dragging GE away from its electrical roots, but interestingly, the RCA acquisition reunited GE with a company it had helped found. In 1919 Franklin Roosevelt, then assistant secretary of the Navy, encouraged GE to help create RCA so that the United States would no longer depend on foreign suppliers for its international communications as it had during World War I. GE held patents on long-distance transmission equipment, so it made sense that GE would become RCA's first major shareholder. For more than a decade GE and RCA maintained a close bond. They developed the first crystal set radios and set up NBC in 1926. In the 1930s, under a Justice Department antitrust ruling, the companies were dispatched their separate ways. Very quickly the former allies became fierce rivals.

In the 1960s and 1970s, however, RCA seemed to lose its focus, acquiring such companies as Hertz car rental and a consumer finance company, while neglecting its flagship property, NBC.

The network's ratings fell. The company's circumstances improved when Thornton Bradshaw, former chairman of Atlantic Richfield Company, took charge of RCA in 1981. He appointed Grant Tinker—former husband of actress Mary Tyler Moore—head of NBC. Tinker encouraged the development of shows like *Hill Street Blues*, *Cheers*, *St. Elsewhere*, and a half-hour comedy show starring Bill Cosby. The improved business performance made RCA a more visible takeover target.

Welch was attracted to RCA precisely because of NBC, which he liked because television networks generated so much advertising revenue and because at that time they had no foreign competition. As alluring as the acquisition was to Welch, it was equally terrifying to RCA employees because of Welch's reputation as a costslasher. The NBC staff was especially uneasy, and with good cause. Before long, late-night talk show host David Letterman was lofting verbal grenades at his own employer—on the air no less. Undeterred, Welch wasted no time telling the managers that he expected NBC, its sacred news operation included, to be as profitable as other GE divisions. Several tense years passed before that would happen.

In the summer of 1987 one-third of NBC's angry workforce went out on a strike that lasted 110 days. When it was over, the union had won few concessions. David Letterman, after he was passed over as Johnny Carson's replacement, moved to CBS. NBC's *Tonight Show with Jay Leno* became the leader among late-night talk shows. The television industry became more competitive after Welch bought the network, but despite that, NBC did make a lot of money, as explained later in this chapter.[6]

A BUYING SPREE

GE acquisitions may be big news in trade and regional presses, but seldom make national headlines. A great many of the deals are carried out through GE Capital, using complex structures including preferred stock, convertible stocks or bonds, or other mechanisms that must be set up and then interpreted by teams of accountants and lawyers. Such was the case in June 2000, when GE acquired Harmon Industries for $425 million in stock and assumed debt to add new lines of railroad signals and controls to its locomotive unit. GE combined Harmon with the GE Harris Railway Electronics, a venture between GE Transportation and Harris Corporation.

Nearly all of the remarkable expansion of GE Capital is attributed to the practice of allocating excess earnings to new acquisitions. GE Capital dates back to the Great Depression when in 1933 the financial operation was established to help Depression-era consumers finance the purchase of refrigerators and other household appliances. It now is a collection of 27 separate companies united by little more than the fact they report to the same owner. If it were an independent entity, GE Capital would rank around 17th on the Forbes Sales 500 list, ahead of Citicorp. In 1993 GE Capital surpassed General Motors Acceptance Corporation in total assets and two years later was twice as large as GMAC. GE Capital's after-tax profits put it ahead of Hewlett-Packard, Berkshire Hathaway, and Microsoft.

Some credit analysts worry that GE Capital has taken too dominant a position in the Welch family of companies. They say GE Capital should produce no more than 40 percent of GE's earnings, because a higher percentage would make the parent too reliant on Capital's earnings. Capital in turn relies on GE's triple A credit rating to gain access to low-cost funds. This is important to Capital, since for several years it has done business in the perilous sub-prime lending field, which serves borrowers with a poor record of repaying loans. If GE's credit rating should ever be compromised, both the parent and all the subsidiaries, including Capital, would suffer.[7]

A SAMPLE OF WELCH'S
GE ACQUISITIONS

1984—One of Welch's first big acquisitions was the purchase of Employers Reinsurance Corporation, which GE bought for just over $1 billion.

1985—GE announced it would buy the Radio Corporation of America, including its NBC properties, for $6.3 billion in cash. That acquisition added glamour to the new GE.

1988—GE acquired Montgomery Ward for $3.8 billion, Roper Corp. for $510 million, and Borg-Warner's plastics business for $2.3 billion.

1990—GE completed the purchase of Tungsram Co. Ltd., a lighting manufacturer, for $150 million from the Hungarian government. Later that year GE spent $138 million to buy the British-based lighting operations of Thorn EMI.

1993—GE picked up a majority stake in an Italian energy company, Nuovo Pignone.

1998—GE Capital, by then already the world's largest nonbank financing company, bought Colonial Pacific, the Pitney Bowes lending unit, for $800 million. Colonial Pacific finances leases for computers, copiers, small office equipment, and medical and construction equipment.

In 1999, a year when GE made 108 acquisitions for $21 billion, Welch told shareholders, "Every one of those acquisitions had a perfect plan. But we know 20 percent or 30 percent will blow up in our face. A small company can only make one or two bets or they go out of business. But we can afford to make lots more mistakes and in fact we have to throw more things at the wall. The big companies that get into trouble are those that try to manage their size instead of experimenting with it."[8]

The majority of GE's acquisitions have gone well, and in some miraculous way a mind-numbing number of companies have been integrated into the GE family and have adopted its culture. Yet it's a good thing GE can afford to get into trouble with a certain number of acquisitions, because it has.

MISGUIDED ACQUISITIONS

Welch will be the first to explain that, at best, business is about trying things, and if they don't work, trying something else. Welch says his biggest mistake at GE was related to what he didn't try to do—not being fast or bold enough in making acquisitions. "We didn't buy a food company in the early 1980s because I didn't have the courage of my convictions. We thought about it, we discussed it at Crotonville, and it was the right idea. I was afraid GE wasn't ready for a move like that."[9]

Yet there were a goodly number of problems with the companies he did buy. Blighting Welch's record in the late 1980s were several acquisitions that either turned out not to be what GE expected or turned sour after GE entered the picture. One such unpleasant experience was the bankruptcy of retailer Montgomery Ward, a subdivision of GE Capital. In 2000, just after Christmas, Ward's gave up the ghost and closed its stores. Because GE Capital has 28 different business segments, the company claimed Montgomery Ward didn't have a large effect on earnings.[10] Nevertheless, the event was worrisome, coming at a time when the United States appeared to be entering a recession.

Another famous misstep was the purchase of Borg-Warner Corporation's chemical operations, which produced a plastic product similar to GE's other plastic products but not used in exactly the same way. Borg-Warner had expended its financial resources trying to avoid a hostile takeover, and in the late 1980s Borg-Warner's management had few choices left except to sell off its parts to repay debt. GE moved in quickly to bid against several large competitors for the Borg-Warner chemical group. Glen Hiner, who headed GE's plastics, took a leading role in the bidding against Dow Chemical, Bayer of Germany, and the Exxon Corporation. GE won the contest, paying a startling $2.3 billion, about $1.5 billion more than the company's book value. In the year of the acquisition, 1988, Hiner was hailed as one of the six best managers in corporate America by *Business Week*. Soon after the deal was consummated, Hiner announced plans to construct a $1.7 billion plastics and silicones complex in Spain. Almost everyone thought plastics would continue to be the phenomenally growing industry it had been in the 1960s and 1970s. But the Borg-Warner business was already wavering, a situation made worse after most of the experienced and well-entrenched sales force was dismissed.[11] Hiner tried various management and accounting tricks to turn things around, but the division's earnings fell far below the target that he and Welch had set earlier, much to Welch's extreme irritation. It wasn't long before Hiner left the company.

ACQUISITIONS ABROAD

Two other major acquisitions, the Tungsram lighting operations in Hungary and Thomson's medical imaging business in France, initially were money losers and required huge infusions of capital before they revived.

Just a week after the 1989 fall of the Berlin Wall, GE announced it would purchase Tungsram for $150 million. The end of the Cold War meant the opening of whole new markets and the availability of cheap assets for cash-laden companies like GE. The lighting company seemed an ideal fit with GE. A state-owned enterprise, Tungsram was desperately in need of modernization, and yet it turned out to be in worse condition than anyone at GE had imagined. Its communist-era accounting procedures did not conform to U.S. standards, or standards anywhere, for that matter. Because checking accounts were a rarity in Hungary, some 150 Tungsram paymasters each week stuffed 17,000 pay envelopes with cash.[12] In 1993 GE had to invest $200 million to keep the company running, upping GE's investment to a total of $550 million.

The situation with GE's medical imaging business was quite different, but even more distressing. Welch traded GE's consumer electronics business (part of which it had received in the RCA acquisition) to Thomson for Cie. Generale de Radiologie (CGR), one of Europe's largest makers of X-ray machines. This was done, reportedly on one of Welch's famous snap decisions, when he visited Europe in 1987. Welch was high on the acquisition, and it was, in fact, GE's largest purchase outside the United States until that time. He put Vincenzo Morelli, at 30 GE's youngest vice president since Edison himself, in charge. Not long afterward it was discovered there had been a miscalculation of CGR's earnings. In the summer of 1989 Welch learned that CGR wasn't doing as well as he had been led to believe. While consumer electronics had annual sales of $3 billion and made money, CGR was selling only about $800 million of X-ray and other diagnostic equipment in Europe and was on shaky ground.

But worse yet, in 1991 the company was sued after the X-ray equipment used in the treatment of cancer gave radiation overdoses to 27 patients at a Spanish state hospital. Twenty of those people died, and in 10 cases the death was attributed to the radiation overdoses. Although the tragedy resulted mostly from hospital employees' errors in calibrating the machines rather than from the equipment itself, CGR's reputation was devastated. Morelli, like Hiner before him, left the company.

The medical imaging business survived that trauma, thanks to its strong product line. Its magnetic resonance imager is one of the best-selling in the world, and the imaging business has been one of the factors that accounted for GE's 20 percent earnings growth at the end of the twentieth century.

"If I'd had a successor then," said Welch, "he would have no doubt closed down both operations, taken a huge write-off, and wondered publicly how anyone could have bought such crap. Well, we took our lumps, had the patience to work through our mistakes, and today both companies are flourishing, profitable operations that have vastly strengthened our market stature in Europe."[13]

FACTORY OF THE FUTURE

The very day after Welch took office he unveiled plans to tap into the emerging market of factory automation with a $500 million investment called "Factory of the Future." It was his intention to preserve GE's role as a technology leader, making it the prime supplier of factory automation systems, including computerized gear and industrial robots. "Automate, emigrate or evaporate" was the division's slogan. Considerable financial resources were expended to poise GE at the front edge of the electronics revolution, hoping to take advantage of the tremendous potential of the microelectronic chip. To fill in the gaps where GE lacked knowhow, Welch bought two companies. Intersil was a producer of metal oxide semiconductors and cost $235 million. Calma, a fast-growing Silicon Valley maker of computer-aided design (CAD) equipment, came with a price tag of $150 million. "These chips are changing the way we live, work, and play," Welch observed, "making possible everything from industrial robots and other 'intelligent' machines that will revolutionize the factory, to advanced medical scanners that will let physicians see into the body without X-rays, to smart home appliances, to highly sophisticated home entertainment centers."[14]

The microchip indeed was a revolutionary development, but the factory-automated system never gelled into the $25 billion market that GE hoped for. By the end of 1983 GE had lost $40 million on the project, and two years later the loss had ballooned to $120 million. To make matters worse, GE and Silicon Valley didn't quite hit it off and both Calma and Intersil faltered as businesses, as did a ceramics division that GE acquired from Minnesota Mining and Manufacturing (3M). In each of these cases, GE management's initial enthusiasm ran out of control and they overestimated the potential market.

THE KIDDER PEABODY BLOOPER

"I've made more mistakes in the 18 years I've been doing this job than probably any human being in America has made," said Welch in 1999. "Of course, when I screwed up Kidder Peabody I get on the front page of everything. But if I make small mistakes, no one sees them."[15]

An irresistible opportunity arose in 1986, just at a time when Welch was nudging GE in the direction of financial services. The New York brokerage house Kidder Peabody found itself in need of a capital infusion and GE was there to be the white knight. Welch paid $600 million to acquire an 80 percent interest in the Wall Street firm. Even though it was a pricey orchid, Kidder was a slow grower from the start, and GE was compelled to sink another $800 million into the company. Finally in 1990 GE paid $550 million for the remaining 20 percent of Kidder it didn't own.

Several problems made the deal a little too exotic for GE's blood. Within months of GE's acquisition of the company, Kidder found itself at the center of the Ivan Boesky insider-trading scheme. Kidder's former merger chief, Martin A. Siegel (who left Kidder prior to GE's acquisition of it) pleaded guilty to peddling confidential information to Boesky, which he in turn used to clean up in the stock market. Both Siegel and Boesky served jail time.[16] GE tried to install its own management and run the company, but the people Welch put in place were seriously disadvantaged because they did not have investment banking experience.

A MALADY THAT INFECTED
THE FINANCIAL WORLD

This was a particularly dire problem since GE bought into Wall Street at a time when it was operating in a casino culture, one far different from GE's even under a mover and shaker like Welch. It was an era when several young hotshot traders, beloved by their bosses for the high numbers they delivered, either fully or nearly brought down companies. At Salomon Brothers, a 34-year-old trader placed an illegal $12.2 billion bid on U.S. Treasury bonds, and his bosses failed to report the incident, largely because the young man had made the company so much money in legal trading that they hoped to somehow protect him. When the scandal came to light, federal regulators nearly closed the investment banker down until Warren Buffett, chairman of Berkshire Hathaway, stepped in to guard his $700 million investment. Salomon did survive, but the British bank Barings did not when in 1995 young Nick Leeson precipitated a securities trading crisis in Asia. Barings, banker to the British monarchy including Queen Elizabeth II, was sold in 1995 to the Dutch banking and insurance behemoth, ING Group, for one British pound. Even at that token price, ING Barings, as it was renamed, had trouble making a go of it and five years later ING was exploring options for either selling or closing down some of the Barings operations.

Kidder's emperor-with-no-clothes was a young black bond trader named Joe Jett. Because Jett's numbers looked so good, and that made his immediate bosses look smart, they gave him enormous latitude and independence, and dallied even when his superiors suspected something was amiss. Kidder's managers, who also were collecting commissions from his work, didn't want to face the awful truth—that most of his trades were bogus. It is estimated that Jett created $350 million in phantom profits, which eventually forced GE to take a $210 million charge against earnings.

Dennis Dammerman, now vice chairman of GE, recalled his own involvement. "It blew up, and I was named chairman and CEO of Kidder immediately afterward—the equivalent of being promoted to captain of the *Titanic* one hour after the iceberg."[17]

The troubles kept escalating until it cost GE $1.2 billion. Before the episode was over, Welch was forced to fire old friend and longtime associate Michael A. Carpenter, whom Welch had put in charge of Kidder shortly after the acquisition. Ultimately, Kidder was liquidated and what remained—$50 billion of customer assets, its brokerage network, and its investment banking operations—was sold to PaineWebber. In a stock swap deal valued at $670 million, GE got a 23 percent stake in PaineWebber and a seat on the board. The deal gave GE 21.5 million shares of PaineWebber common stock; 1 million shares of 6 percent convertible preferred stock, which were valued at $100 million; and 2.5 million shares of 9 percent redeemable preferred stock, valued at $250 million.[18]

Dennis Dammerman was senior vice president for finance before taking over Kidder, and he recalled Welch's reaction. "He yelled, and I yelled, and people yelled back. Were any of us calm for the whole (first) weekend? No, you would've thought we were weird if we had been."[19]

The Kidder story and its $1.2 billion loss was not a pleasant memory for Welch, but it confirmed one of his management principles. Kidder was not a market leader, it didn't hold first or second position in its industry, and therefore it could not withstand the combined pressures of the frauds and weak trading markets.

Three and a half years afterward, the sale to PaineWebber looked like a brilliant move on Welch's part. Thanks to a bull market rally that profited brokerage stocks, GE's 23 percent stake in PaineWebber was valued at $1.65 billion. And that didn't count the $130 million in dividends and the $219 million GE received in 1997 when it sold a portion of its PaineWebber shares. By 1999 GE's stake in PaineWebber, counting dividends received and the stock-sale proceeds, represented a gain of $700 million.

NO FEAR

A few trying experiences aside, Welch is not afraid to go into businesses with which he personally is unfamiliar. "I don't know how to build an aircraft engine," he says. "I don't know what should run on NBC at 9 P.M. on Thursday nights. We're in the cat-and-dog insurance business in England. I don't really want to be in that business, but the guy who brought me that idea wanted to be in it, and I trust him. He'll take it and make it work."[20]

THE HAPPY ACQUISITIONS

The NBC television network, as mentioned earlier, was another acquisition that got off to a rocky start but turned out nicely. It was the top-ranked network when GE first bought it, but it fell into third place and losses piled up. In 1992 Welch seemed to have had enough and nearly completed a deal to sell NBC to Paramount. Talks later were held with Time Warner, Disney, and Sony. The various offers didn't suit Welch, so he decided to keep NBC. In 1993, he announced the network was not for sale, and went to work fixing it. Later, hits such as *Seinfeld*, *ER*, *Frasier*, and, in 2000, *The West Wing* moved NBC back into a leading position in prime-time viewing.

The situation comedy *Seinfeld*—which ended in 1998—was the most successful television series up to that time. *Seinfeld* was the first show to command more than $1 million a minute for advertising, a distinction that previously belonged only to the Super Bowl. By the end of the 1990s NBC, along with its CNBC and MSNBC units and its 13 owned-and-operated stations, was making more money than any other network. In 2000, for the seventh consecutive year, NBC posted record earnings, with a 17 percent increase over the year earlier. Though *Seinfeld* spin-off sitcoms weren't hits and the network retreated to number three in prime time, its evening news show and *The Tonight Show with Jay Leno* carried a lot of weight. Even though its coverage of the 2000 Olympics was panned and profits weren't as high as hoped, the Olympics did account for a 76 percent rise in revenues the quarter they were played. Robert C. Wright, NBC's chief executive, predicted that earnings would keep on rising.

NBC has been innovative in its expansion and now owns CNBC and stakes in MSNBC, A&E, Bravo, American Movie Classics, and several regional sports networks, in addition to interests in Internet companies such as the Snap portal company and the iVillage web site. In 1998, it was reported that Welch and GE were considering spinning NBC into a separate entity as a way to push into the cable business.

AN OPPORTUNISTIC STRATEGY

GE's successful acquisition strategy is based on constant watchful-
ness. A lot of time is spent analyzing deals that never come to
fruition. But often, as was the case with Honeywell, when a decision to buy is made, the company is quick and confident. GE
managers made both opportunistic and strategic acquisitions
south of the border, in Asia, and in Europe at bargain prices. Many
of the acquisition opportunities, such as Tungsram, were presented
by political or economic situations. Even in those circumstances,
the purchases often fit nicely into a plan. GE Power Controls, for
example, is an $800 million operation composed of 10 acquisi-
tions in eight countries. This unit represents about half of GE's
European revenues.

HOW LONG UNTIL AMERICA
IS BOUGHT UP?

There is a limit to how much GE can grow by acquisition. The
Wall Street Journal pointed out that if the pace of mergers of the
late 1990s continued, the United States would be left with only
one company by 2010.[21] GE has been acquiring foreign subsidiaries at a rapid pace for more than a decade, and the world
may be big enough to allow that to continue. Of the non-U.S.
jobs GE added in the past five years, about 80 percent came
through acquisitions.[22]

Opportunities to make purchases abroad will continue for
many years, claims Welch. "Mexico is booming, with a government dedicated to open markets, with imports that will grow
from $40 billion last year [1991] to $115 billion by 2000. From
New York or Raleigh, Mexico is a shorter flight than Los Angeles,
and it is a market America can't miss. Southeast Asia has a GNP

that is doubling every decade with enormous infrastructure and technological needs made for American businesses that can compete. India, with close to 125 million middle-class consumers and an exciting new government commitment to market liberalization, represents a vast opportunity for the next century. Sure they are far away. Sure the cultures are different. And that's why only those passionately devoted to growth are going to share in the huge rewards of winning in these markets."[23]

Whether Welch's growth-by-acquisition plan seems brilliant or addle-brained depends on whom you ask. The fact that the greatest growth for GE came in acquired businesses, and not from research and development or internal expansion, has been offensive to some. "What is his formula and how would one seek to imitate it?" queried business writer Robert Reno. "Well, I guess you would find yourself an exceedingly bright chemical engineer with boundaryless ambition and minimal soul, put him in charge of an old, established electric company and tell him to go out and buy everything he can lay his hands on that has little, if anything, to do with electricity, chemistry, or engineering. Unless I'm missing something, this is about as unscientific as the boundaryless financial formula of a housewife who sets out for Bloomingdale's to shop till she drops. The Welch formula seems to suggest that electricity has a limited future."[24]

chapter five

Building from Within

If you know the enemy and know yourself, you need not fear the result of a hundred battles. Sun Tzu, *The Art of War*

And here is the prime condition of success, the great secret: concentrate your energy, thought, and capital exclusively upon the business in which you are engaged. Having begun in one line, resolve to fight it out on that line, to lead in it; adopt every improvement, have the best machinery, and know the most about it.
Andrew Carnegie, *The Road to Business Success*[1]

GENERAL ELECTRIC IS THE HOLDER OF more than 67,588 patents and its scientists have won two Nobel prizes, in addition to hundreds of other prestigious awards for their work. For decades GE scientists and engineers had a reputation for turning up their noses at any technology that was "NIH," or not invented here. What irritated outsiders most about NIH was that GE's arrogance often was justified. Long after the light-bulb and the radio and television were perfected and commercialized, GE continued to be involved in some of the most impressive scientific accomplishments of all time:

* In 1954, while Jack Welch was still an undergraduate studying chemistry at the University of Massachusetts, GE designed the first jet engine that could propel an airplane at twice the speed of sound.
* Just as Welch took the top office in 1981, GE scientists developed three-foot-long fused-quartz ingots that could be drawn into fiber-optic strands 25 miles in length, thus firing off the fiber optics revolution.
* GE led the team that built the Mars Observer spacecraft in 1992, which was launched from a Martin Marietta Titan 3 launch vehicle for a 1993 rendezvous with Mars.

GE was famous for its scientific and engineering prowess, and much of the company's early growth was based on in-house intellectual creativity. Although GE maintains a research and development center in Schenectady, New York, and although Welch has said he takes pride in GE's R&D innovations, these activities no longer claim center stage at GE. In the spotlight instead is the improvement of productivity through management skills and use of the Internet, plus globalization. General Electric's company values, which are printed in Appendix B, are entirely focused on customer service and management principles, and even if a commitment to innovation is implied, it is never stated directly. Even though he was trained as a scientist, Welch's references to innovation often are vague. "The job for big companies, the challenge that we all face as bureaucrats," Welch is prone to say, "is to create an environment where people can reach their dreams—and they don't have to do it in a garage."

Tom Peters, the ubiquitous management consultant, at one time worked with GE. Insiders say that he and Welch parted ways after Peters described Welch's style as "management by fear." Peters groused to the *Wall Street Journal* in 1988 that once "the most glorious technology company of the century, GE has become a hodgepodge."[2]

Considering that Welch came up through the ranks by building a new business using original technology from within GE, it may seem puzzling that he doesn't place more emphasis on research and development when he promotes goals and accomplishments. But the reason Welch focuses less on R&D is because he knows the process can be a drag on profits. He understands from experience the costs and risks associated with in-house inventions.

LOTS OF OOPS!

The notion of washing clothes by harmonic vibrations may sound like a New Age joke. It didn't start out as one, but it ended as a laughing matter at GE. In 1978 when Welch was sector head of the appliance group, he approved a concept for a revolutionary waterless washing machine that indeed used harmonic vibrations. Four years and nearly $20 million later, GE had a washer that has been described, perhaps with exaggeration, as the size of a Titan missile booster. The machine did everything except get clothes clean. The idea was finally relegated to the scrap heap. "I was new to the business," said Welch sheepishly. "The case was persuasive and well-documented and I supported it. It's not the only failure I've had."[3]

When GE ended its dismal attempt to take the lead in the emerging factory automation industry, Welch admitted that the fundamental ideas were good, he endorsed everything the team did, but the execution of the strategy was all wrong. The automation business was folded into a joint venture with Fanuc of Japan in the late 1980s and eventually became profitable.[4]

The failures were disappointing, explained vice chairman Dennis Dammerman, and they presented a challenge regarding how to encourage GE's people to keep trying. "One of our early efforts was to develop a revolutionary new lightbulb, a potential game changer called Halarc, and after a fair amount of time and resources invested, we failed. But rather than have the employees hear a series of muffled revolver shots in the basement of the lighting business as the Halarc team was executed, we celebrated a great effort. Management awards were distributed, promotions and new jobs were given to the Halarc veterans, and everyone in every business across the company was made aware that GE loved people who took big swings in pursuit of growth, even if they didn't connect every time."[5]

WHEN VALUES CONFLICT WITH PERFORMANCE

Unfortunately a lot of the disappointing results have occurred when Welch applied his sweeping leadership concepts to old-line businesses. The rush to speed, for example, has sometimes clashed with the quest for quality. Such was the case when GE set out to upgrade, modernize, and make more efficient its refrigerator manufacturing. The centerpiece of the drive would be a new factory to manufacture a rotary compressor for the fridge. The new motor had fewer moving parts than its predecessor and was quicker and cheaper to build. Plans were approved in September 1983 to go forward with the engine and the construction of a $120 million factory in Tennessee, 50 miles south of Nashville.

Responding to Welch's mandate for speed, managers had the factory up and running by March 1986. To meet the deadline GE managers set for themselves, only limited testing was done on the rotary compressor. This was a mistake. A year later reports started trickling in of compressor failures, and soon the trickle grew to a deluge. Lawsuits followed that alleged that the defective refrigerators, through their excessive heat and inadequate refrigeration, had caused fires, injuries, and food poisoning. An Indiana man filed a complaint contending that he had suffered a heart infection that led to a stroke as the result of eating contaminated food.[6]

Welch insisted that there were no real safety issues, but GE's team reacted quickly nonetheless, replacing compressors in millions of large-capacity GE and Hotpoint refrigerators at a punishing financial cost of $500 million. The replacement compressors were purchased outside the company from manufacturers in Singapore, Japan, and Italy. It was a situation in which simplicity and speed didn't work without thoroughness and attention to quality. (Note: All this happened before Welch embraced the Six Sigma quality initiative.)

Welch repeats, however, that the luxury of being a company the size of GE is that you can go to bat often, take a lot of swings and miss a few, and still remain in the game. "I don't mind being wrong," he says. "The key is to win a lot more than you lose."[7] Welch and GE earn kudos for persistence. The division unveiled a new "global" fridge in January 2001.

PROBLEMS THAT JUST
DON'T SEEM TO SOLVE

Appliance Park in Louisville, Kentucky, was one of General Electric's shining accomplishments when it was built more than 40 years ago. It was a state-of-the-art facility constructed to build kitchen ranges, clothes washers and dryers, refrigerators, and dishwashers. With more than 1,000 acres of land, 140 acres of building space, 20 miles of railroad track, and 12 miles of paved road, it's another of the GE-owned small cities. The warehouse alone, one of the largest in the world, occupies 47 acres or more than 2 million square feet. Like the facility in Schenectady, it provides most of its own services, including a volunteer fire department, emergency medical service, sewage treatment plant, and power plant.

Appliance Park, however, is a beleaguered little city. While its various appliances usually are first or second in their business and for the most part are money makers, the operations often are not profitable *enough* to meet Welch's ambitious growth targets. GE repeatedly threatens to cut back work, close down product lines, or transport the work to Mexico or some other offshore location with low labor costs. The start of Appliance Park downsizing actually predates Welch. The cuts began in the 1970s when employment peaked at more than 17,000 people. Today the Park has fewer than 6,000 workers.

One of the most dramatic episodes at Appliance Park occurred in 1992 when Welch considered drastic steps to make major appliances a strong contributor to the bottom line. Though GE was ranked number two in domestic sales of dishwashers, the plant was losing $45 million a year and GE was about to reduce costs by outsourcing its domestically built laundry line to a plant in another country. Workers worried that if the washer manufacturing emigrated, the remainder of the appliances might as well start packing up. What happened next has become a casebook management study in certain business schools.

The employees at Appliance Park—then 9,000 strong—launched a "Save the Park" campaign, pleading to be allowed to restructure the washing machine manufacturing process, make labor union concessions, and turn the plant into an efficiency star among GE's businesses. The washing machine design hadn't been upgraded in more than three decades. A design team was given 20 days to come up with a new washer that could be built faster and more easily, and be competitively priced. They met the deadline with a blueprint for a washer than was 60 pounds lighter and used 380 instead of 800 parts. The effort demanded a reward. Perhaps against his better judgment, Welch kept the appliance plant going.

GE committed a $100 million investment in the laundry manufacturing facility, and although employment levels at the park fell overall by one-third, the employee-led work-out seemed effective. In 1996, operating margins rose to 11.8 percent compared to an industry average of 5.7 percent. Major appliances reported sales of $6.4 billion.

But rumors and cost problems persisted in other lines, and GE's top-mount refrigerator business alone was $40 million in the red each year. In 1998 GE announced that it might stop making dryers and ranges at Appliance Park. Again, the work was likely to be transferred to Mexico. This was alarming news not only to GE workers, but to all of Kentucky. More than 80 companies in the state were GE suppliers. A year later the company again reached a tentative agreement with employees to invest $200 million in the Park and save 800 jobs, provided labor unions would help GE reduce costs by about $80 million annually. GE's appliance division also won state approval for almost $10 million in tax breaks (spread over 10 years) that are part of a package to persuade GE to make the refrigerator line secure for Louisville. One stipulation made by state and local governments was that employment at the facility would continue at the level of at least 80 percent of the current 5,640 hourly workers.[8]

All the work seems to be bearing fruit, albeit underdeveloped fruit. In the year 2000 GE's earnings were up about 20 percent, and appliances, though the segment did less than the company as a whole, achieved a highly respectable 16 percent growth rate. Nevertheless, based on net income, appliances is not one of GE's top 20 businesses.

SIX SIGMA

Despite its record and its entrenchment in American industrial history, GE was dogged by a reputation for lackluster quality, especially in its small and major appliances. Yet when Jack Welch threw his infectious enthusiasm behind the Six Sigma quality control process, it wasn't in the name of quality. That was a benefit to be sure, but he was motivated by efficiency and the possibility of substantial cost savings. In the mid-1990s Jack Welch learned from his buddy Larry Bossidy, then still at the helm of AlliedSignal Corp., about Six Sigma. When he looked it over, Welch saw a concept that appealed to his inner engineer. Six Sigma is a statistical term—and now a catch phrase—for products that have a 99.9998 percent perfection rate.

SIX SIGMA WAS "NOT INVENTED HERE."

The Six Sigma concept was developed at Motorola in 1985 when the company was facing extinction, having lost its radio and TV business to Japanese competition. Motorola has since positioned itself in integrated communications and embedded electronics.

More simply put, Motorola is a major presence in, among other things, cell phones, pagers, computers, and networking peripherals markets. Critics say that Six Sigma is really statistical process control (SPC) dressed in new clothes. Others say the notion goes back to the 1950s when it was called multivariate analysis.[9]

With Six Sigma, there is heavy emphasis on measurement sciences, business analysis, and achieving measurable bottom-line results. It requires a solid knowledge of statistics. One person described Six Sigma this way: "Rather than just striving to, say, make a better cup of coffee, Six Sigma requires testing thousands of variables such as the temperature of the water and the strength of the grounds to find out why some pots are good, others sour," says AlliedSignal quality expert Carl Berry. "It halts guesses and gut instincts about what makes good coffee."[10]

Welch adopted the concept at GE with such a fervor that he practically set GE, and the thousands of suppliers for whom the process became mandatory, on fire. At GE, a defect could be anything from the misbilling of an NBC advertiser to faulty wiring in a locomotive. In 1995 GE analysts figured out that the company was averaging 35,000 defects per million operations, or about 3.5 sigma. A sigma represents a standard deviation on a bell curve, so the fewer defects, the higher the sigma. Most companies have between 35,000 and 50,000 defects per million operations, or about 3 sigma. GE's starting record was better than average, but not good enough to satisfy Welch. His goal: 2.4 defects per million, or Six Sigma.

Six Sigma has been successful at GE because it has flat-out, unrestrained support from the highest level of management, and the techniques were drilled all the way down through the organization. Certainly few people dispute the idea that shooting for perfection in the original manufacture of a product makes excellent sense. Doing it right the first time invariably costs less than fixing it later and paying for the damage, downtime, and other costs of failure.

GE Capital in 1998 alone generated hundreds of millions of dollars in net income from Six Sigma quality improvements. By 1999, Welch credited the program for raising the company's operating profit margins from 13.6 percent in 1995 to 16.7 percent.

When Six Sigma was implemented at GE Medical, the division discovered it could save money by making X-ray tube bolts from aluminum and steel, rather than the costly titanium and tungsten that had been used. Savings at the Medical Systems division alone hit $40 million by 1997. Companywide, savings were expected to be around $6.6 billion, 5.5 percent of sales.[11]

One of the advantages of the GE acquisition of Honeywell is that the Six Sigma process is already entrenched there, though GE puts its own spin on the management tool, which Honeywell employees will need to understand and assimilate.

Said Welch, "The methodologies of Six Sigma were learned from other companies, but the cultural obsessiveness and all-encompassing passion for it is pure GE."[12]

Like other management concepts that get elevated to fad status, companies can now buy Six Sigma off the shelf and put it into operation at their own companies. It isn't cheap, however. The Six Sigma Academy in Scottsdale, Arizona, is run by former Motorola quality experts Mikel Harry and Richard Schroeder. Their fees start at $1 million per corporate client. The American Society for Quality has attempted to make Six Sigma training affordable to small and midsize companies. Even though trainees from different companies are grouped together, the ASQ course costs $35,000 to $40,000 per person.

Incidentally, although Motorola said Six Sigma saved $2.2 billion between 1987 to 1991, the company since has stumbled, which only shows that Six Sigma can't control events outside the company such as an economic crisis in Asia and collapsing semiconductor demand. Once the world's undisputed leader in mobile phone sales, Motorola fell into second place behind Nokia. Motorola was a major backer of the failed Iridium satellite network. After disappointing financial results in 1998, Motorola seemed to be on the rebound. Even in the face of trouble and while implementing Six Sigma, Motorola holds to values that have been abandoned at GE. Very employee oriented, the company avoids laying off any worker who has been with the company 10 years or longer.[13]

A BLASTING GOOD BUSINESS
IN BIG, POWERFUL ENGINES

Although GE's dedication to innovation may be in question, most of GE's internal growth has evolved from old-line businesses: medical systems, financial services, and aircraft engines. In terms of that growth, financial services has been both a means and an end. Not only has it pulled through other products and services, it expanded to become a major owner and lessor of capital goods equipment. Medical services has benefited both from high-tech innovations and the opportunity to make strategic acquisitions. Aircraft engines, for the most part, has remained a traditional, grow-from-within business providing 9 percent of GE's revenues but 13 percent of its profits. Aircraft engines is a highly competitive, capital-intensive business where Welch encouraged new approaches to the way business is done. In fact, as Welch faces retirement, he leaves GE a major player in the aircraft industry. Even before he acquired Honeywell, Welch had secured a backlog of engine business that, if it plays out as expected, should last for years.

In 1999 GE blew away its main jet engine competitors, Pratt & Whitney and Rolls-Royce, when it won an exclusive deal with Boeing to supply engines for the 777-200ERs, the long-range version of the 777. This was accomplished by readdressing GE's jet engine business, as an aftermath to an embarrassing failure for GE.

ANOTHER OOPS

During a time when GE was being deeply saturated with Welch's Six Sigma quality program, the company developed a jet engine specifically for the long-range Boeing 777. The workhorse 777 entered service in June 1995, and since then has become the best-selling airplane in its class. The 777 family of aircraft travels at a cruise speed of mach .84 and is the most technologically advanced airplane in production. Boeing claims the plane is unmatched in its economic advantages. However, the new long-range engine, called the GE 90, failed several critical tests during certification. As a result, rivals Pratt & Whitney and Rolls-Royce together won more than 70 percent of the long-range engine orders for the 777. GE came in third, and in 1998 took a $275 million write-down on the GE 90 program. Indignant, Welch told his engineers to go back to their fancy high-tech design programs and start again. The new General Electric GE90-94B engines were developed with a computer design and analysis program, 3-D Aero, which delivered improved fuel burn, and hence greater fuel efficiency.

Welch met with Boeing's chairman and chief executive officer, Philip Condit, and told him that GE was willing to spend the additional $500 million or so it would cost to develop an enlarged version of the GE 90. However, Welch made two demands. First, Boeing would have to move forward quickly on developing a

300-plus passenger version of the 777 that could fly up to 8,700 miles. The current version carries 350 passengers, but flies only 5,600 miles. Second, Welch demanded that GE be the exclusive engine supplier for the enhanced 777. The plane would be sold by Boeing as a package—aircraft plus engines—which is a departure from the normal practice where airlines buy airplanes separately from the engines that power them, then choose a power package for a new plane from among the engine makers.

A PACKAGE DEAL

GE offset the hard edge of its demands by offering the airlines fixed-price, off-wing maintenance of the GE 90 engines, including spare parts, at a present cost of so many dollars per flight-hour. Additionally, the package would include financing by GE Capital. The deal is called "power by the hour." The arrangement removes from airlines the risk of high maintenance costs, should they occur.

While Boeing had something to give, the Seattle-based company also had something to gain from GE's offer. In return for a share of the revenues, GE would pick up as much as half of Boeing's $1 billion development costs for the long-range Boeing 777. By crafting the deal, GE reduced some of its own risk. The only plane the GE 90 is suited for is the 777. If GE had not won this deal, Welch might have had to write down the $2.2 billion already invested in development. And the long-term rewards are substantial for GE. The new engine sells for around $12 million each, and could draw $20 billion in revenues lasting to around 2020.

In interviews after the deal was announced, Welch said the GE/Boeing agreement wasn't as unusual as it appears. "This is a system to sell a plane and an engine as one package, one deal," said Welch. "And unlike many other transactions in this industry where you sell the plane and then the separate transaction takes place for the engine, this will be a total system sale. And there will be one sales force pushing the product, telling the story, and offering the value."[14]

Though the arrangement was hailed in the media as innovative, such arrangements have occurred in the past. GE had been the exclusive provider on the Boeing 737 since 1985, and did the same with an early version of the Airbus A340. Other manufacturers have negotiated exclusive agreements, including Pratt & Whitney with the early 727 and 707. Rolls-Royce has a monopoly on Airbus Industrie's new long-range A340, which will be the 777-200ER's main competitor.

Boeing's chairman, Philip Condit, said that his company reduces costs when there is a single engine provider for one aircraft, since it isn't necessary to constantly tailor the aircraft under construction to a different engine.[15]

By mid-2000, 480 777s (including the new longer-range version) were ordered by 31 customers. Additionally, in September 2000, Boeing announced that Air France signed a definitive agreement to exercise options for four more 777-200ER airplanes. This means that Air France's 777-200ER fleet would total 23 airplanes by spring of 2002. Air France would use the planes on its worldwide routes.

Following the news-making deal with Boeing for 777 jet aircraft engines, reporter Susie Gharib of the PBS *Nightly Business Report* asked Welch if, based on this closer relationship, it was not just a matter of time before GE bought Boeing outright?

"I don't think that has ever been in the cards. It sort of is a fantasy rumor every now and then, which both Boeing and we deny. That isn't the game. We have a very valid customer relationship with Airbus [Boeing's only remaining competitor]. We have more than half of the A320 family of Airbus engines.

We've [got an] exclusive on the A340, smaller A330. So we're in both camps."[16]

THE TREND TOWARD SERVICES

The fact that GE (and AlliedSignal) has applied Six Sigma to every aspect of its business, from manufacturing to customer service, is crucial as Welch makes services an ever greater percentage of GE's business mix. By 1996, nearly 60 percent of GE's profits came from services—up from 4 percent in 1980. "I wish it were 80 percent," said Welch.[17]

GE's horizontal spread into services related to the products it develops and manufactures has led to antitrust problems. In August 1996, the Justice Department charged GE with placing illegal restrictions on hospitals that use its remote diagnostic software for CAT scans. GE does not allow customers to use its software to service rivals' equipment. This has worried independent service providers, but GE claimed the as yet-unresolved CAT scan accusation was without merit.

Some of the complaints about GE falling behind in innovation are a matter of degree, or perhaps percentage of total work. After all, GE did show an innovative streak when NBC launched CNBC, a financial cable television network. Between 1980 and Welch's retirement, corporate research and development at GE developed groundbreaking tomography medical X-ray equipment, a new class of high-performance plastics called ULTEM, and gem-quality artificial diamonds that are the world's best heat conductors. GE's work on artificial gemstones and the enhancement of natural gemstones threatens to alter the entire precious gem industry, especially the diamond business. In 1999 the company spent $2 billion overall on R&D and was awarded 798 patents. But there is no question: Scientific innovation is not among the corporate goals that Welch promotes.

However, in the penultimate year of Welch's chairmanship, he announced that GE would invest about $100 million to expand its research and development center in Bangalore, India, making it GE's largest research facility anywhere. The center will increase its workforce to 2,600 scientists and engineers. Research will be conducted in areas of advanced chemistry, polymer science, mechanical engineering, electronics, information technology, ceramics, metallurgy, and e-business. Just as has happened with financial services and software development at GE, the center was placed in India not only to have access to low-cost labor but also to nurture a more interactive global flow of business. The center will be named for Welch.

chapter six

The Globalization
of General Electric

Money speaks sense in a language all nations understand.
Aphra Behn[1]

The world is larger than our views of it.
Henry David Thoreau

* IN 1988, JACK WELCH TRAVELED TO INDIA, VISIT-
ing dignitaries, hoping to sell airplane engines and electricity
turbines. Aides to then Prime Minister Rajiv Gandhi turned
the tables on him, impressing upon Welch a slide show about
the country's potential usefulness as a software supplier. Soon
after, Welch sent a scouting team who contracted for services
with four different companies, and within a few years, GE
put India's software industry on the map. N. R. Narayana
Murthy, head of one of the Bangalore contractors, Infosys
Technologies Ltd., explained the fundamental importance of
the software business to India's economy. "I realized that this
is the only solution for India, if we were to solve the problem
of poverty, as Mahatma Gandhi wanted." The solution he en-
visioned was to generate wealth legally and ethically, "because wealth must be created before it can be distributed."[2]
India, since Welch's 1988 visit, has become a prime software
producer for various U.S. companies, including the software
pioneer, Microsoft.

* If you wander the streets of Tokyo, Osaka, or Kyoto, you are
likely to notice that vending machines are ubiquitous in
Japan, featuring everything from funky, collectible telephone
debit cards to cigarettes. Among the strangest kiosks is one
that resembles a high-tech public toilet. It would be one of
the 1,000 unmanned "automated credit machines" or ACMs
owned by one of a group of Asian firms acquired by General
Electric in the late 1990s. Anyone with a driver's license can
have their credit checked, sign a loan contract, and within
half an hour receive a cash loan from one of 15,000 automated teller machines that accept GE debit cards. In 1996
about 70 percent of GE's Japanese customers applied for
credit through traditional brick-and-mortar branches, while
30 percent used ACMs. By 2000 the percentages were re-

versed, which was advantageous to GE, since the ACMs are operated at half the cost of the branches.

* August, 2000: Responding to unyielding industrial deflation cost pressures and global competition, GE Aircraft Engines of Evendale, Ohio, said that in 2001 it would double its reliance on offshore manufacturers. Global outsourcing for the GE engine group would reach $400 million, twice the amount in 1999. The company will procure castings from Asia, airfoils from Eastern Europe, tooling from Mexico, and design engineering from India. The global outsourcing trend reflects a progressive shift in the company's supplier base, which may be appropriate considering that more than half of its engine sales are outside the United States. Globalization was further accelerated when in 2001 GE Aircraft launched its "extranet" Internet sites with capabilities for remote diagnostics and interactive technical and repair manuals.

Giant international corporations have become so central to the work of professional investors that in 1999 Dow Jones launched the Dow Jones Global Titans Index (DJGTI), a 50-stock benchmark of the world's largest multinational companies. These companies are truly worldwide organizations, with an average of 40 percent of revenues flowing from outside their home markets. For that reason, sophisticated investors think of these giants' stock as a distinct asset class. "Global Titans are companies that will dominate the world's economy well into the twenty-first century," said Michael A. Petronella, managing director of Dow Jones Indexes. "With no national borders to define their territories, they defy traditional asset categories."[3] At least two investment companies, John Nuveen and Nike Securities, speedily launched derivative products based on the index.

It is no surprise that General Electric was among the 10 largest companies in the Global Titans Index, along with Microsoft, IBM, Wal-Mart Stores, Exxon Mobil, Royal Dutch/Shell, AT&T, BP Amoco, Coca-Cola, and Intel.

GE has several characteristics that almost ensure its dominance as a global leader. First of all it is American, and U.S. companies have an advantage in worldwide markets. They hold leading positions in the most global of industries from pharmaceuticals to aerospace to computer software. According to a 1997 poll by the United Nations, 30 of the 100 largest multinational companies, ranked by their assets, are American.[4]

Larry Bossidy claims that American society has bred the very qualities that make U.S. companies successful in the face of international competition. These traits include the creative thinking that comes from a tradition of political freedom, plus the qualities of "ingenuity, resourcefulness, and determination" that stem from its immigrant and pioneer heritage. Because American society is fairly open and pluralistic, said Bossidy, it is able to draw talent and ideas from a larger, more diverse pool.[5]

Don Davis, chief executive of Rockwell International, a maker of avionics and manufacturing automation equipment, says that the U.S. business community has been moving gradually toward a more international position. "This didn't start the day before yesterday. Globalization is a journey, a process, and it's ongoing."[6]

There is little doubt the political influence of the United States has been helpful, but GE also benefited from its longevity, brand name recognition, dominant market share in a variety of businesses, massive size, and an early start in its expansion abroad.

Indeed, GE has been a precocious traveler. By 1935, GE owned 40 percent of Tokyo Electric, 29 percent of Germany's Osram, 44 percent of France's Compagnie des Lampes, 34 percent of Britain's General Electric Company, 10 percent of Philips in Holland, and 100 percent of China's Edison Electric.

"GE is very strongly placed in the infrastructure of emerging nations, electric utilities for example," said Michael Allen, a former GE strategist who now is a consultant to the company. "That's one reason why it's placed in India."

Welch himself has long understood the importance of sales and manufacturing abroad, said Daniel Natarelli, former head of GE plastics and silicone products. "Jack started saying 'the world is the store' back in 1972."

A GLOBAL NATURE IS NOT ENOUGH

GE's expansion overseas got started because of the wish of cities everywhere to have electric power systems. The early globalization occurred naturally; the wave to global expansion that occurred in the last two decades of the twentieth century has been by design. Over the past 15 years GE has transformed itself from a company that derived 80 percent of its business from the United States into a global corporation with more than 40 percent of its operations outside the country.[7] Before the Honeywell acquisition about 42 percent, or 143,000, of GE's employees lived and worked outside the United States.[8]

GE's demographics shifted for a whole range of reasons—because of the changing nature of the world economies as they recovered from World War II, because of technological advances, because of opportunity, because GE became so big, and because it had so much money to buy up assets that it just spilled over the U.S. borders.

Larry Bossidy explained that at one time, U.S. companies "had a vast domestic market that consumed what you were able to produce. And if sales were good here, you could make them even better by exporting your products to Europe, which was getting hungrier for anything we made."[9]

As late as 1990, GE, for the most part, was still treating Europe as an export market. The company had some European operations, notably its aircraft-engine manufacturing joint venture with Snecma of France, formed in 1974. And way back in 1970 when Welch ran the plastics division, he started a greenfield, or from-scratch, plastics operation abroad. A dramatic change began in 1987 at a time when 44 percent of GE's overseas sales were exports from the United States. That was the year Welch swapped his consumer electronics business for Thomson-CGR, the medical equipment division of France's Thomson, which at the time was state owned. This gave GE a European foothold in Medical Systems, though it took a long time to get that business in good shape. As mentioned earlier, in 1989 GE bought the Hungarian government-owned lighting manufacturer, Tungsram.[10] Again, the transition to the GE way was slow and painful. Approximately 10,000 people were let go, 40 percent of them management, and Tungsram went through several managers before things settled down.

Those early acquisitions were so unprofitable, though, that from 1992 to 1994 Welch shunned further purchases in Europe. But the businesses started improving and he was able to learn from experience. Between 1994 and 1995, European revenues ramped up from $9.1 billion to $14.1 billion as GE gobbled up companies in every line from reinsurance to power controls.

What business could be mature, asked Welch, when you have economies with more than two billion people in India, China, and Southeast Asia and they are just beginning to need and use your products and services?[11]

JUST A NEIGHBORLY TELEPHONE CALL

Telecommunications have led to astounding changes, especially in service-related companies like GE Capital, which manages credit cards for clients such as retail chains, credit unions, or alumni associations. If you live in Texas and get a telephone call from a person with a strange accent asking why your credit-card payment is late, it's probably because the call is coming from as far away as India. The telecommunicators assume Western names and even try to pick up the accent or colloquialisms of the region they cover.

And there's more to it than telephone boiler rooms. At GE Medical Systems, employees tell the story of an injured child who needed an X-ray late at night in California, but the hospital's machinery was malfunctioning. When the call for help came into GE's service center it was routed to Paris, where a software engineer repaired the computerized scanner over a telephone line in half an hour.

High-tech infrastructure, explains Trinity College's Professor Gunderson, has helped collapse political borders. "We're calling it globalization because the cost of dealing at a distance has gone down so much. The cost of phones, e-mail, shipping, containerized freight is relatively small compared to cost of products. We've now got icicle lights all over the country—a cheap, attractive product made in China. This sort of thing will go on regardless of any one person. Yet the person—such as Jack Welch—who takes advantage of these conditions, and brings down costs and expands markets, will get credit."

GLOBAL GROWTH BY OPPORTUNITY

Most of GE's big spurts of global growth occur when there is blood in the streets. When economies anywhere were suffering, GE used its significantly large and secure capital base to bulk up its business portfolio. Domestically, GE Capital loaded up on real estate during the savings-and-loan crisis of the late 1980s.

In Mexico, the company cut deals after the peso collapse of 1996.

"You've got to go to bat every time and take chances . . . where no one wants to be," explained Welch, referring to GE's rapid acquisition of companies in Mexico, Japan, and Eastern Europe after those regions suffered financial reverses.[12]

Over a very short time, Welch noted, the pace of global business speeded up:

"In the late seventies and early eighties, we experienced the Japanese inroads into many of our traditional businesses, realized that our future was no longer in many of them, and moved into businesses that were immune to this assault while we restructured the company. We did this, but we had almost a decade to get it done.

"When Europe experienced doldrums and dislocation in the early nineties, we moved quickly to partner with European firms whose future we believed in. The best opportunities this time were around for only two or three years," said Welch.

During the 1990s GE forked out nearly $30 billion for 133 European acquisitions, and by 1998 its revenue had grown fourfold to $24.4 billion, of which only 11 percent represented exports from the United States.

"Then Asia in the late nineties—again economic dislocation and again sudden opportunities to partner with great companies with great futures from Japan to Thailand. The very best of these opportunities were gone in a year," Welch continued.[13]

Although 1998 was fraught with risk in Asia, prices were irresistibly low, with values down 50 to 75 percent from what they had been 18 months earlier.[14] GE Capital arranged a string of deals that built a solid Asian base. GE now has 20 or so businesses in China alone, including the first synthetic plastics factory in that country. That plant opened in Shanghai's Pudong economic zone in 2000. The $30 million plant will produce 30,000 tons of high-quality plastics to be exported to the United States for use in computers, mobile telephones, cars, and other equipment. In Thailand, the American giant acquired a majority stake in a charge-card issuer, boosted to 100 percent its ownership in an auto-financing business, and bought a 49 percent stake in a consumer-finance company.

GE has done business in Japan for more than a century, but that presence expanded so dramatically that GE now has 17,000 employees in Japan who generate 6 percent of GE's global revenues. In 1999, GE put $575 million into a joint venture with the troubled Toho Mutual Life Insurance Co., its largest investment in Asia. That same year, GE Capital bought Japan's number 2 leasing company, which had gone bankrupt.

Despite continuing hard times in the country, Japan is GE's fastest-growing national market, and for that reason GE Capital focuses much of its Asian effort there. With $12 trillion in personal financial assets (80 percent of Asia's total), the world's largest life insurance market, the world's fastest-aging population, and an underdeveloped financial system, Japan is ripe with opportunity. It also is a profitable place to do business. GE's Japanese loan portfolio yields a remarkable 28 percent annual return.

FOUR STAGES OF GLOBALIZATION

There usually are four stages in a multinational corporation's development: The first phase is corporate colonialism, when companies use foreign outposts to distribute goods made at home. In the second stage, manufacturing is integrated along global lines, most often to save labor costs and get nearer to markets. At stage three, foreign subsidiaries become sources of ideas as well as production.

Finally, corporations reach the fourth, or multicultural, truly multinational state where the country of origin of the staff ceases to matter. The *Financial Times* of London has observed that in almost all industries, the first and second stages of corporate behavior, when multinationals act like empires and foreign operations are run like colonies, are giving way to structures in which more decisions are being made overseas.[15]

For the most part, GE has matured to stage three, though some divisions remain in stage two, and Welch has been trying to advance the entire company to stage four.

The campaign is underway to develop a corporate culture, led by a group of managers, that is fully attuned to what is going on beyond U.S. borders. Fairly early in his tenure, Welch put all operating units into global product groups with regional managers left to coordinate such activities as acquisitions and local public relations. There is no GE French or British or Chinese operation with a lone person responsible for what happens in that country. There is a plastics unit with activities in Europe, a major appliance division with operations in Mexico, and so forth. The foreign operation is managed by the division itself.

When Welch first started talking about the "boundaryless" company he seemed to be thinking about the sharing of ideas within GE, between divisions, the movement of employees up, around, and sideways. Now boundaryless also seems to mean operating as if national borders do not exist, a concept that has vast economic, social, and political implications. As goes GE, so goes the world?

GOING WHERE THE BRAINS ARE

In 1999 Welch expressed his commitment to globalizing "the intellect of the company," which means seeking out talent anywhere in the world where the smartest and best-educated workers are located. "It means using Russian engineering and Indian software—not to arbitrage labor costs, but because these are the best people you can find."[16]

The real challenge, the most difficult one, says Welch, is to globalize the mind of the organization. "When you start talking about globalizing intellect and building massive laboratories in Bangalore and building foundries in the Czech Republic, you start really challenging the organization, because moving intellect out of the home base is a tremendously threatening thing." But, he adds, until you eliminate intellectual borders, you don't have a genuinely global corporation.

GE isn't the only U.S. company experiencing this type of transition, but it is one of the largest. The results are evident: The clever bits of GE's new Spanish plastics factory, for example, were designed by a multinational team of mainly Japanese and Dutch scientists.

The way GE's global business is structured—business line by business line, headquartered from wherever that business line is, rather than country by country—helps break down the barriers. GE now is focusing on promoting management from within the country in which it operates, rather than importing its own people from the parent company. At the turn of the twenty-first century, GE increasingly was sending American executives home and turning over businesses to locals.

Though GE without question is bringing American methods, products, and values into the country where it sets up, globalization to some extent is de-Americanizing GE. Jeffrey Immelt, when he headed GE Medical Systems, was from Cincinnati, Ohio, but 10 of his 21 direct subordinates were not U.S. citizens. Of the 23,000 people in GE's international consumer finance division, fewer than 200 are American. Every national consumer-finance business unit is run by native-born managers.[17]

Despite GE's large global presence, the *Financial Times* complained that it has few foreign representatives on its 17-member board, though it does have several. Italian Paolo Fresco for a decade was vice chairman of GE and worked out of corporate headquarters in Connecticut. He's now the top officer at Fiat. Board member Claudio X. Gonzalez is chairman and CEO of Kimberly-Clark de Mexico, the paper products company. Frank H.T. Rhodes, president emeritus of Cornell University, is British-born, but is a naturalized U.S. citizen. One drawback of foreign board members, claims GE, is the difficulty of traveling long distances to attend frequent board meetings.

THE ROMANCE WITH A NEW COUNTRY CAN END FAST

Since 1986, Welch has cut GE's domestic workforce by almost 50 percent while nearly doubling the number of workers employed abroad. Today, barely half of GE's total workforce is based in the United States.[18]

"Ideally, you'd have every plant you own on a barge, to move with currencies and changes in the economy," Welch said when asked to describe his business philosophy during a Cable News Network (CNN) interview.[19]

In recent years GE has focused particular attention on Mexico, encouraging suppliers to do the same. GE has sponsored what it calls "supplier migration" conferences to pressure its business partners with U.S. operations to move them into proximity with GE's Mexico factories: "This is not a seminar just to provide information. We expect you to move and move quickly," the company declared.[20]

Despite the urgency of the message, GE's sojourn south of the border is likely to last only as long as Mexico can produce suitably lower costs. In a 1999 interview Welch gave an example of what could happen. "We were getting steel casings for turbines in Mexico, which was making them for 40 percent less than they make them for here [in the United States]. Within 45 days our team had moved those casings out of Mexico to Korea, which was 40 percent below Mexico. That took just 45 days."[21]

GE has been under attack from social activists who say GE is exploiting local workers, accused even of firing workers in Mexico to quell a unionization drive, a tactic that is forbidden under the North American Free Trade Agreement (NAFTA).[22] Some union leaders now contend that the major unions should move toward worldwide bargaining, putting domestic and foreign workers on the contract negotiating table at the same time.

Whether it is U.S. union workers who lost their jobs to Mexican factories or it is activism within the host country, wages are always a sticky issue. Writing in the *National Catholic Reporter* in 1998, writer Brian O'Shaughnessy described meeting with a young mother who worked at one of GE's plants in Mexico. Her pay stub showed that for the week of May 11, 1998, Maria Elena earned 332.60 pesos gross, about $42.50. She worked the normal 48-hour Mexican week, plus Sunday, for which she received overtime pay. After taxes and other deductions, she took home 203 pesos, or approximately $25. Even in Mexico a family cannot live on that amount. With inflation and devaluation of the peso, Mexico's food costs are increasingly similar to those north of the border. O'Shaughnessy reported that Maria Elena and her coworkers implored, "Just help us get a fair wage from your U.S. companies. We don't expect companies to solve all of Mexico's problems. We want a wage we can live on, not charity."[23]

Defenders of globalization claim that local people might have no work at all if they didn't work for a global corporation. Despite pay rates that are lower than the U.S. standard, the pay may be higher than what otherwise was locally available. For example, Nike's subcontractors in Vietnam pay an average monthly wage of about $65, more than twice what a teacher earns and considerably above the salary of a young doctor at a state-run hospital.[24] Furthermore, when corporations spread work out in developing nations it helps solve difficult immigration issues. Workers may not feel as compelled to leave their own country if the work is brought to them.

POLITICAL AND OTHER RISKS

What more evidence is needed than the violent demonstrations at the World Trade Organization meeting in Seattle in 2000 that globalization has become a hot political topic? Social and political disruption have always been a risk for companies working on foreign soil. Suspicion always runs high that multinational corporations are manufacturing abroad so that they can use materials or practices that would never be allowed in their home country. Even when no such situation exists, foreign corporations are at risk.

"As Coca-Cola found out," said Michael Allen, "a change in power structure can get you kicked out. To make GE's alliances with nations constructive rather than antagonistic is very critical. It is always the case that you get a triangular relationship between the host nation, GE, and the United States, which has a stake in political, human-rights, and other issues."

A former GE executive said he learned that lesson when Rosalynn Carter, wife of President Jimmy Carter, went to Brazil and inquired of the country's president regarding the whereabouts of missing priests. For several years afterward, GE supposedly lost millions of dollars of business in Brazil, business that went to Germany instead. And yet in terms of political issues and progress toward greater human rights, Mrs. Carter's trip was hailed as a great success.

The globalization of business raises many ethical and moral questions. It would be cowardly for American political leaders to play blind to human rights abuses just to protect trade. On the other hand, some internationalists sincerely believe that the best way to improve human rights practices is to maintain a watchful presence and to help build an economy that allows local citizens the better education and middle-class economic status that invariably leads to reform.

Globalization requires that Americans change as well, that we give up antiquated grudges based on political differences, such as those with Cuba and Vietnam. To some American Vietnam War veterans—though not all by any means—the reestablishment of diplomatic and business relations with Vietnam is a dismaying slap in the face. But by the time the United States normalized relations with Vietnam, dozens of U.S. businesses, including GE, either were planning to do business there or already had operations in Vietnam. Many of the company representatives in Southeast Asia were Vietnam War veterans who were glad to be able to revisit the country in happier times.

SPREADING AMERICAN VALUES ABROAD

When in 2000, for the third year in a row, GE topped *Fortune* magazine's Global Most Admired list, it was an indication that his peers thought Welch was doing something right. Indeed, GE represents the quintessential American business, and just as important, Jack Welch represents the quintessential American businessman. The company and the man are prototypes, paradigms, models—often idealized, but never underestimated in their stature and power. Professor Joseph Bower of Harvard Business School was doing research in Europe in the 1980s, and saw that the business executives there were beside themselves with envy for American companies, which were able to operate without the social and legal constraints that bind Europeans. "Americans had the freedom to go about their business, laying off people, restructuring, buying, and growing, and Europeans couldn't," said Bower. "That's American, it's not just GE." Bower said that the reaction of European managers was to move away from their home country, to invest and expand into the United States, which ultimately had a crippling effect on the success of the European currency, the euro. Siemens CEO Heinrich von Pierer announced in the fall of 2000 that Siemens, a German company and a fierce GE rival, now did more business in the United States than it does in its home market. He described this as a "really unbelievable achievement. When I look back five years, that was a vision—not even a target."[25]

ANTITRUST DEFENSES

GE, like the software megacorporation Microsoft, raises many questions about the role of antitrust in an economy with no national borders. Those issues are playing themselves out in U.S. courts at the moment, and the European Union has been particularly observant in its oversight of mergers when European subsidiaries are involved. GE has been able to steer clear of much antitrust scrutiny by the very fact that it is a conglomerate. Rather than have its business interest concentrated on a single type of business, its activities cover a wide range of industries. Additionally, GE has extensive experience in how to behave itself.

"It is remarkable how high a market share you can get without the antitrust people feeling that they should prosecute you," says Bower. "What it comes down to, if you can avoid abusive practices and still be aggressive, you don't have a problem. Intel is the example of that. GE has done it, especially in its locomotive business." GE, he noted, made a major investment in large DC locomotives, with General Motors being its only major competitor. "Imagine that GM decided 'we're not going to match that' and decided to withdraw or sell. The GE market share would get very large because there are only two competitors. There would be discussion. GE would have to explain what was going on, they would look at GE's papers, look at what GM was doing. GE [has made] an aggressive investment [in locomotives], but there is nothing against the law in doing that."

Bower says that Microsoft is not the right model to study when considering the limits of antitrust. "Gates trashed people. You can do all sorts of things without being abusive." The trick, says Bower, is to read the riot act to managers about how they behave when competing, and to remind executives to be careful about the memos they write. In both the Microsoft case and the IBM antitrust case before it, lawyers uncovered all sorts of "dreadful memos, macho things" that perhaps were only intended to impress coworkers, but didn't fly well in court.

Although GE has been in world markets for many, many years, its global presence and the rethinking of how GE operates abroad made quantum leaps under Welch's guidance. It has been a huge task. Just two years before he was scheduled to depart the company, Welch said he was still at work on it. "I'm 63 and finally getting smart . . . [I] want to hand off global, winning, number one businesses. We've 87 percent to 91 percent of the earnings of the company in that category; 9 percent to 13 percent isn't there. Those are issues I've gotta deal with."[26]

A major challenge for Welch's successor will be to keep connecting the dots between places, people, and products around the globe.

chapter seven

Wired Welch

Risk, risk. That is what this starship is all about. That is why we are aboard her. Captain James T. Kirk, Star Trek

You must never be afraid to go far, for success lies just beyond. Marcel Proust

JACK WELCH ISN'T THE KIND OF GUY TO be left out of anything that is fun, exciting, and new. Yet in the mid-1990s, Welch declared that he didn't use a personal computer. "I don't need one," he said. "I don't know what I'd do with it."[1] But by the end of the decade, a little slower than most Americans, Welch discovered the computer. It happened at Christmas when Welch noticed that his wife and most of the people in his office were doing their holiday shopping using the Internet.

As a chief executive who constantly advises his employees to embrace change, Welch admitted that he, too, had experienced fear of the unknown. "I was afraid of it, because I couldn't type," he said.[2] He actually learned rudimentary typing in high school, yet it wasn't until 1998 that he realized, like thousands of other executives around the world, that the fact that he'd always had a secretary on hand to type for him had become an impediment in the Internet age. He was a dinosaur in the electronic era. "It's a terrible thing to say, but I never really used [typing] much until my tenth wedding anniversary in Mexico two years ago. That's when I really started using the Internet. Since then, I've practiced typing on weekends to get back up to speed."[3]

Welch soon caught on that the value of the Internet is its immediacy and its intimacy, which are lost unless you do the interface yourself. As one wag pointed out, "Come to my office, Harriet, I want to dictate an e-mail" just doesn't work.

Back at the office, using a Dell desktop computer, Welch got further help from his personal assistant Rosanne Badowski. Then, realizing that other GE executives were just as computer illiterate as he was, Welch adopted an idea for a management-level mentoring program from Andrew Haste, a former GE executive based in London. The top 600 GE managers were told to select a coach from within the company, a computer-savvy person they could call on if they lost a file, sent an e-mail sailing into the unknown, or couldn't remember how to write a URL. Welch's own tutor was 37-year-old Pam Wickham from the corporate public relations staff. Junior employees were teaching the senior staff. "What we did with this," said Welch, "was to turn the organization upside down."[4] Welch was now online, though perhaps not with the fastest fingers in town.[5]

Welch was hurrying his top people to catch up to the twenty-first century, but some of them suffered a lingering nostalgia for the old days when the boss's communications were primitive but obvious. "One executive I e-mailed wrote back saying he couldn't stand my new skill. He said, 'How will I know without that big black scribble across the top of the page—with the width of the scribble determining the angst with which you are writing—how you feel?' "[6]

As the sages promise will happen, when the student (Welch) was ready, the teachers came. Welch met Scott McNealy, the 40-ish chairman of Sun Microsystems, and they hit it off. GE already was a major end user of Sun's products, with many of GE's engineers, including those in the medical instruments business, using Sun equipment.

Welch, along with Walt Disney chairman Michael Eisner, Berkshire Hathaway's Warren Buffett, Alcoa's Paul O'Neill, and others, became regulars at Bill Gates's Microsoft summit. There Gates gave his fellow CEOs a crash course in how to use technology to their advantage. Certainly it must have grabbed Welch's attention when he realized that technology has been the most important force behind U.S. economic growth, and by the year 2008 high tech could account for as much as 50 percent of the total economy. Whereas growth in the past was driven by computer hardware and software, the future would depend on Internet sophistication. It wasn't long before Welch began predicting that the big, old-line companies would beat the socks off of the dot-comers when it came to Internet business. "Old companies thought this was Nobel prize-type work. This is not rocket science. It's just like breathing," Welch concluded.[7]

At GE's January 1999 management meeting in Boca Raton, Florida, Welch announced that GE would enter what would be the last revolution under his direction. The first revolution was the internal reform, which involved downsizing and a whole new way for employees to think about business. The second revolution involved the structure of the company itself—the divesting of businesses that didn't work and the global expansion of winning business, both by internal growth and by acquiring complementary companies. Now, just a year before he was to leave office, the Internet revolution at GE was flickering on GE's monitor.[8]

Welch sang praises to the Internet, using words and phrases he'd earlier applied to concepts such as simplification of corporate structure, speed of change, and Six Sigma:

"It will change relationships with employees. We will never again have discussion where knowledge is hidden in somebody's pocket. You will have to lead with ideas, not by controlling information.

"It will change relationships with customers. Customers will see everything. Nothing will be hidden in paperwork. Where is the inventory? Where is that part? They will see it all. Execution is very important. Look what quality will do to the Internet, and vice versa. Every error you make is transparent on the Web, so without Six Sigma quality you can't win.

"It will change relationships with suppliers. Within 18 months, all our suppliers will supply us on the Internet or they won't do business with us."[9]

Again Welch threw all his energy and GE's resources into the campaign. Again he called upon Crotonville, GE's corporate college, to be the catalyst for change. Every business management course—a four-week, action learning program for 50 high-potential managers offered each quarter—was required to do an e-commerce project. Every GE business appointed a "maverick," a designated e-commerce fanatic, who reported to the CEO and was empowered to break every GE rule except the company's core values. Welch announced a 90-day, all-company Work-Out, to be run on the Internet. The subject—how to use the World Wide Web to eliminate bureaucracy and move to electronic commerce.

GE WAS ONLINE LONG BEFORE JACK WELCH LEARNED TO TYPE

As the new millennium began, the media was abuzz with stories that stodgy GE had discovered the Internet because Welch had, which makes for a good story and keeps the Welch mystique spinning. But to say that the company was Internet ignorant until Welch got enlightenment is incorrect. The fact is, almost all employees had been communicating by e-mail for a number of years, and some GE business units were already operating on the Web. By the late 1990s, when Welch woke up, the Internet revolution was well underway, even at GE. Some GE managers had been using the Internet in ingenious ways:

* In 1994 GE created www.ge.com, one of the very first industrial web sites.
* In 1995 GE's Plastics product catalog went on the Web.
* In 1997 GE Plastics began conducting transactions on the GEPlastics.com web site. By 1999, sales on the web site reached $2 million to $3 million a week.
* *Forbes* reported that same year that General Electric and Thomas Register, a leading publisher of industrial parts

catalogs, had created an online mall for business. GE, said the magazine, was actually ahead of most companies in using the Web for its purchases. Because it had such muscle, when GE Lighting put out a request for quotes (RFQ) for a part, suppliers from Europe, Asia, and even Australia submitted bids as easily as small manufacturers in the Midwest.

★ Also in 1997 Peter Foss, president of GE's Polymerland division, showed Welch Polymerland's new web site, where customers could get timely, personalized information about polymer products, about the status of an order, or about customization services. Foss predicted that by 2001 the site would bring in more than $1.5 billion in annual sales. Polymerland's site became the definitive model within GE, a full-scale, fully operational instruction manual for bringing an old-line business into the online arena. Foss traveled to other GE units, sharing his lessons on how to make e-commerce work. Customers were seeking speed, security, and accuracy. In 1998 the web site was upgraded and improved.

★ By 1998 GE had established financial interests in Internet establishments such as the Snap portal company and the iVillage web site.[10]

★ That year *Computerworld* magazine described a medical systems product configurator at GE, a laptop software tool that walks a customer and a salesperson through the product options. Using built-in rules for design, manufacture, and pricing, it allows the customer to determine what configuration of a machine can be delivered and at what price. When the order is complete, the data is downloaded into GE Medical's order-entry system, minimizing any opportunities for defects based on misunderstandings.

DESTROY YOUR BUSINESS

It's not so much that Welch introduced GE to the Internet (he did not). But when he raised the flag and began the charge up Internet hill, the troops followed anyway, guns blazing. The Welch-led Internet exercise within GE was dubbed "destroy your business," or DYB. The goal was to come up with a business plan that a competitor might use to erode GE's customer base, and a counterplan for how to change the existing business model in response to the exterior threats.[11]

Gary Reiner, GE's senior vice president and chief information officer, noted that for many people at GE, the all-out assault on Internet awareness eased a multitude of fears. "We viewed e-commerce with a lot of trepidation. We thought [online marketplaces] were doing something special and mysterious—that they were going to take our customers away or redirect them to somebody else. Now we're a lot smarter."[12]

The DYB exercises produced retooled web sites, new deals with suppliers and partners, better parts, and improved services. One of the retooled web sites was GE Plastics' PlasticsNet, a shoppers' site. Customers of GE's plastics group, who use the raw plastics in such products as cell phones and auto parts, now use the Web to track orders, sometimes right to the location of a delivery van, instantly getting details that once took a dozen telephone calls. GE engineers use the site to describe how its raw plastics can best be used, and to help customers to design the end product.

For example, a product engineer at a cell phone manufacturing company can plug in the dimensions of a phone into GE Plastics' system and may select several plastics that he (or she) is interested in using. GE's system then helps the engineer determine how many molds must be built to make a part. "When he's done in a few hours," said Gerry Podesta, general manager of e-commerce for GE Plastics, "he has a fairly extensive matrix of what products would work and a ballpark figure on costs. It gives him an enormous head start on the process of designing the product."[13]

Even though GE had some experience with the Web, Welch's new and highly energized Internet push generated genuine results. The company estimates that online ordering saves it three to four cents on every dollar, compared to traditional channels. The GE appliance division has been able to reduce costs from $5 to 20 cents by getting people to go to its web site instead of calling a phone-service representative. The division handles 20 million calls a year, so that's a sizable savings.

GE IS THE IDEAL INTERNET COMPANY

Welch figures it this way: Even in the short life of the Web, marketers have learned it is an unsuitable venue for finding new customers, though it is an excellent place to serve customers and enhance your relationship with existing customers. Furthermore, GE's bricks and mortar are an advantage. Start-up companies begin with no revenue and high expenses for advertising, warehouses, and setting up supply channels. The start-ups could go for years without breaking even or without substantial sales, for that matter. But entrenched companies like GE have sales and profits. They simply need to get online to cut costs. Then the profits just pile up, explained Welch. "We have the hard part, hundreds of factories and warehouses, world-leading products and technology. We have a century-old brand identity and a reputation known and admired around the globe, all attributes that new e-business entrants are desperate to get." Then Welch couldn't resist playing his favorite oldie tune. "And we have one other enormous advantage— Six Sigma quality—the greatest fulfillment engine ever devised."[14]

GE'S INTERNET STRATEGY

The toughest thing about operating in an atmosphere of technical change is strategic planning, since it becomes impossible to predict the future based on the past. Often the best planning strategy is to ride the wave of the revolution, taking advantage of those aspects of change that most suit your needs and taxing the imagination in trying to figure out which aspects those may be.

GE's chief information officer, Gary Reiner, has followed this road map to the Internet. He sees GE's Web approach as three-pronged:

1. Buy side, where GE interacts with suppliers.
2. Sell side, in which GE interacts with customers.
3. Make side, where GE interacts within its own operations.

BUY SIDE

Key to GE's Internet development has been its Global Exchange Services (GSX), a business-to-business Internet company. In the past, each of GE's divisions held separate auctions in which they would buy supplies from certain vendors. GXS converts all of those auctions to the Internet. In August 2000, GXS launched a service that enabled trading partners in the United States and Canada to share standardized product information for nearly 60 million items through a Web-based catalog. This cross-border sharing of coded product information should shave costs for retail trading partners through shortened cycle times and reduced overhead. One of the companies using the system is Target Corporation in its department store division (Dayton–Hudson, Marshall Field's, etc.).

Bob Brooks, GE's vice president for marketplace solutions, said, "The Internet gives us a standard way of talking with all our suppliers around the world, and they are all over the world," providing GE with everything from safety goggles to office supplies to factory tools and sheets of metal. "A supplier might have only done business with GE Transportation in the past, but tomorrow they can do Transportation, Medical Systems, and everyone else."[15]

"We're getting price deflation that we never had before," said Reiner.[16] GE now buys many of its $15 billion worth of maintenance, repair, and operations supplies—such as office furniture, screwdrivers, hammers, copiers, lightbulbs, fax machines, and paper—online. Being on the Internet could drive transaction costs down from $50 to $100 each to as low as $5 per transaction.

Sun Microsystem's McNealy, who also is on GE's board of directors, said that GE has been smart in setting up its own exchanges. "Now there's a company that understood that you don't let yourself get disintermediated. Set up your own exchange, don't go and join an exchange."[17]

SELL SIDE

GE also has automated its selling process. Shoppers can log on and check out the specifications on appliances such as GE's latest oven, the Advantium. Appliances alone take 20 million calls a year, counting both orders and customer service. Each customer telephone call that comes in regarding a consumer appliance costs GE about $5 by the time it is answered. The same information disseminated over the Web costs only 20 cents. This translates to around a 90 percent reduction in costs. Working on the Web also should cut down on error rates. Telephone order inaccuracies run at about 45 percent; errors supposedly are reduced to one-tenth of a percent on the Web, if the web site is configured properly.[18]

When GE Power Systems took its business online it made the whole buying and manufacturing process visible for both buyer and seller. While many web sites allow customers to place and even track orders, GE Power Systems takes the next step, letting buyers of turbines write specs and, from their Web browsers, actually watch their machines being built. One of the attractions of such a service is the time savings. Customers in some divisions can place an order on the Web and have production scheduled in minutes.[19]

GE Capital lifted a page from its Japanese subsidiary that operates the consumer loan kiosks when it developed an Internet-based program to process loans and other transactions. The savings here are both in time and money. The Internet was expected to slash the processing time for many deals to 10 days from 60 days, and the program—which cost $3 million to $4 million to create—is expected to save GE $12 million in the first year.[20]

PROGRESS TOWARD E-COMMERCE

Not only did GE rev up its existing operations to go on the Net, it formed new alliances with compatible Internet-based companies and acquired a cadre of new, small companies that might give it a head start. After Welch's vocal commitment, GE began aggressively recruiting e-commerce employees, hiring more than 100 in a single year from such companies as DHL Worldwide Express, PepsiCo Inc., and Snap-On Inc. One analyst estimated that it probably cost GE $200,000 to $250,000 in annual salary to land each e-commerce consultant and practitioner.[21]

Welch says GE has made strategic investments in more than 250 emerging companies, many of them Internet-based companies.

BUYING IN

In the summer of 2000, GE invested in the business-to-business (B2B) start-up software company Asera. Asera planned to use its funding to meet the growing demand for its software products and services, along with expanding its business both in the United States and overseas. The third round of financing brought the company's market capitalization to nearly $1 billion. Asera provides hosted Web-based applications that help companies conduct business and improve communications among their sales channels, partners, and customers via an online marketplace. The company charges on a pay-as-you-go basis.

ALLIANCES

Additionally, GE is partnering with high-tech powerhouses such as Intel and Cisco Systems. In June 2000, GE and Cisco Systems formed a new company to build computerized infrastructure for manufacturing and industrial facilities, in an effort to boost productivity and efficiency on the factory floor. The new company, GE Cisco Industrial Networks, will be more than 80 percent owned by GE. The company, based in Charlottesville, Virginia, expects to begin with about 30 employees. The goal of the new company is to make better use of the reams of data generated by factory automation equipment and more closely link manufacturing sites to corporate offices, suppliers, and customers.[22]

LESSONS LEARNED

Unfortunately, Web marketers everywhere learned two things during the 1999 Christmas shopping season: Internet orders can go as wrong as telephone or direct orders, and while selling costs may be lower, intense competition drives profit margins to the thinness of paper. Projections of cost savings, therefore, may be optimistic.

Some of the service and competition problems will shake out eventually, but some changes require a whole new way of thinking. To switch to an Internet business, explained one strategist, is to switch from managed time to real time. "Traditional organizations run like buses, with routes to follow and schedules to meet; real-time organizations are taxis, responding to a waving arm or a voice crackling on a two-way radio."[23]

STATIC ON THE INTERNET LINE

So despite its shining promise, there are several dangers associated with the Internet. Too many similar sites are chasing after too few dollars. And even if a company reaps benefits from lower supply costs, the Internet also will drive down profit margins for everyone, including GE's own products. At some point, the diminished earnings could slam GE's bottom line. The Internet has been a touchy game and will continue to be so.

Forbes reported that GE's Web efforts have had other negative fallout. Welch's refusal to give his deal makers a piece of the action cost GE dearly. GE Capital Corp. invested $300 million in 45 Weblets, purchasing stakes now worth more than $1 billion. For the Web masters, their options were in GE, not in the firms they helped start.[24] Although at first this bothered some of the entrepreneurs, after the dot-com shake out of 2000, they no doubt were pleased to have blue chip options.

NBCi

In 1999 NBC formed NBC Internet Inc., by combining the NBC-controlled search engine Snap.com with xoom.com, which lets visitors create their own home pages, and several other sites. The idea was to create a family of online properties that could trade traffic and take advantage of the $380 million in free advertising that the NBC television network would contribute. NBC hoped to create an Internet powerhouse that would compete with the likes of Yahoo! Inc. and America Online Inc. NBC (hence GE) owned 43.9 percent of the company. Chris Kitze, the company's first CEO, talked about harnessing the power of the peacock to capture a sizable chunk of the Internet's advertising and electronic commerce. One year later the project was in shambles, reported *Business Week*. NBCi's publicly traded stock, which once sold for $106 per share, had fallen 92 percent to about $8. It was expected that the company would generate sales of only $135 million in 2000, 19 percent less than the $167 million analysts expected. Operating losses were expected to be around $220 million, and by midyear NBCi laid off 170 people, about 20 percent of its staff.

There were various excuses, such as a softness in dot-com advertising and problems integrating the acquisitions. But employees also complained that the start-up was poorly managed and didn't get the support and interaction from NBC that it expected.

In 2000, GE expected to generate more than $5 billion in sales over the Web, out of total projected sales of $125 billion. In mid-2000 William J. Lansing, who started his career at GE, then went to Fingerhut Cos. (which then was sold to Federated Department Stores), took over as CEO of NBCi. The company, based in San Francisco's financial district, was put through a major reorganization, and NBC pledged greater dedication to the project.

Lansing was a likely candidate for CEO, since his former company, Fingerhut, was an early and successful adopter of selling through the Internet. Also, Lansing had been vice president of corporate development at GE, reporting directly to Welch. Kitze stayed on as vice chairman. In August 2000, GE announced that NBCi would showcase NBCOlympics.com, narrowband and broadband multimedia Olympics content and commerce, exclusive Internet coverage of the Sydney Olympic Games. The decision turned out to be a wise one.

NBC suffered tepid ratings and widespread criticism for its coverage of the games because not only was coverage selective and heavily edited during prime time, but many events were broadcast on tape delay from Australia. Since viewers could find the results of the events on the Internet as they were happening, there was less interest in television broadcasting. Even so, NBCOlympics.com did not meet the 10 million visitors forecast before the Olympics. But, there were enough hits on the site to satisfy most advertisers. In fact, NBCOlympics.com had a daily average of 544,000 visitors for the week of the Olympics. The figure represented a 419 percent increase over its previous three-week average.[25]

Within months after its reorganization, NBCi announced its latest "click and mortar" project, an agreement to work with Domino's Pizza to provide a free cobranded Internet access service. The NBCi.com/Domino's service is distributed and marketed by Domino's. It will affix CD-ROM to delivery boxes in some markets, print marketing messages on pizza boxes, distribute door hangers, and promote the access service in its advertising. For its part, NBCi will count user traffic, sell the advertising, and manage the membership.

NO INSTANT GRATIFICATION

There were glitches along the way and some B2B results have been slow arriving, but they arrived nonetheless. By 2000, there was consensus in the business world that GE was writing the book on B2B via the Internet. When Polymerland.com launched its pilot in 1997 as a secure web site for customers to buy products online, less than $10,000 worth of products were sold per week and the site had fewer than 10 regular customers. By 1999 the site still had only about 50 regular customers and sold less than $50,000 online each week. But by the beginning of 2000, sales reached $100 million, or about 13 percent of Polymerland's total 1999 revenue. And six months after that, the site had about 900 customers supporting sales of about $1.5 million a day. If things continue as planned, 60 percent to 70 percent of Polymerland's total sales soon will be online.[26]

GE management thought that through Internet-derived productivity, GE would save from 20 percent to 50 percent of selling, general, and administrative expenses. In 2000, the volume of all Internet transactions was expected to produce more than $5 billion in worldwide revenues for GE.

IF GE IS FULLY ELECTRONIC, EVERYONE ELSE MUST FOLLOW

Elmer L. Winter, chairman of the Committee for Economic Growth of Israel (based in Milwaukee, Wisconsin) circulated a newsletter to Israeli managing directors with the banner "Let me share with you some shocking advice from Jack Welch, CEO of General Electric." The alarming news was that Welch had deemed that GE would do most of its business on the Internet in the future, so any company wanting to deal with GE must be there as well. If GE took this position, other companies around the world would be forced to follow. Winter warned Israeli corporations that they must start immediately to develop globally functioning web sites.[27]

WHAT THE INTERNET MEANS
TO THE FUTURE OF GE

The *Wall Street Journal* described GE as the last far-flung conglomerate. It is not. There are others, such as the German DaimlerChrysler Corporation—but GE is certainly the weightiest
multinational conglomerate.[28] Size is a source of power and pride,
but a conglomerate also can be an unwieldy beast. The Internet
can help relieve one of a conglomerate's worst headaches—its dis-
connection from everything smaller, including parts of its own
body. The Internet should bring GE closer together as a company,
and closer to its suppliers and customers, while at the same time
extending the company's reach.

Once Welch understood the function of the Internet, he
quickly recognized its possibilities. Much of the growth that
Welch orchestrated at General Electric was through efficiency efforts. Briefly, until the Internet light went on, it seemed that
Welch may have wrung the most he could out of cost cutting, labor saving, and time saving. The Internet gave him one more
crack at it, but the actual impact of the Internet remains unknown. This is an area of intense competition. An information
technology arms race is under way, and GE may not have any special advantage over its competitors. The transfer of activity to the
electronic world may be a surefire way to keep pace, but it may
not get GE ahead of competitors.

THE COST AND THE BENEFIT
TO SHAREHOLDERS

Joining the Internet generation cost GE shareholders and it cost
them big: In the spring of 2000, Welch received a $3.3 million
salary, plus a $31.3 million bonus from the company's long-term

incentive plan. (That year he also exercised $48.5 million in stock options.) GE's board of directors said the bonus was to reward Welch's "determination to confront the challenges and seize the opportunities presented by the Internet and e-business," as well as his leadership skills and his focus on customers.[29]

The reward seems big, but it was only in the millions. Welch claims that under the new Internet effort, GE plans to erase up to $12 *billion* from its operating cost by 2002. To put that number into context, a company with $12 billion of *sales* would rank about 150th in the Fortune 500. GE doesn't break out how much of its earnings gains from its Internet moves, but in the third quarter of 2000 earnings rose 20 percent, a record for any third quarter in the company's 108-year history. Investors reacted positively, and GE shares rose by about 40 percent for the year, a performance that analysts said was boosted by the company's steady emphasis on globalization and its expansion into—what else?—electronic commerce.[30]

The *Wall Street Journal* mused that GE may become the first company to truly fuse the rule-busting "new economy" with the "old economy." If GE succeeds, "there will be no more talk of new economy and old economy, for GE will have managed to create a perfect synthesis of old and new. And the most perfectly developed specimen of the industrial age will have become the archetype for the postindustrial corporation—a company that uses its size and operational excellence to crush the upstarts, and its industry-transforming innovations to constantly surprise the old farts. This is a worthy and necessary aspiration for the next leader of America's preeminent corporation."[31]

Welch can wax as enthusiastic about the Internet as the next guy. "It makes the big small, the slow fast . . . It's in our blood today."[32] But in the end, Welch acknowledges that business is still business and the Internet, basically, it just the latest tool. "You have undoubtedly read about the ongoing debate about 'new economy' companies versus 'old economy' companies and the advantages, or penalties, for being one or the other," said Welch. "The fact is the old economy–new economy scenarios are just trendy buzzwords. There is now and will be in the future only one global economy. Commerce hasn't changed. There is, however, a new Internet technology that is fundamentally changing how business operates."[33]

Furthermore, Welch became agitated at the suggestion that the Honeywell acquisition is a departure from his high-tech initiative, declaring it the "silliest" thing he'd ever heard. Honeywell has long used e-business as a primary strategy. Their MyPlant.com web site allows customers to find a single source for plant solutions that include Honeywell's products, but also products from other industrial suppliers. "Somebody threw me a bomb of a question on this: 'Why aren't you doing this with a high-tech company?' My answer is, what the hell do you think Honeywell is? A high-tech company isn't a dot-com. A high-tech company is a company with great fundamental business and technology that can use tomorrow's tools, the e-business tools, to get faster and more global. We're merging two real high-tech companies. With real earnings. Doing real things. And using e-business tools."[34]

chapter eight

The Dark Side of the Legacy

The ultimate measure of a man is not where he stands in moments of comfort and convenience, but where he stands in times of challenge and controversy. Martin Luther King, Jr.

The higher up you go, the more mistakes you are allowed. Right at the top, if you make enough of them, it's considered your style. Fred Astaire

RICHARD ELLSWORTH, A 20-YEAR GEN-
eral Electric watcher who teaches at Claremont Graduate School
in California, credits Jack Welch with transforming GE from a
lethargic and bureaucratic company into the very model of an innovative powerhouse that is quick to seize opportunities. Yet
Ellsworth discerns "a certain hollowness of purpose" beneath
Welch's relentlessly demanding management style. "Welch has
created a cadre of professionals and has given them a focus on
serving their self-interest," says Ellsworth. "He has told them that
GE will make them better professionals, more marketable professionals, and has subjected them to intense pressures to perform.
But he has not given them a sense of loyalty to the organization,
to some higher goal of the organization. He is still hammering
away at being number one, competing and winning, but what he
may not realize is that the message to managers is 'look out for
yourself, win at any cost, do whatever you have to do.' "[1]

Welch's success at GE indeed has come with a price tag. The
price has been a certain number of disgruntled employees and
former employees, some of whom take the company to law
court. Additionally, there have been numerous scandals and scams
associated with Welch, and the company seems to keep up a running battle with environmentalists. Shareholders are happy with
their returns, but many object to egregious CEO compensation
and cite Welch as a particularly dangerous role model in this matter. These and other festering issues can be folded into a question
that has been asked time and again and GE has not fully answered. Does a major corporation have a responsibility beyond
the bottom line?

At the one-hundredth anniversary of the founding of the Edison Electric Light Company in 1978, then GE chairman Reg
Jones (who two years later handpicked Jack Welch as his successor) spoke of GE's culture. "We have roots. We are not merely a

'bundle of assets hastily thrown together in a feverish search for profits,' as somebody once said about one of our competitors. Rather, we are a product of history, shaped and tempered by time. We have our legendary people, places and events, our famous firsts and our famous failures. Out of all these and many other nameless, long-forgotten events we have forged a distinctive set of traditions, values, and beliefs that we call 'the spirit of General Electric.' It inspires great loyalty, it encourages moral integrity, and it honors innovation. In my view it is one of our most valuable assets."[2]

THE COST OF REMAKING GENERAL ELECTRIC

Just as you probably don't want to know how sausage is made, how veal is produced, or how the hen lives that laid the egg you ate this morning, maybe you don't want to know all the details of how Welch remade GE. A lot of guts and gristle went in and a lot of blood flowed from the sausage grinder.

It was only three years before he passed the gavel to Welch that Reg Jones proclaimed that "the spirit of General Electric" had three elements—loyalty, moral integrity, and innovation. Critics say that even with Jones GE didn't always live up to those high standards, but at least he put them forth as ideals.[3]

THE LAST OF LOYALTY

"Welch may be the most brilliant chief executive in America," wrote Robert Reno of *Newsday*, "but he sure didn't get the title creating jobs. GE's workforce has shrunk from 400,000 to 220,000 under his stewardship, even as revenues doubled."[4]

Reno wrote those words in 1994, and since then the layoffs at GE have abated considerably. GE's employee ranks increased by the end of the century to 340,000, but only after many hundreds of companies worldwide were brought into the fold. When GE acquired Honeywell International, the employee level rose to 465,000, but it was expected that some employees would be fired as similar operations, such as the polymer businesses, were merged. More than 500 people work at Honeywell headquarters, which most likely will be closed or drastically reduced in size.

Thomas O'Boyle, author of *At Any Cost*, a book highly critical of Welch, contends, "We as a society have come to believe, mistakenly, that laying off people is what progressive, forward-thinking companies do. The fact that the welfare of people is no longer a consideration in the minds of investors reflects what is perhaps the most far-reaching paradigm shift of the last decade in corporate America, and Jack Welch's actions were instrumental in leading that shift."[5]

Deliberately and with zeal, says O'Boyle, Welch drove the word "loyalty" out of GE's culture, to eliminate any expectation of jobs for life. That, plus a downsizing mania that spread through the entire economy in the 1980s and continues today, has changed the relationship between workers and their companies, and not necessarily for the better. Workers are understandably reluctant to pledge loyalty to a company that offers them none in return.

On one of his many visits to Japan, Welch told business leaders his side of the story. "It's an abuse of management rights to try to keep a weak business going in the name of lifetime employment. It's better for the employees to leave the weak business and have it merged with a stronger company."

Not all departures from GE are based on the need to slash overhead costs. Some, of course, left to seek better opportunity elsewhere. There also is a list of people who left GE in an unhappy state, and dozens who filed wrongful termination suits or some other official complaint against the company. Welch doesn't deny that his standards are tough. "We've been fair and open. That doesn't mean being easy. You perform, or you're gone. There's tension in the rubber band."[6]

In the book *Built to Last*, authors James Collins and Jerry Porras say that when a company's culture is as highly defined as GE's, some discontent is inevitable. "Only those who fit extremely well with the core ideology and the demanding standards of a visionary company will find it a great place to work. If you go to work at a visionary company, you will either fit and flourish—probably couldn't be happier—or you will likely be expended like a virus. It's binary. There's no middle ground. It's almost cult-like. Visionary companies are so clear about what they stand for and what they're trying to achieve that they simply don't have room for those unwilling or unable to fit their exacting standards."[7]

Some rank-and-file employees, especially those less likely to benefit from stock options and performance perks, sometimes resent the pressure put on them by Welch. "No matter how many records are broken in productivity or profits, it's always, 'What have you done for me lately?' " says Stephen Tomrey, who negotiates the United Electric Workers contract for some 6,000 GE employees. "The workers are considered lemons and they are squeezed really dry."[8]

Even so, although union membership has dropped by about two-thirds over the past 20 years, from a high of 120,000, relations between organized labor and GE are stable. GE workers last staged a nationwide strike in 1969. In the summer of 2000, GE and its electric unions reached an agreement that provided a 14 percent increase in salary packages, giving the average worker a raise in weekly pay to $910 from $800. The International Union of Electrical Workers represents GE's unionized workers in the aircraft engines, appliances, industrial motors, power systems, and lighting businesses.[9]

When confronted by the German magazine *Der Spiegel* with the accusation that GE workers get the short end of the stick where compensation is concerned, Welch countered, "We don't go out into the streets and force people into our factories at gunpoint. Everyone who works for us is here because he wants to earn money and develop himself intellectually. The wages I pay are adequate and the atmosphere here is so exciting that they all want to stay. So where's the problem?"[10]

The critics claim that Welch's productivity and cost-cutting pushes may have contributed to some of the defense contracting scandals that have dogged GE, and to the embarrassing Kidder Peabody bond trading fraud that in the early 1990s created bogus profits for the company.

SCANDALS, SCAMS, AND LAWSUITS

General Electric's reputation under Welch's leadership has gained respect in many quarters, but in some ways its name has been tainted. As a matter of fact, GE long held a reputation—warranted or not—for walking within the law but skirting the edge of legality. Between 1940 and 1950, despite a war in which the U.S. military was GE's best customer, the government sued GE 13 times for antitrust violations, charging price-fixing and other anticompetitive practices. Between 1959 and 1961, GE was slapped with 20 indictments from the Justice Department as the result of what *Fortune* magazine called "The Incredible Electrical Conspiracy."[11] The government charged that GE and its accomplice companies had colluded during an eight-year period to fix prices, rig bids, and divide markets on electrical equipment valued at nearly $2 billion each year. Three GE executives went to jail for price rigging and for violating the Sherman Antitrust Act. Following that episode, GE established a strict code of conduct, which remains in place today. Yet in a company the size of GE, it may be inevitable that things still go awry:

* The Kidder Peabody debacle, which was discussed in some detail in Chapter 4.
* The Equal Employment Opportunity Commission, on behalf of employees, sued Kidder Peabody in the late 1980s, charging that Kidder illegally forced out 17 investment bankers based on their age.
* In 1985, GE pleaded guilty to a 108-count indictment brought against the company by a Philadelphia grand jury. The charges stemmed from work done at GE's Space Systems division in Valley Forge, Pennsylvania (which later was sold to Martin Marietta). The guilty plea made GE the first major defense contractor ever to be indicted on charges of defrauding the government on a defense contract. The problem started when GE experienced cost overruns on the Minuteman nuclear missile contract. Welch himself describes this as one of his darkest hours. "The most gut-wrenching thing was being battered in the defense scandal. It hurt, it hurt a lot. We love this place and somebody was throwing stones at it. We went down a lot of paths [figuring out what happened]. It takes a long time because [people] come in with arguments about the complexity of government rules and a lot of other things. Then we got to the point where we concluded that someone did cheat, someone did try to beat the system. Until we got to that point, we were chasing ourselves around in a circle. But it isn't the government's fault. It's basic integrity."[12]
* The Egyptian bribery incident: GE had paid bribes directly and through military officers to win a 1988 radar contract.

GE itself reported the incident and paid fines of $5.9 million to the U.S. government, since it involved the Foreign Military Financing program.

★ The Rami Dotan affair: GE's Aircraft Engines division pleaded guilty in 1992 to diverting $42 million of U.S. government funds to an Israeli general so that the company could win orders for jet engines. That same year the Defense Department suspended GE's Aircraft Engines business from receiving new government contracts. The suspension lasted only five days, at which time GE promised to establish a panel to monitor all foreign arms sales.[13]

★ The diamond price-fixing scandal involving DeBeers of South Africa. Capping a two-year Justice Department probe, GE's synthetic diamond business and the DeBeers cartel were indicted, along with two executives, in February 1994 for conspiring to fix prices. A lawsuit followed but GE prevailed—acquitted by the judge even before the jury met.

★ *Dateline NBC* in February 1993 rigged a GM pickup truck with a rocket so it exploded in a catastrophic fashion to illustrate a news story which prompted GM to sue GE for libel. GM dropped the suit after *Dateline* aired an apology.

★ In 1995, GE's Aircraft Engines division paid $7.2 million to the federal government to settle a whistle-blower lawsuit brought by a GE engineer who charged the company with selling to the U.S. Air Force jet engines that didn't meet contract terms.

In 1989, despite objections from his Corporate Executive Council, Welch pushed through a performance evaluation system that graded corporate officers, the corps of top executives, on how they supported GE values that instructed them to never bend or wink at the truth, to live within both the spirit and the letter of the law, and to remember that teamwork depends on trust, mutual understanding, and the shared belief that the individual will be treated fairly in any environment.

"Excellence and competitiveness are totally compatible with honesty and integrity," insisted Welch, reflecting some of the steely resolve that he often credits to his mother's influence. "The A student, the four-minute miler, the high-jump record holder—all strong winners—can achieve those results without resorting to cheating. People who cheat are simply weak."[14]

Nevertheless, author O'Boyle charges that not only has Welch's profit-driven policy infected GE with misbehavior, but also, since Welch has so many disciples, the situation is contagious. "The constant pressure to 'go get the numbers' has led, inevitably, to aberrant behavior. The impact this Darwinian mentality has had on General Electric is huge; the impact it has had on America is more complex."[15]

A GOLIATH VERSUS THE ENVIRONMENT

Welch was raised as a Catholic, but that cuts him no slack with shareholder activist nuns (he was an altar boy as a child but as an adult he stopped going to church after his mother died). In an effort to pressure GE into disassociating itself from the nuclear weapons business, the Sisters of St. Francis ordered their college, high schools, and 12 hospitals to shun GE products. The boycott deprived GE of $2 million in orders for everything from lightbulbs to CAT scanners. The Dominican Sisters of Caldwell, New Jersey, is just one of several organizations that considers GE the bad boy of U.S. corporations. The Dominicans began buying shares in the 1960s to help support their older members, but their religious values taught them they couldn't be passive owners. Sister Pat Daly attended GE corporate shareholders meetings for more than 23 years, trying to use her leverage as a shareholder to lobby for changes in GE's business practices. Among her objectives was getting GE to clean up toxic PCBs dumped in the Hudson River decades before. In 1999, the Maryknoll Sisters of Maryknoll, New York, also submitted a shareholder proposal regarding the pollution of the Hudson River.

WHO PUT THE PCBS IN THE HUDSON AND HOUSATONIC?

"From 1947 to 1977 General Electric allowed at least 1.3 million pounds of highly toxic PCBs (polychlorinated biphenyls) to enter the Hudson River ecosystem," read the Maryknoll Sisters' shareholder proposal. "An additional large amount saturated the bedrock and soil substrates beneath two plants, from where it is seeping into the Hudson to this day. PCBs persist in the environment for many decades. Women, children, and disadvantaged communities are most at risk. PCBs are not readily excreted, and bio-accumulate in the fatty tissue of fish, mammals, and humans. This has resulted in the destruction of the Hudson River commercial fisheries, which once earned about $40 million annually. Because PCB concentrations in the Hudson River fish exceed the U.S. Food and Drug Administration safe limit, New York state has issued an 'EAT NONE' warning for children and women of childbearing age each year since 1976 for more than 200 miles of the river."

Furthermore, claim the Sisters, the contamination from GE plants at Hudson Falls and Fort Edwards may be spreading north through waterways as far as the Arctic Circle. They point out that the Pittsfield, Massachusetts, plant has polluted the Housatonic River in much the same way. The Sisters, along with the Environmental Protection Agency and a small army of environmental

groups, want GE to pay for cleanup and a massive effort to educate the public and people living along the two polluted rivers as
to the dangers of PCBs.

THE HISTORY

The Hudson River is one of America's grandest waterways and
runs through the most populous city in the world, New York. The
smaller, picturesque Housatonic River flows through the Massachusetts Berkshire Hills, and through Pittsfield, where Welch
spent all of his early career. Eventually the Housatonic travels
south through Connecticut and into Long Island Sound. GE used
polychlorinated biphenyls to make electric transformers at its
Pittsfield plant for some 45 years until 1977, the year the government banned PCBs after animal tests showed them to be a proba-
ble cause of cancer. The company shut down that particular plant
in the 1980s, leaving a 250-acre contaminated site.

The problem of PCB contamination in the Hudson and
Housatonic rivers started before Welch became chairman of GE,
but he was personally involved both as a plant manager and later
after he was promoted to headquarters in a situation that remains
a sore spot, both at the company and throughout New York state.

A DETERMINED, TOUGH NEGOTIATOR

In 1976 the federal government declared the chemical a public
health menace, and a New York state judge deemed GE guilty of
violating state water quality standards. Reg Jones, then still CEO,
selected Welch to negotiate with the state on behalf of GE. Welch
proved to be a tough bargainer, engineering a Hudson River set-
tlement that limited GE's liability to $3 million. It was estimated
in the late 1990s that it might be necessary to dredge the Hudson

River to get rid of the PCBs, a project that would cost at least $300 million.[16]

As for the Housatonic, GE says it spent more than $120 million cleaning up the site. But the oily liquids continue to show up in the river. The EPA wanted to designate an old GE plant and at least 30 miles of the Housatonic as a Superfund site, allowing the government to pay for a massive cleanup and sue GE for triple the cost. GE fought the idea strenuously, saying that it would hurt tourism in the area, and threatening to move the headquarters of its plastics unit out of Pittsfield because a Superfund label would make it difficult to recruit workers. That could cost Pittsfield 700 jobs.

GE has spent a lot of money to remediate the effects of past waste disposal and continues to do so, even though Welch proclaims that PCBs are harmless. He argues that there is no evidence that the chemicals cause harm to humans. The only way to get enough contaminates into the body to hurt it would be to "eat large amounts of dirt."[17]

GE doesn't deny using PCBs, but it maintains a web site where it aggressively defends its environmental record, contending that river dredging is unnecessary since it will not improve conditions significantly faster than is already occurring naturally. GE has commissioned multiple studies of its own and insists that PCBs do not present health concerns to those who swim, wade, and boat in the upper Hudson River, drink the water, or breathe the air nearby. Furthermore, PCB levels in water and fish in the upper Hudson, says GE, have declined 90 percent in the last 20 years.[18]

Furthermore, Welch says that the PCB pollution was an honest mistake and that GE, along with other manufacturing companies, have learned from the errors of the 1950s and 1960s. "There's no question that nobody who polluted in the fifties and sixties knew a thing about the fact that they were polluting. I was a Ph.D.

chemical engineer from a great school. I came to Pittsfield, Mass-achusetts, and *bathed* in phenol in those days. We never had one course from 1957 to 1960 dealing with the environment. I was part of the chemicals we did. We worked in it. We bathed in it. We did things—I can see trucks driving out of my plant now with waste chemicals that I sold to a waste company. I didn't know where the hell they went. Now we say how bad they were, those polluters. It was not mean."[19]

SHAME ON GE

Writing to *Business Week,* John Hoving, grandson of Walter Hov-ing, who served as chairman of Tiffany & Co. for 25 years, protested GE's recalcitrance on the PCB issue, implying that at the very least, it is behavior unbefitting a company that wants to be a good citizen.

"I wonder what Walter Hoving would have done if he had been told his company was responsible for creating 81 toxic Su-perfund sites across the United States through PCB contamina-tion," asked his grandson. "Would he have launched a public relations campaign downplaying the toxicity of fish tainted with PCBs, a compound banned worldwide? Would he have spent large amounts of shareholder money on a lobbying campaign to amend the Superfund law to limit industry liability for the costs of toxic cleanups?"

John Hoving figures not, describing his grandfather's sense of responsibility as one that included a moral conviction to do what is right. "Welch epitomizes the stereotypical corporate leader whose sense of responsibility is driven by the short-term bottom line."[20]

The public shaming did not deter GE, and the company claimed that most of the people of New York are on its side. In

December 2000, the EPA ordered General Electric to spend $490 million in an effort to clean the Hudson by dredging 2.65 million cubic yards of mud containing an estimated 100,000 pounds of PCBs from a 40-mile stretch of the river. The EPA claimed that improved dredging technology would mean minimal disruption of the river. GE described the cleanup proposal as "absurd" and "outrageous" and vowed to fight the plan in every way it could. GE said it would file suit against the EPA, charging that its regulations were unconstitutional.[21]

THE NUCLEAR CONNECTION

Some of General Electric's environmental problems date back to the era when the company was involved in both nuclear weapons and nuclear power generation. GE operated plants in Troy, New York, and Hanford, Washington, that later were found to be contaminated, and was accused by an employee of being negligent with nuclear materials at its Wilmington, South Carolina, plant.

A movie made by the activist organization Infact about GE's history of accidentally and purposefully radiating workers, inmates, and other unsuspecting subjects, especially at the Knolls Atomic Power Laboratory just north of Schenectady, New York, won a 1992 Oscar for best documentary short subject. *Deadly Deception: Nuclear Weapons and Our Environment*, directed by Debra Chasnoff, also won a dozen or so other awards and recognitions. Even so, the film was not often aired in America. Even though the Public Broadcasting Service chose it as one of 12 to represent the United States at an international film festival, PBS did not run the film itself because it had been financed by Infact, which made it ineligible for airing on PBS. Nevertheless, antinuclear activists visited college campuses wherever possible, showing the movie to students, hoping to make an impression. Infact called for a boycott of GE goods until the company got out of the nuclear weapons business.

Although GE said the film had no negative impact on it, economic conditions prompted Welch to distance the company from both nuclear weapons and the nuclear power generating business. In October 1992, when top chief executives gathered in Hot Springs, Virginia, to golf and socialize at the Business Council, Welch approached an old friend, Martin Marietta chairman Norman Augustine, and broached the subject of selling GE's defense business. In the next few weeks a deal was struck, and in the defense sale was included the Knolls laboratory. Martin Marietta, which later merged with Lockheed to become Lockheed Martin, became the leader in the armaments industry. The deal became final in March 1992, and Infact called off its boycott of GE products, despite the fact that GE held substantial stock holdings in Martin.

As discussed earlier, GE also stopped building nuclear power plants for the U.S. market, largely because of diminished demand. GE continues to service its existing plants, and is involved in nuclear generating projects outside the country. When a shareholder petitioned the company to abandon nuclear power altogether, GE's board objected to the proposal. "Nuclear power makes a significant contribution to meeting the world's demand for electricity. In 1999, approximately 17 percent of the world's electricity was generated from commercial nuclear plants," read the statement. The board "believes it is also appropriate for GE to participate in the development of advanced designs for nuclear generating plants for sale, under appropriate conditions and safeguards, to utility customers in areas of the world where a mix of technologies will be necessary to supply a growing and balanced need for electrical generating capacity."[22]

MONEY VERSUS MORALITY

The money versus morality debate such as that surrounding environment and nuclear controversies is not new in America. It dates back to the foundation of the United States, and perhaps was shipped over from England long before the colonies became a nation. Big business often is cast as a villain in the debate, yet there are many employers in the United States that take their social responsibilities as seriously as their economic responsibilities. Welch no doubt would count GE among them.

Some people would have been more convinced had Welch, as one group of shareholders requested, signed GE on to the CERES Principles. These guidelines were drawn up by the Coalition for Environmentally Responsible Economies, a network started by institutional investors who wanted assurance that they weren't financing ruination. The group now consists of more than 50 corporations, including 12 from the Fortune 500. CERES promotes an environmentally sensitive code of conduct for business.[23]

Among the U.S. companies that have adopted the CERES Principles (originally called the Valdez Principles, named for the *Exxon Valdez* oil spill in Alaska's pristine Inside Passage) are Sunoco, American Airlines, Bethlehem Steel, Ford Motor Company, General Motors, Polaroid, The Body Shop, Ben & Jerry's, and Aveda. However, as the CERES organization requests its signers to do, GE provides an annual global environmental report for internal use and makes the report available to the public, shareholders, and the media.

Note: For the full list of CERES Principles, please turn to Appendix C.

WELCH'S SALARY EXCESSES

At the "Executive Pay Watch" web site, the labor union AFL-CIO charged that in 1999 Jack Welch took home more in compensation and stock options than the combined wages of 15,000 Mexican *maquiladora* factory workers. GE also operates factories in such countries as China and India, where workers often are paid even less than in Mexico.[24]

One U.S. union representative said his members didn't want as much as Welch earned, just the same percentage yearly raise that Welch himself receives. On salary alone this would mean a raise of more than 11 percent each year. If salary and benefits are combined, the union raise would be more than 28 percent per year. Typically, union pay increases have averaged 3 to 5 percent per year.

In 2000, Welch's total paycheck was estimated at $75.6 million, with $3.3 million of that in salary and the remainder in bonus and stock options, according to Graef Crystal, a compensation expert who writes for Bloomberg News Service.[25]

The 2000 salary "was 105 percent over the market if you calculate by size, performance, and standards in his industry," explained Crystal. "If there were more emphasis on performance and less on size, it might not be over. If anybody is worth that much money, perhaps he is. But the question is, is anyone worth that much? I would say no."

When asked about the level of his pay, Welch has said that he and other executives like him are paid based on a supply-and-demand market. Crystal contended that if such a market actually exists, it is jiggered because it is set up so that the CEO has enormous power over determining his own salary. In a perfect world, how would the appropriate compensation for the CEO of a company like GE be calculated?

"I couldn't even answer the question," said Crystal. "That would involve my own judgment, which is worth nothing. If you depart from what purports to be a market, it's anyone's guess." Crystal says that there is no standard formula for determining how much a chief executive should earn. "Aristotle says 5 times the pay of the average worker; Peter Drucker says 20 times. Now, it's based on a crazy market where size is everything and performance counts for nothing."

Welch's sky-high pay has set a dangerous precedent, said Crystal. The problem is that GE's compensation figures are used in the general formula to determine what other CEOs should receive. The company "is included in the pay peer groups of virtually every other large company in the land. So Welch's pay jacks up the averages, and a whole lot of companies start paying more because Jack Welch is being paid more." The fact that the other CEOs are running less significant and much less successful companies does not enter into the formula.

"Welch embodies everything that is right and everything that is wrong with U.S. executive compensation." Based on pay for performance, said Crystal, Welch deserves "a ton of money." Yet as fast as Welch puts profits in the pockets of his shareholders, his own pay blooms even more quickly. And because General Electric is prominent in so many industries, his soaring paycheck validates the cycle of ever-rising pay for a swath of CEOs whose performance doesn't justify the money.

THIS IS NOT FAIR, SAY THE NUNS

In 1999, the Sisters of the Blessed Sacrament of Bensalem, Pennsylvania, submitted a shareholder proposal requesting that GE's compensation committee prepare a report that would link executive pay, including Welch's, not just to the company's financial performance, but also to social corporate performance, including treatment of various racial groups, sexual harassment at the company, and so forth. Each year the sisters would like to see a comparison of compensation packages for company officers with lowest-paid company employees in the United States and around the world. Additionally they want the compensation committee to consider whether there should be a ceiling on top executives' salaries to prevent GE from paying excessive compensation. They suggested that compensation should be frozen, with no raises for top management, in the event of massive layoffs.

Franklin Research & Development, a socially conscious investment company in Boston, submitted a shareholder proposal asking that Welch's compensation be limited to an unspecified multiple of the lowest-paid GE worker. Although $100 invested in GE stock in 1980 grew to $4,676 by the end of 1998, the proposal said, "We believe this value has been created not by one individual, but by hundreds of thousands of current and former GE employees." In 1997, Welch's salary was 1,400 times the average factory worker and five times the average CEO, the proposal said. The proposal also charged GE's cost cuts have been disproportionately focused on the factory floor, while ignoring the executive suite.[26]

SPREADING STOCK OPTIONS AROUND— BUT NOT EVENLY

Welch does not deny he has an astronomical salary, but he points out that others inside and outside GE have benefited from his success. He shares the wealth. "This year we will cash $1.6 billion in employee gains in stock options. A billion two of that will be below any senior management level. We have 40 percent of our optionees make $70,000 or less. If they got 1,000 shares the last five years, they would today have a gain of $800,000—12 times, in five years, their annual salary. That's a kick. It can change their lives. And we're having a ball doing it. We're all fat cats, we got it. But now having a lot of other people get it is really a great game."[27]

Again, ordinary employees profited, but their gains were diminutive and disproportionate compared to GE's top officers and directors. The top five executives at GE took home 7 percent of the stock options. Welch took the highest percentage, 3.7 percent. If the remaining 340,000 employees divided the leftover stock options between them, each would receive 0.00027 percent.

But of course the remaining options are not divided evenly. In the 12 months between July 1999 and July 2000, 22 insiders cashed in $326 million in GE shares, an average of $14.8 million each. While not all employees are granted stock options, approximately 30,000 do receive them. This may help account for GE's 8 percent attrition rate among employees, despite the fact that GE-trained managers are in enormous demand by other corporations.

Business Week reported that 73 percent of the American public sees executive pay packages as excessive, and they feel they're not getting their fair share of the riches. Average wages and benefits outpaced inflation by only 7.5 percent since the last recession ended in 1992, while productivity has jumped by 17.9 percent. The gap between the rich and poor is widening, and multimillion-dollar pay packages only inflame matters.[28]

Whether the high salaries are justified or not, whether GE has been careless or even negligent in its business practice, Welch and GE face the risk that the perception of wrongdoing prevails. A public backlash fueled by generalized anticorporate sentiment already was brewing at the end of the twentieth century.[29]

THE LOOMING CORPORATE SPECTER

The saga of GE will continue to be of interest for years ahead, if nothing else because of the size it has accumulated. Size scares people. *Business Week* reported that in 2000, a solid two-thirds of the U.S. public gave companies their due for the current prosperity, and they believed that large corporations make good products and compete well in the global economy. Those polled also said they felt uneasy about the power business has gained over many aspects of their lives.[30]

Business Week wrote that raw anticorporate feelings were on display in the summer of 2000 during the Big Tobacco trial in Miami. "When it ended, the foreman of the jury that delivered a $144.8 billion punitive-damage judgment against the industry took the opportunity to speak out, saying the jurors' deliberate intention was to 'put the companies on notice—not just the tobacco companies, all companies—concerning fraud or misrepresentations of the American public.' "[31]

WELCH ACCOMPLISHED ALL THE GOOD THINGS AT GE: SOMEONE ELSE DID THE BAD THINGS

Welch has been able to align himself with GE's accomplishments, but distance himself from its excesses, scandals, and failures. Unlike Japanese executives, Welch does not make personal apologies for mistakes. Somehow he manages to stand apart from the fray, partly by seldom being seen or heard in near proximity to most GE scandals. In an unusual occurrence, Welch appeared before Congressman John Dingle's subcommittee hearings when GE was indicted for the $14 million fraud in its aerospace division.

Daniel Natarelli, now chief executive officer of Specialty Silicone Products Inc., took over management of the GE Norel industrial plastics plant in Selkirk, New York, after Welch had built and then run the plant for several years. Natarelli feels that the criticism of Welch, especially regarding his relationship to employees, is distorted.

"I was able to see firsthand what he had done. The people he hired worked for me. People still at that plant would keep in contact with him, technical people around the plant. He is a very charismatic leader. There are a lot of bizarre stories. Contrary to what you read sometimes, people who work for him, they love him. They follow him like you would follow any other leader— Patton, Omar Bradley. When he charted a course, they would jump on and follow him. He had it very young and he never really changed."

★ *Part III* ★

The Future

No pessimist ever discovered the secrets of the stars, or sailed to an uncharted land, or opened a new heaven to the human spirit.
Helen Keller

There is nothing impossible to him who will try.
Alexander the Great

*W*hile people worldwide were worrying about millennium problems with computers and the like, at GE the Y2K problem was called NMJ—no more Jack. Or so they thought, until a series of stalls and startling events unfolded.

Welch's retirement would be a big deal—the signal of the end of a certain era, the tenure of CEOs who faced extraordinary challenges in the 1980s and 1990s: globalization, information technology, and the threat to American competitiveness. His peers are the business warriors Larry Bossidy of AlliedSignal, the late Roberto Goizueta of Coca-Cola, and, as odd as it might seem, Bill Gates of Microsoft, though Gates is much younger and adds the glitter of entrepreneurship to his crown. Many CEOs of Welch's era failed, and as a result, have already faded into history, but Welch had become an icon, a name that when spoken, represented all that is good, bad, and fascinating about big business.

The news media wrote and talked about Welch's retirement for years and waited, just short of keeping binoculars trained on corporate headquarters, for the news of when Welch would make his exit. There was a collective holding of breaths in General Electric land, as managers, workers, customers, and suppliers awaited word of the inevitable. Jack Welch would be stepping down as chairman of the company that he spent 20 years reinventing, but when? Who would replace him?

The selection of Welch's successor had been underway at GE for some years and preparations were exhaustive—evaluations, training, shifting of assignments so candidates could be studied encountering different types of challenges. The process took on a sense of urgency in 1995 when Welch suffered chest pain and was admitted to a New York hospital for quadruple-bypass heart surgery. But Welch recovered nicely and the process reverted to a leisurely pace.

MAINTAINING THE GE TRADITION

Historically, GE has been dedicated to leadership continuity, which is one of the explanations for its enduring success as a corporate entity. The traditional pattern is that of a long-serving CEO whose successor immediately sets out to reform the corporation. It has worked for GE. Each new leader has taken the corporation on a steady upward path. GE's commitment to intensive, career-long management training and of promoting from within has helped preserve much the company's fundamental culture and its core values, even in times of change or transition or when the corporation is under pressure for one reason or another.

In taking his time to find his heir, Welch was also walking the GE way. Reg Jones did the same when selecting and grooming Jack Welch. In 1974, seven years before he retired, Jones created a document entitled, "A Road Map for CEO Succession." When Jones started his search, he began with a field of 96 possible candidates, and in the end he chose the one least likely, the maverick.

If the future CEO of GE is like other successful CEOs of our time, he will have the important traits of integrity, vision, an ability to focus, a willingness to take strategic risks, and an unwavering belief in himself and his company.

THE CONTENDERS

Welch says that he tried to guide the picking of his replacement so that competition between the contenders didn't become cutthroat, battle lines weren't drawn, and GE teamwork wasn't impaired. He warned that if anyone was caught backstabbing he would be eliminated from the race. By the fall of 2000, speculation focused on three of the seven possible candidates for the job. The front-runners were Jeffrey Immelt, head of GE Medical Systems; Robert Nardelli, who runs GE Power Systems; and W. James

McNerney Jr., head of GE Aircraft Engines. All three men are married with children, have MBA degrees, and are GE veterans:

* ★ Jeffrey Immelt, 44, was always the favorite in some camps. His father, Joseph, was at GE Aircraft Engines for 38 years, and he met his wife Andrea when both worked at GE Plastics. The former college football player stood out early in his GE career when he persuaded carmakers to substitute plastics for metal on some parts, and later, when he deftly handled the fallout from the recall of refrigerator compressors. At the time he was chosen as CEO, Immelt lead GE's Waukesha, Wisconsin–based Medical Systems where again he showed his mettle. Before he took over that post in 1997, the unit had suffered three years of flat revenues. By 1999, revenues grew 23 percent. Hot on the acquisition trail, Immelt built GE Medical into a $6 billion plus company the size of General Mills.

* ★ Robert L. Nardelli, 52, also the son of a GE engineer, was dubbed "Little Jack" for his similarity to Welch. When Nardelli headed the plant in Schenectady, in addition to running a profitable operation, he worked hard to clean up environmental damage. After he took over Power Systems, the unit installed five times the number of systems as the prior year, pushing profits to twice what they had been even two years earlier.

* ★ W. James McNerney Jr., 51, has no GE genealogy. When he arrived at GE from McKinsey & Co. in 1982 he had to navigate GE waters without it. Although he's said to have the least charisma of the three, he is known for charging up workers and attentiveness to key customers. McNerney made the company a lot of money, turning his group into the most profitable industrial unit at GE. He is particularly responsible for putting together the pact to exclusively supply the GE90 engine for the long-range Boeing 777.

WINNERS NEVER QUIT?

Despite the intensity of the succession planning and a prime selection of candidates, in the late 1990s it seemed as if something was amiss. Welch had always dodged questions about his retirement, a step that is required at GE once a CEO reaches age 65. Because Welch would achieve that benchmark on November 19, 2000, the investment world started expecting an announcement of his retirement date and replacement in 1999. There was no word by the January 1999 Florida GE executive meeting, and none by GE's April annual meeting. Rumors edged the date ahead, month by month. The word didn't come until the fall of 1999; the then 64-year-old Welch would retire after GE's annual meeting on April 2, 2001. Yet Welch and GE's board still hadn't named a successor.

Welch's seeming reluctance to let go of the reins was easy to understand. His entire ego was wrapped up in GE. "I don't *like* this job. I *love* this job," he said in the late 1990s. "If you like business and you like hanging around with bright, enthusiastic people—I love the team because I picked it all. Naturally, having been in this long, they're my friends."

Furthermore, though he looked all of his 65 years, his health was fine and his energy level exceeded that of some men half his age. Welch explained that during one recent week he had worked one day with Power Systems, another with Aircraft Engines, and one with Plastics. During the same week he'd conferred with NBC executives, then acquired a company in the power field and an insurance company, and settled a three-year contract with GE's labor unions. "All weekend we were doing deals and another team was down there doing the union thing. It's a whole series of things, you know. It's such fun."[1]

MAKE UP YOUR MIND, JACK

Nevertheless, five years seemed plenty of time to choose an heir and yet by October 2000, less than six months before he was scheduled to leave, Welch had not done so. Jack was still firmly seated at his desk working when he should have been taking an around-the-world victory lap and saying his good byes. He was extending his stay five months into his 65th year, ostensibly so that he could be certain he handed his successor a global, Internet-active company. It made sense at first that Welch didn't want to name a successor too soon—GE didn't need two alpha-male leaders at the same time. But surely the new CEO deserved some transition time. Questions arose: Was Welch having trouble letting go?

Stories began circulating in mid-1999 that for some unknown reason, Welch was not satisfied with the internal candidates, and that he might break GE code and name an outside replacement. Suspicion turned toward Scott McNealy, the youthful Sun Microsystems chairman who after the two played golf became a Welch sidekick.[2] Welch, nearly 20 years older, has beaten McNealy in their first two golf matches. However, McNealy said that he and his wife beat the Welches in a couples match. "He claims I needed my wife to beat him."[3] McNealy soon afterward was appointed to the GE board of directors.

McNealy, one of the original Silicon Valley wunderkinds who cofounded Sun with a partner in 1982, seemed like the kind of person Welch would like for the job. Sun, which competes with Microsoft, supplies computer hardware and software. The company has a five-year sales growth rate of 21.6 percent and a five-year earnings per share growth rate of 37.2 percent. The drawback to the idea was that McNealy would have to leave his post at Sun, which didn't make much sense unless GE and Sun merged. It wouldn't have surprised some observers if that had happened, but instead, there was a different revelation in store.

THE CHANGE OF HEART

On a late October 2000 weekend, just as the Connecticut autumn leaves were at their peak of color, the Honeywell International board of directors met to make a final decision on a $40 billion acquistion bid from United Technologies Corporation. Imagine the board's shock and then delight when the meeting was interrupted by a telephone call from Welch promising GE would offer nearly $45 billion. And to make sure that the massive combination of GE and Honeywell went smoothly, Welch was prepared to stay on as chief executive until the end of 2001. Imagine the stricken expressions in Fairfield as the succession candidates, who already had been strung out for months, got the news. McNerny may have been the only candidate pleased by the revelation. He'd been advocating the purchase for months, and now, with a heavier aviation component to GE, his prospects of replacing Welch seemed brighter.

THE GUY WHO GOT THE JOB

Welch dodged the retirement bullet briefly, but pressured by reporters and investment houses who wanted to know what was going on, Welch promised to name his successor soon—within a few weeks after the Honeywell acquisition. Perhaps because the contenders were producing such incredible results in their hopes of getting his job, Welch operated in deep secrecy right up to the last moment. On the Friday after Thanksgiving, Welch place a 5:30 P.M. telephone call to Jeffrey Immelt, who was vacationing with his family in South Carolina, asking him to come to Florida to discuss his promotion to the top job. Nardelli and McNerny and others were notified of the appointment that weekend.

Americans were still wondering whether George W. Bush or Al Gore had been elected president when GE hastily convened a press conference for Monday, November 27. Welch shared the news with an interested, but somewhat distracted world. Welch and Immelt showed up for the event at the *Saturday Night Live* set at NBC's New York studio wearing identical navy blue blazers, light blue shirts minus neckties, and gray slacks. Welch called it the "GE uniform." The matching outfits were an accident, he explained, since Immelt had been caught off guard on vacation without much choice of wardrobe. Nevertheless it is a telling point that the heir to the throne would even by happenstance dress exactly like the man who tapped him for the job.

Although it was clear Immelt was delighted to have the job, it was difficult to discern from that press conference what kind of leader Immelt might make. Welch was still clearly in charge, choosing which reporter would ask the next questions and controlling the event. Immelt was polite and somewhat deferential to Welch, giving carefully crafted, politically neutral answers to the queries that went his way. He handily sidestepped some questions by noting that he'd just learned on the previous Friday night that the job would be his. He hadn't made many major policy decisions yet.

Apparently Immelt had youth on his side when competing for the CEO post. Welch has often said that leaders at GE, and indeed at any large company, need time to try things and fail, and time to put innovative ideas into place. Immelt was only 44 years old when he was announced as successor, one year younger than Welch himself was when he took the reins at GE. However, because Welch delayed his retirement, Immelt and he will be co-holders of the title of GE's youngest CEO. While his age gives him time for long service, Immelt's youth also means he is less experienced than the other candidates. A likable, 6-foot-4-inch bear of a man who looks older than his years, Immelt has never worked overseas and has served in only three of GE's major divisions.

Immelt has other characteristics besides youth that appealed to Welch. He earned a degree in applied mathematics from Dartmouth College, training that helped him adapt quickly to the Six Sigma philosophy and to implement the quality assurance program with skill. It helped that Immelt had play basketball at Finneytown (Ohio) High School and lettered in football at Dartmouth, though, unlike Welch, he is not much of a golfer and spends most of his free time with his wife and junior high school–aged daughter. Lest we read too much into his wardrobe selection at his inaugural press conference, Immelt's sports of choice imply that his management style will differ from Welch's. Welch's school-days game, hockey, is a fast, confrontational, opportunistic sport. Though basketball and football are dissimilar in the way they are played, both are brainier and more strategic than hockey.

Earlier, Welch had described the criteria he would be using when he and the board of directors made their final choice: "Obviously anybody who gets this job must have a vision of the company and be capable of rallying people behind it. He or she has got to be very comfortable in a global environment, dealing with world leaders; have a boundaryless attitude toward every constituency—race, gender, everything; have the highest standards of integrity; believe in the gut that people are the key to everything, and that change is not something you fear—it's something you relish."[4]

Certainly Immelt does not lack from good advice from outside the company. The *Wall Street Journal* put forth these three rules for a more successful successor:

★ He must have bigger ideas and more imagination than his predecessor. He must have the vision and foresight to anticipate what the enterprise should become over the next two decades. He won't obsess on how to run the company, but on what the company should become, preparing the company for shifts in businesses, markets, technology, governance, and culture.

* He must lead leaders, not simply manage managers. Process discipline, such as total quality management, Six Sigma, are fine for making things run smoothly and efficiently, but they do not constitute leadership. The super-CEO builds a team of top managers who make his vision and beliefs about the business their own.

* He must have political skills to deal with outside challenges. The bigger a company is, the more of a target it becomes for negative journalism, attack politics, government investigation, and so forth. Microsoft, AT&T, Standard Oil, and GE all have found themselves in government crosshairs.

A CHOICE THAT DEFINES WELCH HIMSELF

No matter how well Welch has done at GE, *Newsweek* columnist Allan Sloan says, and as effective as his leadership has been in guiding GE from an old-line industrial company into a sleek, finance-oriented conglomerate, it will not be clear how fine a manager Welch is until Immelt is tested as GE chief executive. "Because picking a worthy successor is one of the most vital elements of managing. Welch seems to be a shoo-in for business immortality," writes Sloan. "But let's take our lead from sports halls of fame, and wait until well after his retirement to put him among the immortals."[5]

THE NEXT BIG QUESTIONS

At this stage of his life, and for General Electric as well, there are many questions. Welch is considered by many to be a national treasure, a unique embodiment of the American spirit. What will he do when he finally leaves GE? Something big, bold, visible, we might expect.

And what about GE? Before the Honeywell acquisition, the question was this: Has Welch wrung so much performance out of the company, operated it so near the edge, that his successor will have trouble molding Honeywell into the mix, and continuing sales and earnings growth at the Welchian rate?

Among the many questions that remain: Will GE continue to trade so richly on the stock exchange, often as high as 49 times trailing earnings? Was that premium based on Welch's leadership intensity, or was it the merits of the company? How has Welch been able to wield so much influence and power over the most far-flung, complex corporation in the world, and how will Jeffrey Immelt ever measure up? Most managers have difficulty leading and motivating a small workforce, and are happy to squeeze out a just average performance. Welch consistently drew superior response from a business empire with assets of $406 billion and 340,000 employees located in more than 100 countries around the world. With the Honeywell merger, those assets will swell to around $428 billion and there will be more than 460,000 employees. As the U.S. economy takes a breather from its recent roaring growth rate, how well will GE hold up? Will the new GE chairman lose support from the board and shareholders if GE wavers in any way?

There is no mystery about one thing: "I'm not retiring because I'm old and tired," said Welch. "I'm retiring because an organization has had 20 years of me. My success will be determined by how well my successor grows it in the next 20 years. I've got a great management team, and they're ready to get the old goat out of there so they can do their thing."[6]

Several years earlier Welch had made a pledge to let the next generation of GE managers do just that. "The day I go home, I'll disappear from the place and the person who comes in will do it their way."[7]

chapter nine

The Meta-Corporation: General Electric after Welch

The dogmas of the quiet past seem inadequate to the stormy present. Abraham Lincoln

There never was a great character who did not sometimes smash the routine regulations and make new ones for himself. Andrew Carnegie, *The Road to Business Success*

JACK WELCH CLAIMS THAT RUNNING GEN-
eral Electric Corporation is the best job in the world, yet the person who takes over after him may find it the toughest job in the
world, especially considering the size and complexity of the Honeywell deal. Jeffrey Immelt inherited a completely different company than no doubt he expected. To complicate matters further,
shareholders, institutional money managers, the media, and even
GE employees will continually compare his performance and his
vision to that of the much admired, outspoken, fleet-footed Welch.
Even before the Welch replacement was named, people were wondering if it was even possible to manage GE better than Welch had.

"If you can find another guy like Jack Welch," says former GE
manager and consultant William E. Rothschild, "who can do the
leadership job he has and is a portfolio strategist and has an infrastructure that gives you sound strategic intelligence to make decisions, the company can probably continue. I guess my feeling is
that there's no simple answer, but at some point in time you're not
going to be able to find a guy like that."[1]

Taking charge of an organization after a legendary leader is a
treacherous thing to do. George Bush seemed rather a bland president after Ronald Reagan. Following the untimely death from
cancer of Roberto Goizueta, the well-liked chairman of Coca-
Cola, in 1997, Doug Ivester lasted only 25 months. This despite
the fact that Coca-Cola, like GE, had a history of chief executives
who served for life.

To make the situation at GE more perilous, this seems to be in
an era when CEOs get the boot faster than they once did. Jill
Barad made a hasty departure from Mattel after just three years as
top executive; Robert Annunziata lasted at Global Crossing only
53 weeks. Welch's successor will be a battle-tested veteran, but
that does not guarantee success. The pressures of the top job are
greater than at any other corporate level.

CHALLENGES AHEAD
FOR THE COMPANY

The first order of business for GE's next anointed leader will be making certain that Honeywell gets settled into the GE family and begins growing and earning at a rate comparable to the rest of the company. Because Honeywell was going through a bad patch, it is likely to be a drag on earnings at first, a problem that may be exacerbated by all the costs that invariably attend a merger. Because Welch plans to stay for an extra year, the first impact on earnings will come under his flag, and that may be good. The Honeywell situation may prove an advantage to Immelt, who formerly was faced with taking over at the end of a year of record high earnings. If Welch takes responsibility for the first earnings hit, his successor can take credit for future improvements.

Even with that little break, the new CEO will face other immediate problems, including the retention of GE's talent pool and managing public and media perception of his performance.

REBUILDING THE MANAGEMENT TEAM

Welch had expected that the losing front-runners for his job would be so primed and ready to run their own companies that they would want to leave, and that Immelt would be faced with rebuilding the management team.[2] A similar thing happened when Welch became CEO. In part, people left because of a sense of hostility and competition that developed during the fierce selection phase Welch endured. "We lost talent, but I think you'd lose talent if you did it nicely. Because these people are just too strong. I'm going to try to do it different," Welch said early on. "I'm not going to have it quite as glaringly a race. And so far—knock on wood—we don't see any signs of it affecting our teamwork. These things got to a point the last time of becoming very political—with each other, not with Reg [Reginald Jones, Welch's predecessor]. Reg handled it beautifully. The people were all just siding with each other. Camps were being formed in the company. Pray to God that doesn't happen.[3]

Despite that, GE was so completely ready for the management shift that an atmosphere developed in which the two losing candidates, McNerney and Nardelli, were almost compelled to go, and indeed Welch's expectation that GE would lose some top talent came to pass. But it happened faster than anyone expected. The new GE chairman and chief executive officer was announced on Monday, November 27, and on Sunday, just six days later, the board of Minnesota Mining and Manufacturing Co. met to ratify its selection of McNerney as its CEO. For the first time in its 98 years, 3M would be led by an outsider. When asked if he harbored any hard feelings for not getting the top job at GE, McNerney replied, "I was disappointed for about 90 seconds. Now I'm excited."[4] Investors clearly were pleased. 3M's share price leaped 11 percent the day after the appointment.

One day after McNerney announced his departure from GE, Home Depot named Robert Nardelli to become its chief executive. Nardelli said he was contacted by Home Depot just moments after he was told of Immelt's promotion. The news of Nardelli's appointment came late on the afternoon of December 5, but in after-hours trading, Home Depot shares rose 7.1 percent.

MANAGING PUBLIC PERCEPTION

A major challenge for the new CEO will be keeping the external market happy. Over the long term GE is sure to survive and prosper in the post-Jack Welch years. In many ways, GE is too big to be controlled or even damaged much by one man. All of the operating managers know their jobs, so in the long term it should not affect the performance of the business. But as Benjamin Graham explained in his classic *The Intelligent Investor*, "Mr. Market" has an emotionally unstable personality and does not act on logic alone. GE's share price took a dive after Welch announced the Honeywell merger and confirmed his retirement—the so-called "Welch effect." GE's shares reached a high of $60.50 in 2000, but then declined more than 30 percent, then rose to end the year at around $47. A celebrity CEO like Welch draws investors into a company, and those who are impressed by the glitter may be frightened when the star plans to step off the stage. GE could go through a period of turmoil similar to what other corporations experience under similar circumstances. "Different company, different leader, different market, but it is still the same street," wrote a participant on the GE Motley Fool online chat room.

"The stock price is so dependent on how analysts interpret what is happening," said Harvard Business School's Professor Bower. "If for one reason or another, perhaps just because of something happening in the environment, GE's performance were to be unexpected, you could imagine the analysts deciding that [the new CEO] doesn't have it. That possibility strikes me as very real, just because of the way the analysts are—a mindless herd. If that were the way they chose to go, it could be very hard on the next leader. Remember, it took a long time, almost a decade, for Welch to get appreciation from Wall Street. The next leader will face some version of that problem."

GE's vice president Dennis Dammerman said that analysts and investors alike should expect the company to be different, but they both should allow the new CEO some leeway. Not only will the Honeywell merger take time to settle, "It's unlikely that from day one his successor is going to be both a celebrity and the leader Jack Welch is. I happened to be there when Jack Welch took over and he's not the same now as he was then."[5]

LONG-TERM CHALLENGES

At the same time the rookie CEO is dealing with temporary tur-
bulence, he will be forced to address larger issues. He must make
sure the GE/Honeywell business portfolio is configured in a way
that is strong enough to replicate the Welch track record. GE has
always been a strategically led portfolio company with a mix of
businesses in different phases of their life cycles, which enables
GE to deliver consistent earnings. Identifying areas of vulnerability in the new business mix, places where cycles are either fundamentally at odds or temporarily out of whack and compensating
for that, will be a major task.

Welch drives home the message that GE's future is that of an
increasingly postindustrial company in which intellectual capital and information will continue to replace muscle and tangible assets. Products and services must be continuously
revamped, and costs must be endlessly and relentlessly driven
down. The trend toward service has been strong, yet GE still has
a mass of hard assets, including a fleet of 850 aircraft, 950,000
cars and trucks under lease and service management, 13 communications satellites, 186,000 railcars, and millions of acres of
real estate.

GE Businesses	Percent Revenues	Percent Earnings
GE Capital Services	49 percent	28 percent
Industrial	10 percent	3 percent
Aircraft Engine	9 percent	13 percent
Power Systems	8 percent	9 percent
Plastics	6 percent	11 percent
Technical	5 percent	8 percent
Major appliances	5 percent	5 percent
Broadcasting	4 percent	9 percent

Note: A more complete description of GE business units is included at the back of the book in Appendix D.

Honeywell had 1999 revenues of $23.74 billion, and was projected to have revenues of $25.1 billion in 2000. A fair amount of that was nonoperating revenue, but its $900 million plus in sales was derived from the following sources.

Honeywell 1999 sales:

Electronics and avionics	39 percent
Auxiliary power	8 percent
Propulsion	20 percent
Design and services	8 percent
Landing systems	4 percent
Engine systems	11 percent
Environmental controls	10 percent

Honeywell's blend of businesses will tip GE back toward its industrial base, which could provide future balance and stability. Economists surmise that if GE has a structural flaw, it is in the sector that has powered much of GE's growth—GE Capital Services. GE Capital dominated the entire company prior to Honeywell, accounting for 85.1 percent of its assets and 89.6 percent of its liabilities. While GE Capital has been the motor behind the company's rapid acquisition program, in recent years the growth has been achieved at the cost of balance sheet deterioration, often caused by paying a high price for such intangibles as goodwill. "None of this means that the company is likely to go bust tomorrow," wrote John Plender in the British newspaper, the *Financial Times.* "But it is a very slender margin of safety against recession and financial shocks, even in a group as well run as [GE]. In addition, it would only take a 5.7 percent fall in the value of GE Capital's gross tangible assets to make the whole

GE group appear technically insolvent. Since GE has guaranteed only a tiny part of GE Capital's debt, this matters less than it might appear. But it shows that GE's boundaryless culture is at odds with legal reality; there is a boundary protecting GE from insolvency at GE Capital."[6]

GRAPPLING WITH GROWTH

To match the 41 (including dividends) percent compounded annual share price appreciation rate Welch achieved between 1994 and 1999—a growth rate against which GE will be measured for years to come—the company's market capitalization would need to expand to more than $3 trillion by 2005. Honeywell's market capitalization at the time of acquisition was around $300 billion, so even taking into account the biggest acquisitions GE has ever made, there is a long way to go. Ultimately, a company can't grow any faster than its earnings grow. In 1999, GE's earnings rose 15 percent; in 2000, a 20 percent earnings growth seemed on track. Welch was predicting about the same for the future before Honeywell entered the picture, so it will be difficult for a new CEO to push the share price higher at the rate Jack Welch did. While GE's long-term prospects look reasonably healthy (2001 revenues with Honeywell in the mix are expected to be around $176 billion), maintaining the past pace of growth, both in earnings and in market capitalization, will require ingenuity.

The situation is complicated by the fact that prior to the Honeywell acquisition there were subtle signs that GE's growth may have been flattening. Between 1981 and 1990, revenue per employee increased by 187 percent. Yet between 1990 and the end of the century, revenue per employee grew by only 55 percent. After 1996, it was nearly horizontal. Honeywell's average employee generates about $209,000 in revenue, compared to $382,000 at GE.[7]

The next CEO of GE has many alternatives to keeping the company going strong, though there are widely differing opinions of the specific course that should be followed. The best ideas could be right before the eyes of a person who understands GE thoroughly. "What you do know is that when someone's been there for 20 years, there have got to be problem areas," said Professor Joseph Bower, referring to Welch's tenure at GE. "It's inevitable. But we don't know where the problems are. The next CEO may have some idea where they are and will move to deal with them. He may decide the benefits of scope are no longer worth the cost of being that big and complicated and might decide to manage it very differently. Everyone speculates on selling some things, but that's not really changing GE. If they've got someone as good as Welch, GE five years from now won't look like the GE of today."

Bower made that prophetic remark before Welch acquired Honeywell, not realizing that Welch would leave the company in such a state of flux that a CEO couldn't avoid having a different company five years out. Nevertheless, Bower's comments on areas of vulnerability and opportunity apply to GE, pre- and post-Honeywell.

SOLUTIONS TO GE'S CHALLENGE

In the coming century, GE has said that it plans to grow through e-commerce, globalization, product services, and Six Sigma quality efforts, but those broad strategies are already underway and may not transport GE far into the future. The growth by acquisition ploy, Welch's leading strategy, will be limited by the number of high-quality corporations of the desirable size available for purchase. Welch's successor may seek growth by creating new companies within the existing GE structure or by returning to GE's former position of an innovator and creator of new technology. A final strategy, as mentioned earlier, might actually shrink the size of

GE by breaking it up into smaller parts. This may sound nonsensi-
cal after a two-decade-long buying spree, but the "destroy your
business" strategy Welch called for when implementing the Internet age could promulgate remarkable new value for shareholders.

THE CREATION OF NEW BUSINESSES

Selling laggards and buying better prospects isn't the only way to
grow. The *Wall Street Journal* figures that GE is capable of creating
10 to 20 new businesses over the next few years, with each adding
an average of $5 billion to GE's market value.[8] Although it is a
mammoth company, Welch has encouraged an entrepreneurial
spirit that could serve well if the new CEO decided to focus on
new business creation. "The United States clearly has a comparative advantage in entrepreneurship, meaning creating and running
small and innovative companies is what America does best," said
Professor Gunderson. "GE is really an anomaly. GE sees itself as a
series of niche businesses. If one business doesn't work, sell it, start
up something new. This is very different from most big business,
which is to wring the cash out of the assets as long as you can."

One stimulant for the innovation GE needs would be to break
from Welch's philosophy and give GE executives an equity stake
in the new ventures they start. GE already invests in start-ups
through GE Equity, to the tune of $1.5 billion in 1999. In 1999
GE repurchased $1.9 billion of its own stock, money that could
have been invested in new ventures. The results could be astounding, but there are obvious pitfalls when pinning future hope on
start-ups. New businesses can be slow off the mark, and some percentage of the companies will either fail or deliver unsatisfactory
returns. When you buy a business, a lot of those start-up risks are
in the past and the buyer has a fairly good idea of how the company will perform. GE investors are accustomed to that advantage

and might need to cultivate the patience to allow new businesses to find their feet.

RETURNING TO TECHNOLOGY LEADERSHIP?

GE once garnered more U.S. patents each year for its inventions than any other company, foreign or domestic. In 1965, GE's peak year, the U.S. Patent Office issued the company 1,063 patents. In 1999, GE was twentieth on the patent list, with IBM in the lead. Of the top 13 patent earners, all but three were Japanese companies.

Welch spent decades hacking away at the self-limiting GE mentality that if something was "not invented here" it had scant value. It would be foolish to go back to a chauvinistic way of thinking, but reviving a pride in "invented here" might offer long-term advantages. After all, GE has derived many years, in fact many decades, of profits from inventions such as the lightbulb and the jet engine.

Such a reemphasis would challenge GE's corporate intellect, but the company knows how to proceed. Back in 1963 GE realized it needed to find new areas of growth, so the chairman commissioned a special group to study the problem, the Corporate Growth Council. The council was charged with identifying business opportunities that were growing faster than the U.S. gross national product (5 percent at the time) and which built on GE's strengths. The Growth Council had a powerful influence on GE. It was one of the first adopters and developers of the now common SWOT (strengths, weaknesses, opportunities, and threats) method of business analysis.

Some of the endeavors that the Growth Council recommended became the foundation of significant GE businesses. Among the growth opportunities pinpointed were engines for aircraft, medical systems, polymer chemicals, nuclear, computers, financial and personal services, entertainment, housing and community development, and education. At the Growth Council's urging, GE Credit became GE Capital and evolved into one of the leading financial services companies in the world. Polymer Chemicals was the foundation for GE Plastics and Materials. Aircraft Engines is one of GE's largest and most profitable businesses, and is growing. Medical Systems also remains on the growth path, and is one of the leading suppliers of medical diagnostic systems in the world. As for computers, community development, and education, GE did not fare well in these industries, but they became growth industries nonetheless.

Although GE has succeeded in only about 60 percent of its new ventures, the performance of the winners has been worth the exercise. The Growth Council was disbanded in the late 1960s, but it could be time for it to be reestablished.

THE VALUE OF ALLIANCES

Under Welch, GE has demonstrated its willingness to grow through commercial alliances with other industry leaders, which could help maintain a high level of innovation. In December 1995, Microsoft and General Electric (NBC) joined forces to operate a news network called MSNBC. The cable television network, which debuted in July 1996, shared programming with the Microsoft network for computers. The idea was that the viewing public could glean news from either the television or the computer, or from both at the same time.

Both Microsoft founder Bill Gates and Jack Welch viewed the partnership as a first step toward blending and maximizing the two media. "Business will be done differently," said Welch. "Distribution will be done differently. Who better to hang around with than the company that has done more to change the world than any other?"[9]

GE has experimented with joint ventures in dozens of phases

of its business, each of them very different in nature from the others. For example, GE is partnered with Elamex S.A. de C.V., a 27-year-old company headquartered in Mexico that operates contract assembly plants, or *maquiladoras*. So far that has been a money-losing proposition plagued with accounting foul-ups and late deliveries, but both GE and Elamex management express confidence that it will get sorted out.

TOO BIG TO MANAGE?

The *Wall Street Journal* put forward the notion that GE was too unwieldy to manage, even before the Honeywell acquisition. William E. Rothschild, a former senior corporate strategist at GE and now a consultant, recently wrote that the next CEO must at least consider whether the company's many parts should move forward as a unit. The parts have grown so huge that there are portfolios within portfolios. Rothschild retired in 1984 after 29 years with GE. "I'm not saying it has to break up, but I'm saying it has to be thought through differently. There may be a creative combination of things that allows the company to maintain its identity as a company but recognizes the distinctly different nature of these giant pieces."[10]

As counterproductive to Welch's legacy as it may seem, breakup isn't a new idea. For years after Welch took charge, analysts and pundits urged him to divide the company into more relevant pieces, claiming it was GE's only hope to compete. The outside experts were wrong, of course, but the idea has pluses and minuses. Other large companies, Standard Oil in the 1920s and AT&T in the 1980s, sent flocks of businesses flying from the nest, companies that became such entities as Exxon and Chevron and Lucent Technologies and all the Baby Bell telephone companies. AT&T was forced into its first split for antitrust reasons, but at the start of the twenty-first century the company was planning another spin-off, this one voluntary. The advantage of a GE split-up is that it would give the complex and far-flung company a clearer notion of the kind of business (or businesses) it really is.

One of the most obvious steps would be a media-related spin-off, and rumors of that possibility have been particularly persistent. The *Los Angeles Times* reported in 1998 that GE was considering cutting NBC off into a separate entity as a way to better establish the network in the cable television business. As mentioned earlier, a jump into any new venture with huge start-up costs and uncertain payoffs could depress or dilute GE's earnings, so by moving NBC into an independent unit, the parent company is granted some protection.[11]

Welch also was reported to have had discussions with Barry Diller about merging NBC with Diller's USA Networks Inc. and Viacom Inc. Talks reportedly broke down with USA Networks because Seagram Corp. chairman Edgar Bronfman balked over a stock swap that would quickly reduce his 45 percent stake in USA Networks to 20 percent or less of a combined company. A second problem with these deals, according to some industry analysts, was that Welch wanted an arrangement that would keep GE in control of NBC, but all of his prospective merger partners wanted to be in control themselves.

Fortune magazine has written that it would like to see NBC merge with Dow Jones. "It's clear that these two powerhouses can work together—they've done it at CNBC, must-see TV for [stock] market junkies. If the companies merged, NBC would get further access to one of the best brand names in financial news, and Dow Jones would have more outlets for its content."

In December 1999, Ted Turner was talking publicly about his desire to acquire NBC for Time Warner. Jack Welch denied that GE had offered to release NBC to Time Warner for $25 billion. "We have no intention of selling. I've tried to say that as many ways as I can."[12]

Although there have been frequent reports of GE doing its own breakup analysis, Welch finally disparaged a split as "hooey" because he felt the "boundaryless" company gains from exchanging ideas across businesses. "GE is greater than the sum of its parts because of the intellectual capacity that is generated in the business and the sharing that goes on of that learning and the rapid action on that learning." He describes GE as a "business laboratory, with ideas everywhere that elevate us to be better than a single-product company could possibly be."[13]

A DISSECTION IN THE BUSINESS LAB

Citing the breakup of ITT Corp. in 1995 by Rand Araskog before he retired (Araskog's predecessor, Harold Geneen, acquired 275 companies in 20 years at ITT to create the much praised, much damned largest conglomerate in the world), *Forbes* couldn't resist playing the break up GE game.[14] Even though a spokeswoman for GE called the *Forbes* idea downright "goofy, the journalistic equivalent of an acid trip," it didn't seem all that crazy.

Forbes would split the company into five pieces:

1. The media arm: This would include NBC network, 13 television stations, the CNBC and MSNBC cable channels, and related web sites.
2. Lighting and appliances.
3. GE Capital Services: GE Capital could do well on its own, but would the remainder of the company prosper without GE Capital, which is contributing about 44 percent of GE's profits? It's easier to produce rising earnings from financial businesses than from manufacturing or other businesses because there is the wide latitude—all perfectly legal—in deciding to cash in profits or defer losses.

4. Jet engines, power plants, locomotives, industrial services, and medical systems.
5. Plastics and all its component parts:[15] Under this category, GE has an especially good candidate for spin-off—Polymerland. Polymerland is similar to a company with a huge valuation, Chemdex. Chemdex is a "vertical portal" that brings together buyers and sellers of life science research products on the Web. Chemdex has a $2.8 billion market capitalization on expected revenues of $24 million (1999). Polymerland does a similar thing with polymers and might do very well in a spin-off initial public offering.

Although *Forbes*'s case study was done before the GE-Honeywell merger, it is interesting to note that it would apply just as easily to the merged companies. The main difference would be that the jet engines and the polymer segments would be bigger and stronger than originally thought. There are, of course, dangers to splitting GE into different companies. Because GE Capital is so deeply integrated into the growth process, many analysts feel that the remaining companies are handicapped and worth less without it. Even if Jeffrey Immelt wanted to do so, some time could pass before he disassembled GE. Although Welch made some changes right away, it took him three years at the helm before he instituted deep, serious reforms at GE. His successor might give himself the luxury of time as well.

RAMPING UP FOR THE META-ECONOMY

Jack Welch ordered many of his dramatic changes at GE because he understood the fundamental shifts in the world economy. The Berlin Wall came down, signaling the end of the cold war. National borders were purposefully removed in the European Community and, with the North American Free Trade Agreement and other pacts, began to crumble elsewhere. Other global barriers were eroded by wireless communications and Internet advances. As this was happening, economists began to observe a new economic trend, one that recognized the emerging political reality, transforming technologies, and the need to either integrate the old with the new or create a whole new economic system. The future of GE may depend on how astute its new leaders are regarding "metacapitalism."

As successful as capitalism is in terms of materialism, there is a theoretical camp that says capitalism is not the apex of economic thinking. Even so, the next step of economic evolution—metacapitalism—is not clearly defined. It carries different definitions for different people. For many economists, metacapitalism can be characterized in three different ways: as either refinement, fusion, or replacement.

Refinement thinking says that basic tenets of classical capitalism must be further modified—the economic system simply needs more work. Specifically, there is a call for finer tuning regarding social and cultural issues. The fusion approach is based on the concept that capitalism must be blended with competing theories, such as socialism or even elements of communism. The replacement theorists search for a completely new way of thinking about economics, or even structuring an economic system.

In each case, the calls for reform are based on dissatisfaction with the long-acknowledged trouble spots of capitalism. Among them: the psychological and emotional price of success for individuals and communities; a deficit of social equity in health-care delivery, legal services, and other areas; and the devaluation or undervaluation of those who perform still-essential old-economy tasks, such as house and street cleaning, child or elder care. Unfortunately, the undervaluation often applies to work that is as essential to the new economy as it was to the old, such as teaching, medical nursing, or keeping homes and public places clean.

BREAKING DOWN THE BARRIERS OF THE MIND

Michael Allen, a former GE strategic planner who now runs his own consulting firm, insists that metacapitalism goes beyond functional issues. It is a change in the way people think about business and work. Ideas and concepts will replace things.

"The new-economy companies will not define themselves in terms of products," said Allen. "They will move to consumer- or customer-defined meta markets. Instead of diagnostic medical equipment, it would be health care; instead of NBC, it will be entertainment. I think when the new CEO of GE decides which consumer arenas the company will be involved in, we'll see as big a transformation of GE as the one made by Welch. I think the change has to be massive."

Allen says that rather than undermine or destroy GE, the meta-economy presents vast opportunities for productivity and growth. "We're entering a golden era. There have always been Luddites who think otherwise. Look around. I'd love to have a cure for cancer, wouldn't you? Or arthritis? The opportunities abound. I make the point that Welch has done a magnificent job with businesses he inherited, and for the most part he still has them, but the GE portfolio is not as strong as it should be in such areas as drugs, international communications, and the like. He's got bits, but I would say he's not deep enough into postindustrial industry."

The Honeywell acquisition did not expand GE into the businesses suggested by Allen, but it is quite possible that GE is already in the metacapitalism mode, or at least headed in that direction. "We service airlines rather than just engines," explains Dennis

Dammerman, "railroads rather than locomotives, hospitals rather than CAT scanners. We sell solutions and answers rather than products."[16]

How will GE get past the antitrust issues that will arise with the transition to the meta-economy? Welch does not see antitrust as an impediment to the GE-Honeywell merger, but the deal will be scrutinized by the Justice Department. "There will be a government power struggle with mega enterprises," said Allen. "Government is all about power. As the economy shifts to the new idea-based value creation, old rules of commerce have to be rethought. A leader has to help shape and educate the governments in the new economics so that government regulators help the economy to grow in a so-cially responsible type way, not a Luddite way."

HOW SHOULD THE NEW CEO LEAD?

As Jeffrey Immelt assumes leadership at General Electric he does not lack for advice on how he should behave and how he should manage the company. The ideas for how Immelt should lead hit almost every point on the management philosophy compass:

* *The maintenance engineer.* Perhaps GE's new avatar does not need to be the agent of change that Welch has been. That kind of CEO was needed when Welch took charge, and Welch got the job done. The role of the new CEO will be to consolidate, cement, secure GE's place in the economy of the new millennium, to keep the newly reinvented engine running at maximum performance, not to build a new engine. For example, Immelt could acknowledge the problems that globalization has brought, and strive to create a GE that is less threatening to those who fear the power of dominant gi-ant corporations in a global setting. By initiating and pro-

moting highly responsible manufacturing and labor practices, GE could become a guiding light to other corporations
as they expand worldwide.

★ *The developer:* Perhaps the new CEO should move GE back a
little in time, toward its earlier traditions. During the reign of
Cordiner, management purges were common. When Fred
Borch took over in 1962, the pendulum swung the other
way. The Borch years were characterized by stability rather
than radical change. He was a consensus manager. Immelt
might be well advised, for example, to address some of the
problems that have plagued GE during Welch's leadership.
Specifically, he could quietly call a truce with the Environmental Protection Agency on the Hudson River pollution
and dredging issue, call GE's formidable negotiating skills
into play, and find a win-win solution with the government.
The company can financially afford to take this stance, and
there would be many intangible benefits. Although in many
ways GE is an admirable corporate citizen, environmental
problems have always cast a dark cloud on that image in the
public's mind.

★ *The boxer:* Most people assume that the successor must surpass Welch. Not so, said Michael Allen. "He doesn't need a
surpasser. The challenges coming down the line are different
than the ones Welch addressed." In other words, the successor
must be quick to spot crucial issues and deal with them decisively.

Welch realizes that his successor will get a lot of sideline coach-
ing. "They're all sitting there saying, 'I would like to do this way. I
would like to do that way. And why is that jerk doing that?' That
is the way life is." But his successor must establish his own identity, said Welch, "by being himself and doing it his way. It will take
some time; it takes everyone time. But [GE is] so deep. We have so

many people. This is so much less of a one-man show than the world will ever give it credit for being."[17]

A POWERFUL MOMENTUM

While many different ideas deserve consideration, the fact is GE now operates in a world economy where mega-corporations dominate, and GE is likely to remain a mega-corporation. A company the size of GE is unmanageable unless it is fully decentralized with high-quality units directed to a common goal, which nonetheless are autonomous. Immelt's smoothest course would be to move GE toward being even more of a holding company, with goals and operating principles descending from on high, but all operating decisions made at the subsidiary level. GE corporate structure could be seen as a Lego project, making it easy to snap off subsidiaries and sell them, or to snap on new subsidiaries as necessary. The groundwork is in place for Immelt to do this.

As a pioneering company, GE has put employees in charge of both their own knowledge and their knowledge connections, freeing the managers of GE's companies to follow the course that makes the most sense. This is what GE now does, and what it is likely to continue to do. Such an atmosphere is not just an end state permitted by information technology, but a stimulus for constant progress. Consistent with GE's financial commitments, managers of diverse business units are now encouraged to experiment and tailor their organizations, products, and processes in response to the needs and forces of their particular markets. "We want to be a company that is constantly renewing itself, shedding the past, adapting to change," claimed Welch.[18] GE acts as a clearinghouse for successful new ideas from one part of its vast empire to other parts, not only by providing for the transmission of information, but also by creating an open culture and structure. The system as a whole can thus adapt for the better, thanks to its diverse but interconnected parts.

MANAGING IN THE SPOTLIGHT

Welch understands some of the harsh judgments the next GE leader will face, because he faced them as well. "I hope you understand," Welch said, "that business is a series of trial and error. It's not a great science. Mistakes are made. It's just moving the ball forward, and nobody has any great formula."[19]

Professor Gunderson of Trinity College in Connecticut says that Welch certainly has been an outstanding CEO, but "whether GE's success is due to him, or to its own structure, or to a common culture is difficult to say. My guess is that it's less of him. He's the visible symbol, but there has to be a lot more than that. We'll see. There will be a test of that. No company is great forever. You develop structures around important tasks, things that need to be done in certain environments, and eventually those things change. The classic example is Ford Motor Company. In the early years it was very effective in driving down costs on a particular product. The Model T did extremely well. But as the market changed and Ford had to respond to a whole range of consumer demands it had difficulty. Sooner or later GE will be caught up in that somehow."

chapter ten

Welch after General Electric

The world exists to end up in a book.
The French poet Stéphane Mallarmé

The end is where we start from. T. S. Eliot, *Little Gidding*

IN THE SUMMER OF 2000, JOHN F. WELCH, the soon-to-retire chief executive officer of General Electric Corp., stunned just about everyone in the world who was paying attention by reeling in a $7.1 million advance to write his memoirs. Only senator and former first lady Hillary Clinton and Pope John Paul II have attracted higher advances. To add to the drama, the sum paid Welch was an advance against royalties earned in North American sales only, and his book is expected to sell well worldwide.[1]

Yet to earn out a publishing advance of that heft, Welch will need to sell two million hardback copies. Publisher Time Warner Inc. paid this princely sum despite the fact that so many Americans don't know who Welch is, and once they become informed, quite a few *still* don't understand why he's such a big deal. Welch's book won't reveal insider gossip, help readers lose weight, improve their sex lives, or calm troubled minds. Some have lamented that Welch got this much money for writing a book that he will not even write—it will be written for him. "Who *is* he?" demanded one amazed commentator.[2]

Why would Time Warner's book division place such a wild wager on America's willingness to read Jack Welch's personal account of his life and work? Certainly not because it is a star-studded story or because Welch has risked his life for others or because he has exceptional promotional flair. The *New York Times* surmised that people will buy the Welch book hoping to read the definitive text of modern American business practices. Time Warner hopes Welch's book will surpass Alfred Sloan's *My Years at General Motors* as the most respected business autobiography of all time. Readers may also buy it to get inside the mind of a man who represents almost everything dear to the American psyche—rising from humble beginnings to a place of power and influence, leading an over-aged business to world dominance, and—to paraphrase Frank Sinatra—"doing it his way." There is another possibility: The publishing house may be betting that the sexiest thing in the world isn't sex or spirituality, political or military might. It is money, and Welch is a master at making money.

ON THE BOOK TOUR

There is speculation as to what Welch will do when he finally retires. At least for a while, he will be working on the book, which is expected to be a memoir and more. Welch went about negotiating the book contract with the same fervor he has applied to GE's business deals. At 9 A.M. on July 7, 2000, in Welch's office on the 53rd floor of GE's building overlooking New York's Rockefeller Center, Laurence Kirshbaum, Warner Books CEO, and other Warner executives made a 90-minute pitch to Welch, his writer John Byrne, and agent Mark Reiter. Kirshbaum then followed up with a handwritten note stressing how much faith and passion Warner had for Welch's ideas. Their $7.1 million bid won the Welch book in a contest that involved HarperCollins, Doubleday Broadway, and Simon & Schuster. Reiter is a literary agent at Mark McCormack's International Management Group, the same agent that represented Pope John Paul II when he sought a book contract. McCormack, a prominent sports agent, also has handled the promotion of some of the pope's trips abroad.

Kirshbaum says the Welch book will sell for about $30 for hardcover and about $19 softcover, and $30 and $20 for unabridged or abridged audiotapes. The first printing will be between 1 million and 1.5 million hardbacks, the largest first printing for a Warner book. One of Warner's most popular books, *Simple Abundance* by Sarah Ban Breathnach, sold three million copies in 1999, getting a big boost from being picked for Oprah

Winfrey's book club. The company's most successful business book is Bill Gates's *Business at the Speed of Thought*, which sold 500,000 hardback copies and 300,000 in softcover. Microsoft itself bought massive numbers of copies to be given away at various software developer conferences and other events where Gates was speaking. GE no doubt will use Welch's book in a similar way. The Welch book also will be heavily marketed to business schools, and pushed in nontraditional book retailers such as Home Depot and Wal-Mart. The marketing effort will employ all of Time Warner's formidable weapons, including its magazines and cable outlets, and even America Online, to extend the marketing reach for the book.[3]

One of the perks of receiving a dazzling advance is that Welch got lots of early attention for the project, including writing advice from almost everyone who had ever been involved in publishing. Harriet Rubin, a former publisher at Doubleday and founder of its Currency imprint, gave Welch a list of problems to look out for and warned him—and his hired-gun writer John Byrne—that turning out a book would be tough:

"My heart goes out to everyone connected with the Welch memoir. They will suffer. After the thrill of winning the auction dies down, the Warner Books folks will wake up and say 'We have to sell how many copies? It's impossible.' They will order Welch (who intends to donate his book proceeds to charity) to write about things he would rather forget. They will send pages back to him, red-lined and blue-penciled. Some nervous editor may even scrawl 'Repetitious!' 'Pretentious!' or even 'Huh!' in the margins. These are words Welch has probably not had directed at him in decades."[4]

The book originally was to be published in the spring of 2001, about the time Welch was expected to retire. His sudden cancellation of retirement plans could delay the book as well. Because he's already changed his mind once and because it appears that merging Honeywell into GE will be a major task, there is some doubt as to when Welch actually will retire from GE. He has said it will be at the end of 2001. When he does leave, Welch will have other postretirement obligations as well, including contractual commitments at GE, but there are plenty of other things he might do.

Welch promised that when he hangs up his CEO hat, he will walk away from GE and leave his successor to run the company in any way he wishes. To a certain extent, however, Welch will stay connected. His contract with GE calls for him to be available up to 30 days a year as a consultant for the remainder of his life, to be compensated on a daily basis based on his salary at the time he retires. He also will have lifetime access to company facilities and services.

VOLUNTEER WORK

The Edison Preservation Foundation announced in late 1999 that Jack Welch would lead a campaign to raise $80 million to conserve and preserve the Thomas Edison legacy. Edison's heritage includes seven locations around the United States where the inventor lived and worked. Probably the most notable is the Edison National Historic Site (home of the main laboratories and manufacturing facilities in West Orange, New Jersey). Although they became part of the National Park system in 1962, the New Jersey labs are considered one of the nation's most endangered special places. Dating to 1887, the laboratory complex, considered the first research and development facility in the world, features Edison's chemistry lab, machine shop, library, and the world's first motion picture studio. It includes 3,500 original Edison notebooks that document each Edison experiment, idea, failure, observation, and business activity. Among the other sites covered by the project are the Edison birthplace (Milan, Ohio), his winter estate (Fort Myers, Florida), the Thomas Edison Memorial Towers (Edison, New Jersey), the Port Huron Museum (Port Huron, Michigan), parts of the Henry Ford and Greenfield Village (Dearborn, Michigan), and the Edison Plaza Museum (Beaumont, Texas).

The project is a worthy one, and Welch believes in it. "Today it is impossible to imagine a world without the electric lightbulb, street lights, recorded music, or film," said Welch. "Edison's accomplishments and values will inspire our natural sprit of innovation and entrepreneurship into the next century and millennium."[5] On the other hand, the Edison project hardly seems demanding enough for anything other than a part-time activity.

KEEPING AN EYE ON E-COMMERCE

Welch has said that he doesn't want to amass a bunch of directorships and go from one board meeting to another. He does, however, sit on the boards of Fiat and NBC Internet, Inc. (NBCi). Welch also is on the board of Idealab, a Pasadena, California–based venture capital company founded by Bill Gross. Idealab filed for an IPO in April 2000 with plans to raise $300 million to be used to finance start-up companies. All of Idealab's holdings are dot-coms: CarsDirect.com, Cooking.com, Etoys, Eve.com, FirstLook.com, FreeMusic.com, iExchange.com, Jackpot.com, jobs.com, MyHome.com, PETsMart.com, Swap.com, Ticketmaster Online-CitySearch, Tickets.com, Utility.com, WeddingChannel. com, Z.com, PayMyBills.com, Sameday.com, and others.

Idealab and other personal investments imply that Welch will continue his avid interest in e-commerce. Along with heavy hitters like Deutsche Bank Ventures and the Bank of Montreal, and an impressive list of individual investors, Welch invested in Ya-daYada Inc. (a company that took its name from a catchphrase made popular by Welch's favorite television show, NBC's *Seinfeld*), the first fully integrated wireless service provider. Basically, YadaYada makes possible a wireless connection to the Internet through laptop and handheld computers. Welch also contributed $1 million of his own money to ZixIt, a company that supposedly has the most secure software available for transmitting e-mail. ZixIt has an all-star group of capitalists behind it, including Bill Gates of Microsoft, Michael Dell of Dell Computer, and Wayne Huizenga, founder of AutoNation and Welch's neighbor on Nantucket. Other investors include four GE executives, CFO Keith Sherin, CIO Gary Reiner, general counsel John Samuels, and Dennis Dammerman, vice chairman. Also in the group are Sprint CEO William Esrey and Sprint president Ronald LeMay (approximately $1 million each).[6] Together, the group invested $44 million in the company. As part of the transaction, Huizenga became ZixIt's vice chairman.

THE LONG, LEISURELY GOLF GAME

Welch is passionate about sports, golf in particular. He and his wife recently built a new home in Fairfield near the golf course. They are frequently visited by his four children and numerous grandchildren, and Welch has been teaching golf to the youngsters. He is a member of several prestigious golf clubs, including the Augusta National Golf Course. Among his proudest achievements was a Florida golf match in 1999 with The Shark, Greg Norman. Norman shot 70 and Welch shot 69. It is likely that Welch will continue to spend a lot of hours on the links because he's been playing since high school and it has been his best sport, and especially because his second wife Jane took up golf as well so that the couple could spend more time together. She's become an accomplished golfer.

HANGING OUT AT NANTUCKET

Welch owns several homes, most of them near golf courses. His favorite may be on the island of Nantucket, 30 miles off the coast of Cape Cod, Massachusetts, where in the past Welch has spent most of the month of August. Nantucket is a small island, three miles wide and 15 miles long, and more remote than its sister island, Martha's Vineyard. The island has 82 miles of shoreline and a small, bustling harbor, and although at high season the population swells to about 55,000, there is plenty of open space, including meadows and moors. Nantucket is an exclusive community where the price of a home starts at around $600,000 and with very little effort a buyer can find property selling for $1 million. The island has a treasure of an old town center with about 800 historically preserved sites, among them seventeenth-, eighteenth-, and nineteenth-century homes, shops, inns, bed-and-breakfasts, most reached by cobblestone streets. In the 1970s the entire island was declared a historic district. There are no stoplights on Nantucket, and in fact there is little need for an automobile because the entire island is accessible by foot.

Unlike Martha's Vineyard, only a few luminaries have homes on Nantucket. In addition to Welch, it boasts Mr. (Fred) Rogers and AutoNation's Wayne Huizenga.

AMBASSADOR TO ANYWHERE
HE WANTS TO GO

If he so desired, Welch could continue to make a public contribution through politics. It isn't unusual for retired business leaders to become ambassadors to important or picturesque countries, and certainly Welch would be welcomed in many nations. His name has even been mentioned in regard to higher office. In the 1990s, he came up as a possible candidate for U.S. president. At the next presidential election in 2004 Welch would be 69, but with a history of heart problems, he is an unlikely candidate. On the other hand, there are other important offices, including one in the president's cabinet. In his book, *The America We Deserve*, Donald Trump wrote that if he assembled a cabinet as president of the United States, he would ask Jack Welch to be Secretary of the Treasury.

What type of federal administration would Welch be willing to join? He has visited the White House during the administration of Ronald Reagan and practically every president while he was GE's chief executive. He's played golf with Bill Clinton and met with George W. Bush before his inauguration for a summit on economic issues. "I'm to right of center fiscally and to the left of center socially. I used to be left of center fiscally. When I first got this job, I thought—with the exception of Reg Jones—there were a bunch of raving right-wingers running this company. As you stay with the company a long time and deal with government, fiscally you move to the right. I hope I don't sound as bad as they did, but I sound more like them 17 years later than I did when I started."[7]

WATCHING THE COMPANY
OVER HIS SHOULDER

Reg Jones gave up all official titles at GE when he retired, including his seat on the board of directors. Welch will do the same. Yet because Welch has sizable shareholdings in GE, he could continue to have considerable influence over the board when he leaves the company. At the end of 1999, he held 4.3 million unexercised option shares with a paper profit of $436 million. Combine that

$436 million with the $340 million value of the shares he actually owns, and it adds up to a personal stake of more than $800 million. Welch says that all of his and his family's wealth is tied up in the company. While the shareholdings will give him extra influence at GE, it does not give control. No GE director owns more than one-tenth of 1 percent of the total outstanding shares.

Even without a board position and Welch's shareholdings aside, says Daniel Natarelli, a former GE executive who left to start a company of his own, Welch will continue to have influence. "He doesn't need to be on the board. If he's not on the board and the stock goes down, he will telephone the chairman anyway and bellow, 'What the hell's going on here?' "

Jack Welch really should have some meaningful, even gut-wrenching work to do when he leaves GE. The events of 2000 show that he's got all the piss and vinegar he ever had and he's up to a tough challenge. On a *60 Minutes* interview he admitted that he wouldn't mind running another company, as long as it was large enough for him to continue to paint in big, broad strokes.

Warren Buffett, chairman of Berkshire Hathaway, thinks another company would be lucky to get Welch as a CEO. Buffett is quirky about keeping heads of his companies in place long beyond the typical retirement age. Mrs. B. (Rose Blumpkin), the inimitable founder of the Nebraska Furniture Mart, stayed on the job until just short of her 100th birthday. Buffett says that the mandatory retirement age for corporate CEOs should be at least 70, rather than the usual 65. He used Jack Welch as a specific example of how much use a person could be in this extra five years. "I'll guarantee that Jack Welch has never been better," he said. "I'd rather hire the Jack Welch of today than the Jack Welch when he was 50 years old."[8]

The story goes that Buffett and Welch were having a late-night gab session with Microsoft founder Bill Gates at his home, when the subject turned to Welch's pending retirement. Buffett and Gates told Welch that they would love to back him in anything he decided to do. "We were joking around with Jack saying we will give you a blank check," said Gates. "You can buy whatever business you want when you retire."[9] Welch has yet to take them up on their offer, but the account does raise a question. Buffett has announced that Berkshire Hathaway will be run by a triumvirate, with his son Howard Buffett as chairman of the board, former GEICO cochairman Louis Simpson running the investment operation, and a third, secret person, to run the operating side of the massive holding company. The speculation as to who that secret person might be so far has focused on people within Berkshire. So far Welch's name hasn't come into play. Yet both Buffett and Welch have surprised the business world before. Buffett is in good physical and mental health, and his retirement does not seem imminent. But whatever happens, Welch could very well be back in the business world in some interesting capacity.

chapter eleven

Welch's Place in History

We can chart our future clearly and wisely only when we know the path which has led us to the present.

Adlai Stevenson

History will be kind to me. I intend to write it.

Winston Churchill

THE EVENTS LEADING UP TO THE RETIRE-
ment of John Francis Welch, 20-year chairman of General Electric Corporation, have been entertaining, and his final bow will
be a business event of theatrical proportions. GE, the world's most
profitable company and the largest in terms of stock market capitalization, has won dozens of corporate honors under Welch's
leadership, and it generally is regarded as the most admired and
respected company in the world. But it isn't just GE that is admired. Welch took the helm of the mega-national conglomerate
at a time when the competitiveness of American businesses in the
world economic order was in question. Ronald Reagan had just
been elected president. Inflation was running in the double digits
and it looked as if the United States would fall from grace as the
world's preeminent business leader. With all the starch of a military leader, Welch led the corporate war to reestablish economic
power and influence, and he triumphed. GE's dominance was
firmly established, and America's self-esteem was restored. In the
American way, Welch was a hero who rose from the grass roots,
from the ranks, from the people. GE is the ultimate American
company and Welch himself is as American as baseball and apple
pie. He grew up in a working-class New England neighborhood,
attended public school and then a state college. Afterward, he
went to work for a company in which he had no family or financial connections. During the time he was rising as a business
leader, Welch skied, golfed, and played as hard as he worked. He
married, had a family, divorced, and remarried.

On the business level:

* He has not been bound by tradition or old ways of thinking.
* He faces reality.
* He welcomes change and sees clear opportunities in trans-
  ferring scientific technology into the everyday world.

* He encourages freedom of movement, whether it be social, political, geographic, or economic in nature.
* He rewards success, and treats losers respectfully, though he expects them to deal with their situation without resentment or rancor.
* He strives to be the biggest by being the best.

Unlike some other business leaders, Welch has focused on his role at GE with no attempt to use his office for personal fame. His face doesn't appear in GE ads and, until a new-millennium research facility in India was dedicated to him, his name never was plastered on a building. He seldom talks about his four grown children and his grandchildren, preferring to protect them from the spotlight as well.

On a personal level:

* He rose from a railroad conductor's son to being the most influential business leader in the world, using his own brains and resources.
* While Welch has a Ph.D. in chemistry and could be called Dr. Welch, he is unpretentious. Most people inside and outside of GE simply call him Jack.
* Although he is small in stature, he is athletic and health-conscious. Even when faced with a pending heart attack, he made a practical and quick decision to have surgery. He took the necessary steps for recovery, but gave no ground on his leadership at GE.
* He's outgoing, optimistic, and cheerful, albeit a little like sandpaper around the edges.

Not everyone's idea of a hero, Welch also is accused of having the stereotypical American faults. He can be overly competitive, brash, outspoken, and unconcerned—even hard-hearted—about the impact that change has on those left behind. For example, Welch boldly distanced GE from the nuclear energy business because he said Americans had spoken, and they said they did not want nuclear power plants. Engineers and other workers at GE nuclear facilities complain, however, that while they are paid well to run the facilities that remain, it is depressing to work in a business that has been pronounced dead in the United States and has a bleak future elsewhere. There is no way for them to shine, no future for them at the company. Well, get over it, said Welch. That's the way the world is.

"What does Welch prove," management guru Tom Peters once asked, "except that among six billion people there's a real freak?"[1]

Management professor and Welch biographer Noel Tichy contends that "opinions of Welch range from 'Jack Welch is the greatest CEO GE ever had' to 'Jack Welch is an asshole.' The two views are quite compatible. Leadership makes it necessary to be an asshole at times. All the great leaders, from Martin Luther King Jr. to Gandhi, could become assholes at the drop of a hat."

In his drive to downsize GE and make it as profitable as possible, Welch gave redundant workers generous farewell packages, but he did not hesitate to wave a quick good-bye, even to people he liked and admired. Capitalism is capitalism in Welch's view, and harsh economic measures are good for the American people, who are used to rolling with the punches and landing on their own two feet. There is no question that Jack Welch played a rough-and-tumble game.

BUILDING ON THE BEST

There also is little doubt that Welch's performance as a chief executive officer was made possible by the exceptional company he inherited. He grew up playing team sports, and again at GE he became the captain who built a strong, winning team. The year 2000 purchase of Honeywell International was his final touchdown, guaranteeing that Welch's mark will be on GE for years to come.

Nevertheless, James C. Collins and Jerry I. Porras, authors of *Built to Last: Successful Habits of Visionary Companies*, insist that Welch's very selection, and his ability to shape GE, evolved from the company's fundamentally excellent architecture: "We cannot deny that Welch played a huge role in revitalizing GE or that he brought an immense energy, drive, and a magnetic personality with him to the CEO's office. But obsession on Welch's leadership style diverts us from a central point: Welch grew up in GE; he was a product of GE as much as the other way around. Somehow GE *the organization* had the ability to attract, retain, develop, groom, and select Welch the leader. GE prospered long before Welch and will probably prosper long after Welch. After all, Welch was not the first excellent CEO in GE's history, and he probably will not be the last."[2]

A *Business Week* reader, Mike Higgins Jr., agreed. "Jack Welch does not motivate people. People motivate themselves. No single person can take a company from $12 billion to $280 billion by himself. It takes an army—such as the army that Jack has built by creating an environment that attracts and retains the best and the brightest. Jack's legacy will not be his ability to motivate, it will be the environment he has created, one that will prosper beyond his time at the helm."[3]

WELCH'S PROUDEST LEGACY

Welch may have been handed a company on a silver platter, but he didn't skate casually through his 20 years at GE's helm. Throughout his entire career, he disproved unproductive, tired assumptions. He showed you don't have to job-hop to rise to the top. Just because a company is old and industrial doesn't mean it cannot compete. Simply because the future is different doesn't mean it has to be worse.

His work has been inspirational. It tells people: Have faith in yourself. Just keep expanding the dream. Grow with the challenges that come your way. Welch proves that an individual can still stand out and make a difference even in a behemoth company like GE. But in order to make any meaningful change, a person has to be persistent, durable, and full of determination.

RESOLVING THE CONFLICTS

Welch's most unforgiving critic has been Thomas O'Boyle, author of the book *At Any Cost: Jack Welch, General Electric, and the Pursuit of Profit.* "Ultimately," writes O'Boyle, "history will judge Jack Welch as the quintessential CEO of the late twentieth century, symptomatic of our times, no more, no less. He will be seen as an executive who made the trains run on time, who did one thing and did it well in the context of the times but never embraced a bolder vision, never achieved the greatness that could have been his. The fact that he was lionized in his time will matter little to future generations and likely will be seen as indicative of how cutthroat and vicious an era it was, a time when there was virtually no vision in the mainstream of American business. Money is always what matters most to Welch, that and running the most profitable corporation on the planet. History, I believe, will judge him harshly for that."[4]

There are grains of truth to what O'Boyle says. As visionary as his leadership has been, Welch also has ushered in many ugly problems. Loss of U.S. jobs to foreign countries; discomfort with a new world order that many feel is too big to recognize the needs of individual citizens; a personal greediness on the part of top corporate management that is breathtaking in its scope but almost impossible to limit. Companies the size and scope of GE invariably raise questions about the way they affect lives everywhere, and though Welch has defended himself and the company, troubling conflicts exist. Welch vowed to get GE out of the nuclear business and to help maintain those nuclear facilities that remain in service, and yet the company still does nuclear work in Japan and other parts of Asia. Additionally, the challenges of globalism and technology loom large. Nobody has figured out how to build a world in which all people live in a just, humane society that rewards them adequately for the work they perform. On a simple and personal level, Welch has led the movement to raise productivity to the level that Americans tend to work so hard for their companies that in many cases, their personal and family lives suffer terrible stress.

Owen D. Young, who served two stints as chairman of General Electric, surely would have been disturbed to know that GE's corporate philosophy has distanced it from the human condition. "Business, since it serves people, must live with them from day to day, and hence its plans cannot be impersonal. Which is as it should be, for if we were to permit statistics and the cold logic of economists to act without the disturbing factor of the human being there, then life could not be worthwhile."[5]

Tom Brown, who wrote a manifesto called "The Anatomy of Fire," insists GE will be a great business only if it is an honorable company: "To be sure, GE must strive to be ahead technologically, politically, socially, and commercially in a very diversified spread of businesses. It must face the challenge of change just like any other company or organization; if it invents washing machines (or whatever) that are different from the past, but not better; if it maneuvers to cozy up with governments that assure GE guaranteed business while also oppressing people, if it guzzles vast profits from society without acknowledging through contribution and charity that it is a guest of society, not its treasurer; and if it becomes a beast of a company to do business with, one that treats its base of customers as an encumbrance, or, worse, mere patsies to twirl for profit—then it is safe to say that GE's days in the sunshine of success will be an easy, and small, number to calculate."[6]

And yet when considering GE's impact on its major constituencies—shareholders, customers, employees, and society at large, Welch would say that he added substantial value to the company he inherited, and the value may have been won by tough measures, but not by actions that were unthinkingly cruel.

POSTER BOY FOR CAPITALISM

Jack Welch is the walking, talking, living prophet of capitalism. If you believe in capitalism, you will appreciate Welch. If you have trepidation and fears about bare-naked capitalism, you will feel uncomfortable with Welch's work. Capitalism has been a tremendous boost to American well-being. Although it isn't always an easy economic system in which to live, when linked with a strong democracy it seems to produce the best long-term results. Take for example the city of Ontario, California, one of the places that earned Welch the name "Neutron Jack," when he shut a clothing iron plant that seemed profitable. Workers in Ontario suffered job losses in the short term, but when the U.S. economy strengthened due to the reorganization of many of its businesses, so did Ontario. Now, at the turn of the century, Ontario is a thriving city with a busy airport and streets that are bustling with the construction of new homes and businesses. So many jobs are available that nobody even notices that GE irons are no longer manufactured there.

WHAT HISTORIANS WILL RECALL

Welch will have left the legacy of steering American business—like an easy-to-misguide supertanker—into the twenty-first century and allowing the United States to maintain a stand tall in the global economy. Welch recognized the importance of speed, competitiveness, and making the best of new technology. He furthered the globalization of all business in the United States and abroad by clever use of GE's big bank account and by mobilization of high technology, including satellites and the Internet. Ultimately, Welch hopes his legacy will be the business itself. He intends to leave behind "a company that's able to change at least as fast as the world is changing, and people whose real income is secure because they're winning and whose psychic income is rising because every person is participating."[7]

Appendixes

General Electric and Jack Welch: The Chronology

1878—Edison Electric Light Co. was founded with $300,000 to commercialize Thomas A. Edison's breakthrough in electricity, the incandescent lamp.

The first practical application of the technology was the lighting of the steamship *Columbia* in 1880. Soon afterward Edison Electric built an individual lighting system for the Holborn Viaduct in London and the Pearl Street Station in New York City.

1885—Albert Butz patented the furnace regulator and alarm and another device called the "damper flapper," and this was the very beginning of the Honeywell Company.

1889—Several Edison Electric operations were consolidated to form the Edison General Electric Co.

1892—Edison General Electric and Thomson-Houston merged on April 15. The combined company was incorporated in New York state as the General Electric Company. One thousand shares were issued and sold for $100 per share. GE traded on the New York Stock Exchange for the first time on June 28, 1892. There was a single trade of 50 shares at $108 per share. Edison was disappointed that the company did not retain his name and attended only one board meeting. He continued to serve as a consultant and to collect royalties on his inventions.

1895—GE manufactured the largest electric locomotive in the world.

1896—Dow Jones Industrial Average created. General Electric was among the original companies and is still in the DJIA today.

1899—GE paid its first quarterly dividend. Dividends have been paid each quarter since.

1900—GE Research Laboratory was established.

1905—GE made the first toaster.

1915—GE produced the first electric refrigerator.

1925—GE's first hermetically sealed domestic "Monitor Top" refrigerator was unveiled.

1928—WGY broadcast the first television drama.

1930—The plastics department was created at GE.

1932—Consumer credit division was formed to finance refrigerators. The first washing machine was rolled out.

1935—John Francis Welch Jr. born November 19 in Peabody, Massachusetts, to John Francis and Grace Welch.

1942—GE manufactured its first jet aircraft engine. To supply the U.S. military in World War II, factories worked to capacity.

1953—Lexan polycarbonate resin was developed by GE.
   Honeywell introduced the T-86, the familiar round thermostat that adorns the walls of millions of homes around the world.

1954—GE designed first jet engine to propel an airplane at twice the speed of sound.

1956—The GE Management Development Institute at Crotonville was established.

1957—Jack Welch graduated from the University of Massachusetts with honors, B.S. in chemical engineering.

1959—Welch married Carolyn B. Osburn, November 1959.

Several senior GE executives were found guilty of a price-fixing scheme with Westinghouse. The executives were fired, but the incident raised questions about CEO Ralph Cordiner's aggressive "management by objectives" program.

1960—Welch earned a doctorate in chemical engineering at the University of Illinois.

Welch joined General Electric's plastics division in Pittsfield, Massachusetts. He was responsible for the technical development of Noryl, a plastic resin.

1961—Following a lukewarm raise at GE Plastics, Welch accepted a position as a chemical engineer in Chicago. Before he started the new job, GE induced Welch back with a salary increase and a higher title.

1963—Welch was placed in charge of the chemical development operation.

GE commissioned the Growth Council and challenged it to find opportunities that were growing faster than the GNP and which would build on GE's strengths.

1968—At age 33, Welch became GE's youngest general manager ever. He was given charge of the plastics business department, which included new products like Lexan and Noryl.

1970—General Electric sold its computer business to Honeywell. That business later became Honeywell Bull, a joint venture with Compagnie des Machines Bull of France and NEC Corporation of Japan. Honeywell gradually decreased its ownership level until 1991, when it was out of the business entirely.

1972—Welch was promoted to vice president.

1973—At age 37, Welch became group executive for the $1.5 billion components and materials group, which included all of GE Plastics, plus GE Medical Systems.

1977—Welch was named senior vice president and sector executive for the consumer products and services sector. At the same time he became vice chairman of GE Credit Corporation.

1978—GE built the largest nuclear power plant ever—Tokai-Mura in Japan.

1979—Welch was named vice chairman and executive officer.

The Three Mile Island nuclear power plant accident destroyed already shaky consumer confidence in nuclear energy. Orders evaporated for GE-built nuclear reactors.

1980—GE opened a new dishwasher plant in Louisville, Kentucky, the first phase of a $1 billion investment in major appliances.

1981—On April 1, John F. Welch, 45, became the eighth chairman of GE.

GE's shares, adjusted for splits, were trading at around $4 and the company's market value was $12 billion, 11th in the stock market. Earnings were $1.65 billion on sales of $27.24 billion.

1982—Welch's Phase I or "hardware" restructuring began.

GE invested $300 million in automating its locomotive business and another $130 million to expand the R&D center in Schenectady, New York. The air-conditioning business was sold.

The television show *60 Minutes* criticized GE for shutting down a clothes iron plant in Ontario, California, that seemed to be making money.

1983—GE sold its housewares division to Black & Decker for about $300 million.

The magnetic resonance imaging system was developed for medical diagnostic use.

1984—*Fortune* magazine called Welch the "Toughest Boss in America."

GE sold Utah International mining operations to BHP of Australia for $2.4 billion, and acquired Employers Reinsurance Corporation for $1.1 billion.

1985—In December, GE announced it would buy NBC from the Radio Corporation of America for $6.3 billion in cash.

The hardware phase of the Welch revolution was completed. As a precursor to Phase II, Welch began "delayering" and then reshuffling top management.

Welch and his wife Carolyn divorced after 28 years of marriage, an apparently amicable separation.

1986—GE bought Kidder Peabody for $602 million, and later pumped $800 million into the company.

GE bought RCA, including NBC, for $6.4 billion.

1987—GE acquired a Miami television station for $270 million, bought D&K Financial for $100 million, swapped the medical equipment business of Thomson S.A. for GE's consumer electronic business, and acquired Gelco Corp. for $250 million.

GE sold North America Co. For Life & Health for $200 million.

1988—Welch began the "software revolution" at GE in earnest. GE initiated its trademarked Work-Out program.

The semiconductor business was sold to Harris Corporation. GE also sold RCA Global Communications for $160 million and five radio stations for $122 million.

GE acquired Montgomery Ward for $3.8 billion, Roper Corp. for $510 million, and Borg-Warner's plastics business for $2.3 billion.

1989—In April, Welch married his second wife, investment banker Jane Beasley.

NBC launched CNBC, a financial cable television network.

1990—GE purchased Tungsram Company Ltd., a lighting manufacturer, from the Hungarian government for $150 million.

1991—GE passed IBM as the nation's most valued corporation.

1993—Joe Jett's phantom trading scheme bilked Kidder Peabody of $210 million in net income.

GE got out of the defense business by selling its aerospace division to Martin Marietta for $4 billion in cash and preferred stock.

GE acquired a majority stake in the Italian energy company Nuovo Pignone.

1994—Kidder Peabody's trading operation was liquidated and the investment firm was swapped for 25 percent equity in PaineWebber. The sale created a major write-off for GE.

GE created one of the first industrial web sites with www.ge.com.

1995—Welch underwent triple bypass heart surgery.

GE launched its Six Sigma quality control effort, initially with 600 projects and an intensive training program. By 1997 the company had 9,000 Six Sigma projects underway.

GE's market valued exceeded $100 billion for the first time.

1996—GE achieved $150 billion market capitalization, largest of any company in the world. It was the most profitable company in the United States.

NBC and Microsoft launched MSNBC, a 24-hour television and Internet news service.

1997—Welch was inducted into the National Business Hall of Fame in Cincinnati.

GE became the first company in the world to exceed $200 billion in market value.

1999—GE launched e-business as its fourth growth initiative under Welch's leadership.

AlliedSignal acquired Honeywell, and the company became Honeywell International.

2000—If an investor had purchased one share of GE stock prior to 1926 and never sold, thanks to stock splits the investor would own 4,608 shares.

Friday, October 20, Welch put in a surprise $45 billion bid to buy Honeywell International, and assured Honeywell's board he would stay on the job for another 14 months to make sure the merger went smoothly.

2001—Jack Welch has promised that he would retire from General Electric at year-end.

GE Values

GE Leaders . . . Always with unyielding integrity . . . :

* Are passionately focused on driving customer success
* Live Six Sigma Quality . . . ensure that the customer is always its first beneficiary and use it to accelerate growth
* Insist on excellence and are intolerant of bureaucracy
* Act in a boundaryless fashion . . . always search for and apply the best ideas regardless of their source
* Prize global intellectual capital and the people that provide it . . . build diverse teams to maximize it
* See change for growth opportunities it brings . . . i.e. "e-Business"
* Create a clear, simple, customer-centered vision . . . and continually renew and refresh its execution
* Create an environment of "stretch," excitement, informality and trust . . . reward improvements . . . and celebrate results
* Demonstrate . . . always with infectious enthusiasm for the customer . . . the "4 E's" of GE leadership; the personal Energy to welcome and deal with the speed of change . . . the ability to create an atmosphere that Energizes others . . . the Edge to make difficult decisions . . . and the ability to consistently Execute.[1]

The CERES Principles

The Coalition for Environmentally Responsible Economies (CERES) has been a leading advocate of corporate environmental responsibility since the group's inception in 1989. In order to become a corporate CERES member, businesses must agree to the CERES Principles, submit annual environmental reports, and support and practice the ethic of stakeholder engagement. The following precepts were formerly called the Valdez Principles because they were developed as a response to the Exxon-Valdez oil spill in Alaska.

Principle #1: Protection of the Biosphere—*We will reduce and make continual progress toward eliminating the release of any substance that may cause environmental damage to the air, water, or the earth or its inhabitants. We will safeguard all habitats affected by our operations and will protect open spaces and wilderness, while preserving biodiversity.*

Principle #2: Sustainable Use of Natural Resources—*We will make sustainable use of renewable natural resources, such as water, soils, and forests. We will conserve nonrenewable natural resources through efficient use and careful planning.*

Principle #3: Reduction and Disposal of Wastes—*We will reduce and where possible eliminate waste through source reduction and recycling. All waste will be handled and disposed of through safe and responsible methods.*

Principle #4: Energy Conservation—*We will conserve energy and improve the energy efficiency of our internal operations and of the* *goods and services we sell. We will make every effort to use environmentally safe and sustainable energy sources.*

Principle #5: Risk Reduction—*We will strive to minimize the environmental, health, and safety risks to our employees and the communities in which we operate through safe technologies, facilities, and operating procedures, and by being prepared for emergencies.*

Principle #6: Safe Products and Services—*We will reduce and where possible eliminate the use, manufacture, or sale of products and services that cause environmental damage or health or safety hazards. We will inform our customers of the environmental impacts of our products or services and try to correct unsafe use.*

Principle #7: Environmental Restoration—*We will promptly and responsibly correct conditions we have caused that endanger health, safety, or the environment. To the extent feasible, we will redress injuries we have caused to persons or damage we have caused to the environment and will restore the environment.*

Principle #8: Informing the Public—*We will inform in a timely manner everyone who may be affected by conditions caused by our company that might endanger health, safety, or the environment. We will regularly seek advice and counsel through dialogue with persons in communities near our facilities. We will not take any action against employees for reporting dangerous incidents or conditions to management or to appropriate authorities.*

Principle #9: Management Commitment—*We will implement these Principles and sustain a process that ensures that the Board of Directors and Chief Executive Officer are fully informed about pertinent environmental issues and are fully responsible for environmental policy. In selecting our Board of Directors, we will consider demonstrated environmental commitment as a factor.*

Principle #10: Audits and Reports—*We will conduct an annual self-evaluation of our progress in implementing these Principles. We will support the timely creation of generally accepted environmental audit procedures. We will annually complete the CERES Report, which will be made available to the public.*

DISCLAIMER

These Principles establish an environmental ethic with criteria by which investors and others can assess the environmental performance of companies. Companies that endorse these Principles pledge to go voluntarily beyond the requirements of the law. The terms "may" and "might" in Principles 1 and 8 are not meant to encompass every imaginable consequence, no matter how remote. Rather, these Principles obligate endorsers to behave as prudent persons who are not governed by conflicting interest and who possess a strong commitment to environmental excellence and to human health and safety. These Principles are not intended to create new legal liabilities, expand existing rights or obligations, waive legal defenses, or otherwise affect the legal position of any endorsing company, and are not intended to be used against an endorser in any legal proceeding for any purpose.

Note: For more information on the CERES Principles, contact the organization at www.ceres.com or you may reach the organization at its New York office.

General Electric Businesses

GENERAL ELECTRIC'S BUSINESSES, SUBSIDIARIES, PARTNERSHIPS, AND JOINT VENTURES

GE Aircraft Engines is the world's largest producer of large and small jet engines for commercial and military aircraft. It supplies aircraft-derived engines for marine applications and provides aviation services. Throughout the 1990s, more than 50 percent of the world's large commercial jet engine orders were awarded to GE or CFM International, a joint company of GE and Snecma of France.

Airfoil Technologies International, UK, Ohio, California, Singapore
Garrett Aviation Services
GEAE Services Ltd., Wales, UK
GE Accessory Services
GE Aviation Materials LP (formed by acquiring the assets of TPI
    Aviation Ltd.)
GE Caledonian Ltd., Scotland
GE Celma S.A., Brazil
GE Dallas LP, Texas
GE Engine Leasing
GE Engine Services
GEES Malaysia, Sdn. Bhd., Malaysia
GEES Inc. (Ontario), Canada
GEES Inc. (Strother), Kansas
GEES—Wales, UK, Indiana, Ohio (5), Yokoshiba (Japan),
    Veresgyhaz (Hungary), Singapore

GEES Xiamen Co., Ltd. China
GE Harris Group (joint venture with Harris Corporation and GE)
GE-IAI Aviation Services International (joint venture with GE
   and Israel Aircraft Industries)
GE On-Wing Support
GE VARIG Engine Services S.A.
Middle River Aircraft Systems

GE Appliances is one of the largest manufacturers of major appliances in the world, producing Monogram, Profile Performance, Profile, GE, and Hotpoint brands as well as several private-label brands. An industry innovator, products include refrigerators and freezers, speedcook ovens, electric and gas ranges and cooktops, microwave ovens, washers and dryers, dishwashers, disposals and compactors, room air conditioners, and water purification systems. GE Appliances serves the world's fastest-growing markets, including India, China, Mexico, and South America.

GE Capital Aviation Services is one of the world's largest aircraft leasing companies, with an owned/managed fleet of 850 airplanes and an additional 150 firm Boeing and Airbus aircraft orders. GE Capital Aviation Services began its involvement in aircraft finance in the United States over 30 years ago. Today, it has numerous longstanding customer relationships globally and has significant expertise in both aircraft hardware and complex financial/aircraft trading transactions.

GE Accessory Services
GE Capital Aviation Services (GECAS)
GE Capital Aviation Training Ltd.
GRA Inc.
Carmen Systems (Sweden)
Corporate Aircraft Group
Garrett (partner)

PK AirFinance
QuickTurn (pilot training)
SimuFlite (partner)

GE Capital Business Asset Funding offers real estate, franchise, and equipment financing as well as leasing programs. The Franchise Express Program provides financing quickly and easily for smaller franchises: McDonald's Franchise Program, hospitality franchises, convenience store franchises, and restaurant franchises.

GE Capital Card Services provides credit services to retailers and consumers. Issues corporate cards for commercial customers, including purchasing, travel, and fleet credit cards.

GE Capital Commercial Equipment Financing provides innovative solutions to the ever-changing equipment financing and asset management needs of growing companies around the world. Through government guaranteed Small Business Administration loans, direct-source tax-exempt financing programs, and a wide variety of lease, loan, and sale-leaseback offerings, Commercial Equipment Financing provides companies with low-cost alternatives to cash as well as debt, tax, and balance sheet management.

GE Capital Commercial Finance is a leading global provider of innovative financing solutions primarily for non–investment-grade companies. GE Capital Commercial Finance was created in 1994 and consists of several customer-focused business segments:

Auto Fleet Leasing
Commercial Equipment Financing
Commercial Real Estate
Credit Card Services
Transportation Services

GE Capital Corporate Aircraft Group offers financing for corporate aviation.

GE Capital Energy Services Group participates in the structuring and financing of equipment installations, including HVAC, backup generators, variable speed drives, district energy products, energy management systems, gas conversions, and central steam plants.

GE Capital Fleet Services is a worldwide leader in commercial vehicle financing, offering integrated resources to provide total vehicle finance solutions.

GE Capital Global Consumer Finance is a provider of credit services to retailers and consumers in 29 countries around the world. Global Consumer Finance offers private-label credit cards and proprietary credit services to some of the world's leading retailers and manufacturers, automobile financing solutions through auto dealers, and diversified financial programs directly to consumers.

GE Capital Global Energy provides specialized equity, debt, and structured solutions for the construction, acquisition, and/or financing of assets and companies throughout the energy industry. Investments extend from oil and gas reserves to power plants worldwide.

GE Capital IT Solutions is an IT solutions integrator. It is segmented into three business units: GE IT Product Solutions, GE Managed Service Solutions and GE Net Solutions.

Nexgenix (strategic alliance)

GE Capital Modular Space offers a wide range of mobile office and site trailer structures combined with a nationwide service and support program.

GE Capital Rail Services provides railcar equipment and maintenance and repair services to rail businesses worldwide, and offers the industry's most diverse railcar fleet and flexible leasing solutions.

IntelliTrans, Inc. (joint venture partner)

GE Capital Real Estate finances and invests in a broad range of commercial and residential properties. Real Estate provides financing for the acquisition refinancing and renovation of income producing properties such as office buildings, rental apartments, shopping centers, industrial buildings, mobile home parks, hotels, and warehouses. Financing includes intermediate to long-term senior or subordinated fixed and floating rate loans, as well as equity on a joint venture basis. Loans range from $2 million for single-property mortgages to several hundred million for multiproperty portfolios. Real Estate also offers loan servicing and asset management expertise to other real estate investors and advisory services for pension fund clients through GE Capital Investment Advisors.

GMH Associates Inc. (joint venture with GE Capital Real Estate)
UIC (major holding—France)
UIS (France)

GE Capital's SeaCo, formed in 1998 through the merger of London's Sea Containers and GE Capital, is the world's leading container lessor. The company's modern fleet includes refrigerated containers, tanks, swapbodies, flatracks, and standard boxes as well as ventilated containers and the new two-pallet-wide Sea-Cell, an intermodal container. The company's SeaCover damage insurance and SeaWorthy repair cost limitation programs are additional customer services.

GE Capital's Trade Payables Services provides working capital solutions to alliance partners and their suppliers.

GE Capital Structured Finance Group is a leading equity investor and provider of innovative financial solutions for clients in the global commercial and industrial, energy, telecommunications, and transportation sectors. With more than 30 years of experience, Structured Finance Group meets the needs of its clients by combining industry and technical expertise with significant financial capabilities. It delivers a full range of sophisticated financial products and services and participates in development projects, partnerships, and joint ventures. In the past five years, Structured Finance Group has financed over 200 transactions in excess of $8 billion, and has assets of over $11 billion.

Magnum Hunter (strategic alliance)

GE Capital Telecom provides private capital through a broad offering of financial products. Clients include broadband wireline and wireless, mobile, and telecom infrastructure providers serving the United States, Europe, and selected countries in Asia Pacific and Latin America.

GE Capital Vendor Financial Services is a global leader in providing financial solutions and services to equipment manufacturers, distributors, dealers, and end users. Vendor Financial Services has built and managed successful private-label and outsourced sales financing operations by creating flexible programs that sell where our customers need to sell: directly to end users of all sizes, through channel distribution, in the not-for-profit arena, and to local, state, and federal governments. And every commitment is undertaken to help our customers generate more revenue and enhance their brand equity through innovative, tailored programs. With approximately $12 billion in served assets, Vendor Financial Services works with our customers to drive new business and make existing customers repeat customers through superior service, a commitment to quality and fairness, and the application to the latest technology.

GE Capital Colonial Pacific Leasing
GE Capital Energy Services
GE Capital Office Technology Financial Services
GE Capital Telecom Financial Services Leaseconnect Reseller Site
GE Capital Trade Payables Services
GE Leasing Solutions, a provider of credit services to retailers
    and consumers in 29 countries around the world

GE Employers Reinsurance Corporation (ERC) is a world leader in risk management solutions. ERC provides risk transfer to insurance companies, Fortune 1,000 companies, self-insurers, health-care providers, associations, and other groups.

ERC Group Healthcare
ERC Life
First Specialty Insurance Corporation
GE Frankona RE (ERC Group's European operation)
GE Reinsurance Corporation
Industrial Risk Insurers
Insource Limited
The Medical Protective Company
Westport Insurance Corporation

GE Equity is the private equity arm of GE, and is a subsidiary of GE Capital. GE Equity offers innovative deal structures, which includes the use of preferred stock, convertible debt, subordinated debt, and common stock. With a portfolio of over 150 companies located throughout the United States, Latin America, Asia, and Europe, GE Equity provides creative, flexible, and innovative deal structuring designed to satisfy the needs of its clients. GE Equity was formed in late 1995 as part of GE Capital. With 120 investment professionals, and five business units, GE Equity continues to create value for its clients by providing them with the strength of the GE brand name, distribution channels, technology support, business training, portfolio company networking, sourcing discounts, GE knowledge, and operating experience.

Circon (investment along with GE Industrial Systems)
Keystone (investment along with GE Capital Commercial
    Equipment Finance)
McHugh Software (investment)
Silvertech (investment along with GE Industrial Systems)
Truck-Lite (investment along with GE Capital Transport
    International Pool)

GE Financial Network is an integrated family of investment and insurance companies, that includes nine business units. GE Financial Network provides financial security solutions that help consumers accumulate, preserve, and protect wealth over a lifetime.

GE Global eXchange Services (GXS) combines innovative Internet commerce technologies with Six Sigma process disciplines to create intelligence for business supply chains around the globe. Managing the world's largest electronic community of more than 100,000 trading partners, GE Global eXchange Services is part of GE Information Services, Inc., a wholly owned subsidiary of the General Electric Company, USA.

GE Integration Solutions (EAI)
GE Interchange Solutions (IDE)
GE Marketplace Solutions (Exchanges)
Active (VAR [Value Added Reseller] partner)
Baan (software partner)
bTrade.com (software partner)
Cyclone (software partner)

Enterworks (VAR partner)
iPlanet (VAR partner)
Lucent (software partner)
Oracle (software partner)
PeopleSoft (software partner)
SAP (software partner)
Telcordia (software partner)
TPN Register (technology partner) (joint venture between GE
   Information Services and Thomson Publishing Company)
Vitria (VAR partner)

GE Industrial Finance covers the globe, providing finance across a wide range of products, currencies, transaction sizes, and durations. Active in multiple sectors of the broad chemicals industry, including bulk chemicals, agribusiness, life sciences, industrial gases, waste management, water treatment, and specialty chemicals.

GE Industrial Systems is a supplier of products used to distribute, protect, operate, and control electrical power and equipment, as well as services for commercial and industrial applications. Major products and services include circuit breakers, switches, transformers, switchboards, switchgear, meters, relays, adjustable-speed drives, control and process automation systems, a full range of AC and DC electric motors, and comprehensive technical engineering and power management solutions.

American Superconductor (alliance)

GE Lighting is a supplier of lighting products for global consumer, commercial, and industrial markets. Products include incandescent, fluorescent, high-intensity discharge, halogen, and holiday lamps, along with portable lighting fixtures, lamp components, and quartz products. GE also manufactures outdoor lighting fixtures, residential wiring devices, and commercial lighting controls.

GELcore (joint venture between GE Lighting and EMCORE
   Corporation)
GE Lightnet Services
GE Quartz Worldwide
Thorn EMI

GE Medical Systems provides medical diagnostic imaging technology, services, and health-care productivity. Products include computed tomography (CT) scanners, X-ray equipment, magnetic resonance imaging (MR) systems, nuclear medicine cameras, ultrasound systems, patient monitoring devices, and mammography systems. Its global operations provide sales, service, engineering, and manufacturing in more than 100 countries.

CardioDynamics (joint technology development agreement)
Clinical Services Company
Critikon
EG&G (collaboration pact)
EMC (joint agreement)
Fonar Corporation (technology and distribution agreement)
GE Healthcare Financial Services
GE Marquette
Imarad Imaging Systems Ltd.
Lunar Corporation
MECON Inc.
Micro Medical Systems
OEC Medical Systems
PinPoint Corporation (strategic alliance)
Pronosco (strategic alliance)
Syncor International (joint agreement)

GE Mortgage Insurance Corporation is a provider of private mortgage insurance, which enables borrowers to obtain home financing with a down payment of as little as 3 percent, rather than the standard 20 percent. Mortgage Insurance also makes loan origination safe and profitable by minimizing risk for lenders and investors by protecting against default risk.

GE Petrochemicals is a major supplier of styrene monomer, a product that is used internally to manufacture ABS plastics, and externally sold to the domestic merchant market and to international customers.

Atofina Petrochemicals (joint venture)

GE Plastics produces versatile, high-performance engineered plastics used in the computer, electronics, data storage, office equipment, automotive, building and construction, and other industries. GE Plastics components include GE Silicones, GE Superabrasives, GE Electromaterials, GE Specialty Chemicals, and GE Polymerland.

GE Bayer Silicones
GE Silicones
GE Silicones Americas
GE Toshiba Silicones
Shin-Etsu Chemical (joint venture with GE Silicones)

GE Power Systems designs, manufactures, and services gas, steam, and hydroelectric turbines and generators for power production, pipeline, and industrial applications. Power Systems also provides nuclear fuels and services. Nuovo Pignone, GE's Italian manufacturing affiliate, also produces turbines, pumps, compressors, and related equipment. GEPS's customers can be found in 119 countries around the world.

GE Aeroderivative and Package Services
GE Distributed Power

GE Energy and Environmental Research Corporation
GE Energy Rentals
GE Enter Software LLC
GE Glegg Water Technologies
GE Harris Energy Control Systems LLC
GE Hydro
GE Inspection Services
GE Microgen
GE Nuovo Pignone
GE Nuclear
GE Power Systems Energy Consulting
GE Smallworld
GE Syprotec
GE Welding Specialty Services
Paiton (joint venture between GE Power Systems and Mitsui
    & Co.)
Reuter Stakes, Inc.
S&S Energy Products
Turbine Blading Ltd.

GE Transportation Systems manufactures more than half of the diesel freight locomotives in North America, and its locomotives operate in 75 countries worldwide. Other products include passenger locomotives, diesel engines for marine and stationary markets, electrical propulsion and control systems for rapid transit cars, motorized electric wheel systems for large mining trucks, and advanced railway signaling and control systems.

NBC—In the United States, NBC owns and operates the NBC television network (13 television stations and CNBC), operates MSNBC in partnership with Microsoft, and maintains equity interests in a wide array of entertainment and sports cable channels and ValueVision International. NBC is the leader among traditional media companies in Internet and new media business and owns 47 percent of NBC Internet Inc. (NBCi). NBC also holds equity stakes in a wide range of new media companies and operates CNBC/Dow Jones Business Video with Microsoft and Dow Jones. Internationally, NBC owns and operates CNBC: A Service of NBC and Dow Jones in partnership with Dow Jones & Company in Europe and Asia. In partnership with National Geographic and Fox/BSkyB, the network owns and operates the National Geographic Channel in Europe and Asia.

CNBC
MSNBC
Paxson Communications

HONEYWELL INTERNATIONAL'S DIVISIONS, BUSINESSES, AND SUBSIDIARIES

The Honeywell businesses will be merged into the new parent company, General Electric.

Aerospace Electronic Systems Division
Aerospace Equipment Systems
Aerospace Services
Aircraft Landing Systems
Amorphous Metals
ASEC Manufacturing
Automotive Aftermarket
Burdick & Jackson
Defense & Avionics
Electron Vision Group
Electronic Materials Division
Engines & Systems Division

Federal Manufacturing & Technologies

Fluorine Product Division

Heat Transfer

Home & Building Control

Industrial Control

L-3 Communications Corp./Ocean Systems Division

Microelectronics & Technology Center

Oak-Mitsui Inc.

Polymers

Raytheon Systems Company/Identification & Command Controls Sector

Research & Technology Center

Truck Brake Systems Co.

General Electric—Nineteen-Year Performance Figures: 1980–1999

A comparison of the 19-year cumulative total return among GE, and the Dow Jones Industrial Average (DJIA), and Standard & Poor's 500 (S&P 500).[1]

Year	GE	DJIA	S&P 500
1980	100	100	100
1981	99	96	95
1982	171	123	116
1983	219	155	142
1984	220	157	150
1985	293	209	198
1986	357	266	235
1987	375	281	248
1988	394	326	289
1989	586	432	380
1990	538	430	368
1991	739	534	480
1992	851	573	517
1993	1,073	671	569
1994	1,076	705	576
1995	1,563	965	793
1996	2,194	1,245	975
1997	3,315	1,555	1,301
1998	4,676	1,837	1,672
1999	7,183	2,339	2,024

Notes

Part I The Jack Welch Legacy

1. GE Honeywell Press Conference, October 23, 2000, Media Transcripts Inc.
2. Ibid.
3. Carol Hymowitz, "In the Lead," *Wall Street Journal*. October 31, 2000, p. B1.
4. Diane Brady, "Jack Welch: One Big Pair of Vacant Shoes," *Business Week*, November 15, 1999, p. 54.
5. Gary Strauss, "Daimler Chief Lives and Works in Overdrive," *USA Today*, May 7, 1998, p. 3B.
6. Peter Landers, "In Japan, the Words of Chairman Jack Are Revolutionary," *Wall Street Journal*, February 9, 2000, p. A1.
7. David C. Gompert and Irving Lachow, "Transforming U.S. Forces: Lessons from the Wider Revolution," Rand Issue Paper 193, 2000.
8. *"Fortune* Selects Henry Ford Businessman of the Century; GE's Jack Welch Named Manager of the Century," Business Wire, November 1, 1999.
9. James C. Collins and Jerry I. Porras, *Built to Last: Successful Habits of Visionary Companies* (New York: HarperBusiness, 1994), p. 3.
10. Jim Rohwer, "GE Digs into Asia," *Fortune*, October 2, 2000, p. 170.
11. Collins and Porras, *Built to Last*, p. 3

Chapter One   The House of Magic: How Welch Became an American Icon

1. Jack Welch, speech to the 50th anniversary annual meeting of the North Carolina Citizens for Business and Industry, Raleigh, North Carolina, March 18, 1992.

2. Gerald Gunderson, "Letters to the Editor," *Wall Street Journal*, January 22, 1999, p. A11.

3. Marilyn A. Harris and Christopher Power, "He Hated Losing—Even in Touch Football," *Business Week*, June 30, 1986, p. 65.

4. Jack Welch, interview with author, Fairfield, Connecticut, July 3, 1997.

5. Ibid.

6. Dennis Dammerman, speech presented at the Durland Memorial Lecture, Cornell University, April 1, 1998.

7. "Passing the Torch," *Monogram*, January–February 1981, p. 6.

8. John A. Byrne, "Jack," *Business Week*, June 8, 1998, p. 90.

9. Janet Lowe, *Jack Welch Speaks: Wisdom from the World's Greatest Business Leader* (New York: John Wiley & Sons, 1998), p. 47.

10. "The Latest Perk: 70 Years Ago in *Forbes*," *Forbes*, June 1, 1929, as reported in *Forbes*, June 14, 1999.

11. James C. Collins and Jerry I. Porras, *Built to Last: Successful Habits of Visionary Companies* (New York: HarperBusiness, 1994), p. 69.

12. "A Conversation with Roberto Goizueta and Jack Welch," *Fortune*, February 5, 1996.

13. Graef Crystal, "GE's Welch Is a Master CEO Setting a Bad Example," Bloomberg News Service, March 16, 2000.

14. Byrne, "Jack."

15. Ross Laver, "Corporate Charm School," *Maclean's*, December 7, 1998, p. 49.

16. Tom Peters and Nancy Austin, *A Passion for Excellence: The Leadership Difference* (New York: Random House), 1985, p. 180.

17. Susan Adams, "Corporate Communion," *Forbes*, April 3, 2000.

18. "GE's General Earns Another Star," *Washington Post*, November 3, 1999, p. E1.

19. David Warshaw, "An Interview with Jack Welch," *Monogram*, Fall 1984, p. 10.

20. Byrne, "Jack."

21. Warshaw, "An Interview with Jack Welch," p. 10.

22. Peter Krass, *The Book of Business Wisdom: Classic Writings by the Legends of Commerce and Industry"* (New York: John Wiley & Sons, 1997), p. 122.

23. Ibid.

24. Richard Tanner Pascale, *Managing on the Edge* (New York: Simon & Schuster, 1990), p. 192.

25. "Investor FAQs," GE Investor Relations, www.ge.com, August 31, 2000.

26. Alan Abelson, "Up & Down Wall Street: Next Time Around," *Barron's*, October 11, 1999, p. 5.

27. Collins and Porras, *Built to Last*, p 171.

28. Ibid.

29. "*Fortune* Selects Henry Ford Businessman of the Century; GE's Jack Welch Named Manager of the Century," Business Wire, November 1, 1999.

30. Marilyn Harris, Zachary Schiller, Russell Mitchell, and Christopher Power, "Can Jack Welch Reinvent GE?" *Business Week*, June 30, 1986, p. 62.

Chapter Two   The Gospel of Good Management

1. James C. Collins and Jerry I. Porras, *Built to Last: Successful Habits of Visionary Companies* (New York: HarperBusiness, 1994), p. 194.
2. Noel Tichy and Stratford Sherman, *Control Your Own Destiny or Someone Else Will* (New York: Currency Doubleday, 1993), p. 71.
3. John F. Welch, General Electric Company meeting, Richmond, Virginia, April 26, 2000.
4. Peter Krass, *The Book of Business Wisdom: Classic Writings by the Legends of Commerce and Industry* (New York: John Wiley & Sons, 1997), p. 122.
5. John F. Welch, message to shareholders, General Electric 1983 annual report.
6. Jack Welch, speech at the New England Council's 1992 Private Sector New Englander of the Year Award, Boston, Massachusetts, November 11, 1992.
7. Janet Lowe, *Jack Welch Speaks: Wisdom from the World's Greatest Business Leader* (New York: John Wiley & Sons), p. 61.
8. Harry C. Stonecipher, "Innovation and Creativity," Second Annual Sir Frank Whittle Lecture Series, Royal Aeronautical Society, London, England, February 10, 1998.
9. Janet Guyon, "GE Chairman Welch, Though Much Praised, Starts to Draw Critics," *Wall Street Journal*, August 4, 1988.
10. Marilyn A. Harris, Zachary Schiller, Russell Mitchell, and Christopher Power, "Can Jack Welch Reinvent GE?" *Business Week*, June 30, 1986, p. 62.
11. Collins and Porras, *Built to Last*, p. 172.
12. David Parsley, "Jack Welch," *Times of London*, April 16, 2000.
13. Tim Stevens, "Follow the Leader," *Industry Week*, November 18, 1996.

14. Richard Turner Pascale, *Managing on the Edge* (New York: Simon & Schuster, 1990), p. 211.

15. "Wendt, Once Seen as Possible Heir to GE Chairman Welch, Resigns," *Minneapolis Star Tribune*, December 9, 1998, p. 1D.

16. John Helyar, "Solo Flight: A Jack Welch Disciple Finds the GE Mystique Only Takes You So Far," *Wall Street Journal*, August 10, 1998, p. A1.

17. Nanette Byrnes, "What Really Happened to the Class of GE," *Business Week*, November 13, 2000.

18. Ibid.

19. Marc Nexon, "The Secrets of the Finest Company in the World," *L'Expansion*, July 10, 1997.

20. Christopher Lorenz, "Life under Jack Welch: Opportunistic and Touch," *Financial Times*, May 15, 1998.

21. Holman W. Jenkins Jr., "Exporting the Jack Welch Way," *Wall Street Journal*, March 10, 1999, p. A23.

22. Peter Landers, "In Japan, the Words of Chairman Jack Are Revolutionary," *Wall Street Journal*, February 9, 2000, p. A1.

23. Ibid.

24. Ibid.

Part II General Electric Then and Now

1. John F. Welch Jr., "Shun the Incremental: Go for the Quantum Leap," Hatfield Fellow Lecture at Cornell University, reprinted in *Financier*, July 1984.

2. Nicholas Stein, "Fortune 500," *Fortune*, April 17, 2000, p. 127.

3. Dennis Dammerman, speech presented at the Durland Memorial Lecture, Cornell University, April 1, 1998.

4. Ibid.

5. Jonathan R. Laing, "Riding into the Sunset," *Barron's*, February 15, 1999, p. 23.

6. Michael Finley, "Noel Tichy Redefines Leadership for the 21st Century," The Master's Forum, September 15, 1998, www.mastersforum.com.

7. John F. Welch, speech to shareholders, General Electric annual meeting, Greenville, South Carolina, April 25, 1989.

8. Carol Hymowitz and Matt Murray, "How a Top Manager Makes Things Happen," *Wall Street Journal Interactive Edition*, 2000.

9. "A Conversation with Roberto Goizueta and Jack Welch," *Fortune*, February 5, 1996.

10. Matt Murray, "Last Conglomerate," *Wall Street Journal*, April 13, 2000, p. A1.

11. "GE's Nayden to Report to Welch: Dammerman to Help on Succession," Bloomberg News, June 28, 2000.

12. Mark Haines, David Faber, Squawk Box, "General Electric, Chairman & CEO Interview," CNBC/Dow Jones Business Video, May 7, 1999.

13. Tom Peters, "Contradicting Myself 13 Ways," *Forbes* ASAP Supplement, June 6, 1994.

14. Thomas O'Boyle, *At Any Cost: Jack Welch, General Electric, and the Pursuit of Profit* (New York: Alfred A. Knopf, 1998), p. 374.

Chapter Three   The Companies General Electric Dumped

1. Leta W. Clark, *Women, Women, Women* (New York: Drake Publishers, 1977), p. 43.

2. Jack Welch, message to shareholders, General Electric annual report, 1980.

3. Ikuo Hirata, "The Past Is an Impediment in Changing Times," *Nikkei Business*, November 18, 1996.

4. Mike Wallace interview, *60 Minutes*, March 7, 1982.

5. Dennis Dammerman, speech presented at the Durland Memorial Lecture, Cornell University, April 1, 1998.

6. Worldwatch News Briefing, "Nuclear Power Nears Peak," March 5, 1999, www.worldwatch.org.

7. Ibid.

8. Noel Tichy and Stratford Sherman, *Control Your Own Destiny or Someone Else Will* (New York: Currency Doubleday, 1993), p. 82.

9. "Defense Procurement Fraud: Information on Plea Agreements and Settlements," a report of the U.S. General Accounting Office, Washington, D.C., September 1992, appendixes I–II.

10. Marshall Loeb, "Jack Welch Lets Fly on Budgets, Bonuses, and Buddy Boards," *Fortune*, January 5, 1987, p. 76.

Chapter Four   **The Companies General Electric Acquired**

1. Peter Krass, editor, *The Book of Business Wisdom: Classic Writings by the Legends of Commerce and Industry* (New York: John Wiley & Sons, 1997), p. 123.

2. Matt Murray, Jeff Cole, Nikhil Deogun, and Andy Pasztor, "On Eve of Retirement, Jack Welch Decides to Stick Around a Bit," *Wall Street Journal*, October 23, 2000, p. A1.

3. Jack Welch, GE Honeywell press conference, New York, New York, October 23, 2000.

4. John Huey and Geoffrey Colvin, "The Jack and Herb Show," *Fortune*, January 11, 1999, p. 163.

5. Frank Swoboda, "A Late Realization Draws General Electric into the Net," *Washington Post*, April 5, 2000, p. G17.

6. Robert Slater, *The New GE: How Jack Welch Revived an American Institution* (Hammed, Illinois: Business One Irwin, 1993), p. 142.

7. Thomas F. O'Boyle, *At Any Cost: Jack Welch, General Electric, and the Pursuit of Profit* (New York: Alfred A. Knopf, 1998), p. 42.

8. Carol Hymowitz and Matt Murray, "How a Top Manager Makes Things Happen," *Wall Street Journal Interactive Edition*, 2000.

9. Krass, *The Book of Business Wisdom*, p. 117.

10. Tim Smart, "Jack Welch's Encore," *Business Week*, October 28, 1996.

11. O'Boyle, *At Any Cost*, p. 118.

12. Slater, *The New GE*, p. 238.

13. Jonathan R. Laing, "Riding into the Sunset," *Barron's*, February 15, 1999, p. 23.

14. "General Electric Dedicates R&D Center," PR Newswire, October 4, 1982.

15. Huey and Colvin, "The Jack and Herb Show."

16. Janet Guyon, "GE Chairman Welch, Though Much Praised, Starts to Draw Critics," *Wall Street Journal*, August 4, 1998.

17. Dennis Dammerman, speech presented at the Durland Memorial Lecture, Cornell University, April 1, 1998.

18. Anita Raghavan and Patrick McGeehan, "GE Scores Big with Kidder, 3½ Years After," *Wall Street Journal*, May 14, 1998, p. C1.

19. Betsy Morris, "Robert Goizueta and Jack Welch: The Wealth Builders," *Fortune*, December 11, 1995.

20. John A. Byrne, "Jack," *Business Week*, June 8, 1998, p. 90.

21. Gary Hamel, "Heir to Greatness," *Wall Street Journal*, September 18, 2000, p. A38.

22. "General Electric Unions Likely to Accept Contract," Bloomberg News, June 28, 2000.
23. Jack Welch, speech at the 50th anniversary annual meeting of the North Carolina Citizens for Business and Industry, Raleigh, North Carolina, March 18, 1992.
24. Robert Reno, "Reno on Sunday: Neutron Jack Has Own Idea of Electricity," *Newsday*, March 20, 1994, p. 84.

Chapter Five   Building from Within

1. Peter Krass, editor, *The Book of Business Wisdom* (New York: John Wiley & Sons, 1997), p. 8.
2. Janet Guyon, "GE Chairman Welch, Though Much Praised, Starts to Draw Critics," *Wall Street Journal*, August 4, 1988.
3. Marilyn A. Harris, Zachary Schiller, Russell Mitchell, and Christopher Power, "Can Jack Welch Reinvent GE?" *Business Week*, June 30, 1986, p. 62.
4. "Jack Welch: I Got a Raw Deal," *Fortune*, July 7, 1986.
5. Dennis Dammerman, speech presented at the Durland Memorial Lecture, Cornell University, April 1, 1998.
6. Thomas F. O'Boyle, *At Any Cost: Jack Welch, General Electric, and the Pursuit of Profit* (New York: Alfred A. Knopf, 1998), p. 237.
7. Noel Tichy and Stratford Sherman, *Control Your Own Destiny or Someone Else Will* (New York: Currency Doubleday, 1995), p. 91.
8. "Industry Update, June–July 2000," Appliancemagazine.com, July 21, 2000.
9. Del Jones, "Firms Aim for Six Sigma Efficiency," *USA Today*, July 21, 1998, p. 1B.
10. Ibid.

11. Michelle Conlin, "Revealed at Last: The Secret of Jack Welch's Success," *Forbes*, January 26, 1998, p. 44.
12. "Mastering Six Sigma Excellence," www.bestpractices.com.
13. Jones, "Firms Aim for Six Sigma Efficiency."
14. Mark Haines, David Faber, Squawk Box, General Electric Company, "CEO: The Boeing Company," CNBC/Dow Jones Business Video, February 2, 2000.
15. Ibid.
16. Paul Kangas and Susie Gharib, "GE Chairman and CEO Interviews on *Nightly Business Report*," *Nightly Business Report*, February 29, 2000.
17. Tim Smart, "Jack Welch's Encore," *Business Week*, October 28, 1996.

Chapter Six **The Globalization of General Electric**

1. Aphra Behn, first professional English woman writer, quoted by Leta W. Clark, *Women, Women, Women* (New York: Drake Publishers, 1977), p. 88.
2. Jonathan Karp, "The IT Guys," *Wall Street Journal*, September 27, 1999.
3. "Dow Jones Indexes Launches Global Titans Index," Business Wire, July 14, 1999.
4. "Perspective: America Finds Its Customers in the World," *Financial Times*, October 10, 1997.
5. Ibid.
6. Ibid.
7. Frank Swoboda, "A Late Realization Draws General Electric into the Net," *Washington Post*, April 5, 2000, p. G17.
8. "General Electric Unions Likely to Accept Contract," Bloomberg News, June 28, 2000.

9. "Perspective: America Finds Its Customers in the World," *Financial Times*, October 10, 1997.

10. Thomas A. Stewart, "See Jack. See Jack Run Europe," *Fortune*, September 27, 1999, p. 124.

11. Jack Welch, speech to the Economic Club of Detroit, May 16, 1992.

12. Eric Dash, "GE Honcho Brings Business World to Life at U. Pennsylvania," University Wire, February 22, 1999.

13. Jack Welch, chairman's message, General Electric annual meeting, April 26, 2000, Richmond, Virginia.

14. Matt Murray, "GE Capital Goes Bargain Hunting in Troubled Asia," *Wall Street Journal*, March 12, 1998, p. B4.

15. "Perspective: America Finds Its Customers in the World," *Financial Times*, October 10, 1997.

16. Stewart, "See Jack."

17. "General Electric: The House That Jack Built," *Economist*, September 18, 1999, p. 23.

18. *Business Week*, December 6, 1999.

19. CNN *Moneyline*, December 8, 1998.

20. *Business Week*, December 6, 1999.

21. John Huey and Geoffrey Colvin, "The Jack and Herb Show," *Fortune*, January 11, 1999, p. 163.

22. "Short Cuts," *Newsday*, February 12, 1994, p. 33.

23. Brian O'Shaughnessy, "After 18 Holes, Maria Gets Justice If I Win," *National Catholic Reporter*, September 4, 1998, p. 29.

24. Deroy Murdock, "CEOs on the Globalization Warpath," *Chief Executive*, www.chiefexecutive.net.

25. "US Now Bigger than Germany for Siemens," Reuters, Tokyo, October 30, 2000.

26. Jack Welch, speech at General Electric annual meeting, 1998.

Chapter Seven   Wired Welch

1. Frank Swoboda, "Jack Welch and the Boundaryless Company," *Washington Post*, February 27, 1994.
2. Elizabeth Corcoran, "The E Gang," *Forbes*, August 11, 2000.
3. Brent Schlender, "The Odd Couple," *Fortune*, May 1, 2000, p. 106.
4. Ibid.
5. Frank Swoboda, "A Late Realization Draws General Electric into the Net," *Washington Post*, April 5, 2000, p. G17.
6. Carol Hymowitz and Matt Murray, "How a Top Manager Makes Things Happen," *Wall Street Journal Interactive Edition*, 2000.
7. Corcoran, "The E Gang."
8. Jack Welch, chairman's message, General Electric annual meeting, April 26, 2000, Richmond, Virginia.
9. "Now It's Electron Jack," *Fortune*, September 27, 1999, p. 130.
10. Sallie Hofmeister, "Company Town: Networks Need to Expand Revenue Sources, Panelists Say," *Los Angeles Times*, December 3, 1998, p. 6.
11. "Now It's Electron Jack."
12. Meredith Levinson, "Destructive Behavior," *CIO Magazine*, July 15, 2000.
13. Ibid.
14. Jack Welch, chairman's message, General Electric annual meeting, April 26, 2000, Richmond, Virginia.
15. James F. Peltz, "GE Takes to the Net to Lower Company Costs," *Los Angeles Times*, October 9, 2000, p. C1.
16. Howard Rudnitsky, "Changing the Corporate DNA," *Forbes*, July 17, 2000.

17. Andrew Fisher, "Ardent Advocate of E-Commerce," *Financial Times*, August 2, 2000.

18. Rudnitsky, "Changing the Corporate DNA."

19. Thomas A. Stewart, "Three Rules for Managing in the Real-Time Economy," *Fortune*, May 1, 2000, p. 334.

20. Peltz, "GE Takes to the Net, p. C1.

21. Thomas Hoffman, "GE's Siren Call Lures E-Commerce Leaders," *Computerworld*, August 2, 1999, p. 14.

22. "Industry Updates, June–July 2000," appliancemagazine.com, July 21, 2000.

23. Stewart, "Three Rules for Managing."

24. Kerry A. Dolan, "GE's Brain Drain," *Forbes*, November 1, 1999, p. 52.

25. Jon Friedman, CBS MarketWatch.com, September 29, 2000.

26. Marianne Kolbasuk McGee, "E-Business Makes General Electric a Different Company," *Information Week News*, January 31, 2000.

27. Elmer L. Winter, "CEGI Newsletter to Israeli Managing Directors," www.cegi.org, October 14, 1999.

28. Matt Murray, "Last Conglomerate," *Wall Street Journal*, April 13, 2000, p. A1.

29. Sara Nathan, "GE Chief Picked Up 20 Percent Raise in '99 Rewards," *USA Today*, March 14, 2000, p. 3B.

30. "GE Earnings Rise 20 Percent," Reuters, October 11, 2000.

31. Murray, "Last Conglomerate."

32. Mark Haines, Maria Bartiromo, Squawk Box, General Electric Company, CNBC, December 15, 1999.

33. Jack Welch, chairman's message, General Electric annual meeting, April 26, 2000, Richmond, Virginia.

34. Jack Welch, GE Honeywell press conference, New York, New York, October 23, 2000.

Chapter Eight   The Dark Side of the Legacy

1. John Greenwald, "Jack in the Box," *Time*, October 3, 1994.

2. Reginald H. Jones, speech, reprinted in the GE Jubilee section of the *Berkshire Eagle*, October 7, 1978.

3. Thomas F. O'Boyle, *At Any Cost: Jack Welch, General Electric, and the Pursuit of Profit* (New York: Alfred A. Knopf, 1998), p. 237.

4. Robert Reno, "Reno on Sunday: Neutron Jack Has Own Idea of Electricity," *Newsday*, March 20, 1994, p. 84.

5. O'Boyle, *At Any Cost*, p. 237.

6. "White Paper: Jack Welch Employee Performance," www.ideabridge.com.

7. James C. Collins and Jerry I. Porras, *Built to Last: Successful Habits of Visionary Companies* (New York: HarperBusiness, 1994), p. 9.

8. John A. Byrne, "Jack," *Business Week*, June 8, 1998, p. 90.

9. "General Electric Unions Likely to Accept Contract," Bloomberg News, June 28, 2000.

10. "The Brutal Manager," *Der Spiegel*, July 14, 1997.

11. "The Incredible Electrical Conspiracy," *Fortune*, April, 1961; reprinted in the February 11, 1980, issue, p. 174.

12. "Jack Welch: 'I Got a Raw Deal,' " *Fortune*, July 7, 1986.

13. Robert Slater, *The New GE: How Jack Welch Revived an American Institution* (Homewood, Illinois: Business One Irwin, 1993), p. 248.

14. Noel M. Tichy and Stratford Sherman, *Control Your Own Destiny or Someone Else Will* (New York: Currency Doubleday, 1993), p. 148.

15. O'Boyle, *At Any Cost*, p. 15.

16. Ibid., p. 187.

17. William M. Carley, "Battle of the Housatonic," *Wall Street Journal*, July 27, 1998, p. B1.
18. GE web site: www.ge.com.
19. Jack Welch, interview with author.
20. "Jack Welch: Role Model or Rascal?" *Business Week*, July 6, 1998, p. 9.
21. "U.S. to Order GE to Pay $490 Million for River Cleanup," Reuters, New York, December 6, 2000.
22. General Electric Proxy Statement, 1999, p. 30.
23. O'Boyle, *At Any Cost*, p. 189.
24. "Executive Pay Watch," www.AFL-CIO.com.
25. "Total Pay for 505 US CEOs: Bloomberg Pay Survey," Bloomberg News, June 22, 2000.
26. Del Jones, "General Electric's CEO Earns $97 Million," *USA Today*, March 15, 1999, p. 7B.
27. Geoffrey Colvin, "Web Exclusive: Jack Welch & Herbert Kelleher—Create Great Companies and Keep Them That Way," Fortune.com, January 11, 1999.
28. Aaron Bernstein, "Too Much Corporate Power?" *Business Week*, September 11, 2000, p. 145.
29. Suzanne Koudsi, "Ten Deals We'd Like to See," *Fortune*, April 17, 2000, p. 59.
30. Bernstein, "Too Much Corporate Power?"
31. Ibid.

Part III   The Future

1. Jack Welch, interview with author, Fairfield, Connecticut, July 3, 1997.
2. Geoffrey Colvin, "Would GE Pick an Outsider CEO?" *Fortune*, September 27, 1999, p. 290.

3. "McNealy: Businessman and IT Guru," *Financial Times,* August 2, 2000.

4. Peter Krass, Editor, *The Book of Business Wisdom: Classic Writings by the Legends of Commerce and Industry* (New York: John Wiley & Sons, 1997), p. 122.

5. Allan Sloan, "Judging GE's Jack Welch," *Newsweek,* November 15, 1999, p. 67.

6. Geoffrey Colvin, "The Ultimate Manager," *Fortune,* November 22, 1999, p. 185.

7. "We're Driven by Soft Values," *Business Today,* February 7–21, 1995.

Chapter Nine　The Meta-Corporation: General Electric after Welch

1. Matt Murray, "Last Conglomerate," *Wall Street Journal,* April 13, 2000, p. A1.

2. Jonathan R. Laing, "Three's a Crowd," *Barron's,* June 12, 2000, p. 15.

3. Jack Welch, interview with the author, Fairfield, Connecticut, July 3, 1997.

4. Del Jones, "McNerney Sees No Need for Major Fix at 3M," *USA Today,* December 6, 2000, p. 2B.

5. Andrew Hill, "A Tough Act to Follow," *Financial Times,* September 25, 2000.

6. John Plender, "GE's Hidden Flaw," *Financial Times,* August 1, 2000.

7. Pamela L. Moore and Diane Brady, "Running the House that Jack Built," *Business Week.* October 2, 2000, p. 138.

8. Gary Hamel, "Heir to Greatness," *Wall Street Journal,* September 18, 2000, p. A38.

9. Daniel Gross, "The Greatest Business Stories of All Time" (New York: John Wiley & Sons, 1996), p. 349.

10. Murray, "Last Conglomerate."

11. Sallie Hofmeister, "Company Town: Networks Need to Expand Revenue Sources, Panelists Say," *Los Angeles Times*, December 3, 1998, p. 6.

12. Harry A. Jessell, "Turner Still Primed for Peacock," *Broadcasting & Cable*, December 20, 1999, p. 10.

13. Murray, "Last Conglomerate."

14. Kerry A. Dolan, "The Jack Factor," *Forbes*, December 22, 1999.

15. Ibid.

16. Dennis Dammerman, speech presented at the Durland Memorial Lecture, Cornell University, April 1, 1998.

17. Carol Hymowitz and Matt Murray, "How a Top Manager Makes Things Happen," *Wall Street Journal Interactive Edition*, 2000.

18. Marilyn A. Harris, Zachary Schiller, Russell Mitchell, and Christopher Power, "Can Jack Welch Reinvent GE?" *Business Week*, June 30, 1986, p. 62.

19 Jack Welch, interview with the author, Fairfield, Connecticut, July 3, 1997.

Chapter Ten Welch after General Electric

1. "Along Publishers Row," *Author's Guild*, Spring 2000, p. 27.

2. Jonathan Yardley, *Moscow Times*, June 21, 2000.

3. Keith L. Alexander, "Welch Book Must Sell 1.5 Million Copies to Show Profit," *USA Today*, July 17, 2000.

4. Harriet Rubin, "Traps Await CEOs Who Pen Books," *USA Today*, July 27, 2000.

5. "Preserving the Past to Spur the Future," *Electric Perspectives*, March/April 2000, p. 7.
6. Herb Greenberg, "What's Up With Jack Welch and ZixIt?" www.TheStreet.com.
7. Jack Welch, interview with the author, Fairfield, Connecticut, July 3, 1997.
8. Jon Friedman, "Buffett Calls Online Trading 'Casinos,' " CBS MarketWatch.com, April 30, 2000.
9. Devon Spurgeon, "Warren Buffett Bids and Bill Gate Passes, but It's Only Bridge," *Wall Street Journal*, December 11, 2000, p. A1.

Chapter Eleven   Welch's Place in History

1. Mark Gimein, "Has Tom Peters Gone Crazy?" *Fortune*, November 13, 2000, p. 175.
2. James C. Collins and Jerry I. Porras, *Built to Last: Successful Habits of Visionary Companies* (New York: HarperBusiness, 1994), p. 34.
3. "Jack Welch: Role Model or Rascal?" *Business Week*, July 6, 1998, p. 9.
4. Thomas O'Boyle, *At Any Cost: Jack Welch, General Electric, and the Pursuit of Profit* (New York: Alfred A. Knopf, 1998), p. 374.
5. Peter Krass, editor, *The Book of Business Wisdom: Classic Writings by the Legends of Commerce and Industry* (New York: John Wiley & Sons, 1997), p. 124.
6. Tom Brown, "The Anatomy of Fire," Leader's e-book, www.mgeneral.com.
7. Thomas A. Stewart, "GE Keeps Those Ideas Coming," *Fortune*, August 12, 1991, p. 41.

Appendix B   GE Values

1. General Electric Co. web site: www.ge.com/ibinta18.htm.

Appendix E   General Electric—Nineteen-Year
Performance Figures: 1980–1999

1. *Source*: General Electric 1999 annual report, p. 20.

Index